# SUE
# YOUR
# BOSS

# SUE YOUR BOSS

Rights and Remedies for Employment Discrimination

## E. RICHARD LARSON

FARRAR · STRAUS · GIROUX
NEW YORK

Designed by Irving Perkins Associates
First edition, 1981

Library of Congress Cataloging in Publication Data
Larson, E. Richard.
Sue your boss.
Includes bibliographical references.
1. Discrimination in employment—Law and legislation—
United States.   I. Title.
KF3464.L38      344.73'01133      80–39674

# Contents

# SUE
# YOUR
# BOSS

# An Invitation
# to Use the Seven
# Major Federal Laws
# Barring Job Discrimination

Employment means money. Employment discrimination, as employers are painfully learning, means more money, sometimes vast sums of it. Paid by employers to the people they discriminate against, this money comes in the form of wage adjustments, back pay, double back pay, out-of-pocket damages, and punitive damages—not to mention legal fees.

On August 16, 1979, Bechtel Corporation, the nation's largest privately held construction company, settled two sex discrimination lawsuits in San Francisco by awarding a total of $1.4 million to its female employees. The same day in Detroit, the Detroit Edison Company settled a race discrimination lawsuit, benefiting four hundred black employees, for $4.25 million. In Ohio, a year earlier, the Youngstown Sheet & Tube Co., which hadn't even been sued, paid $295,000 to twenty-seven older employees who had charged the company with unlawful age discrimination. These companies aren't alone. Within the past several years, scores of employers—including such major banks as Chase Manhattan and Bank of America—have agreed to pay from thousands to millions of dollars to settle charges of discrimination made by their employees, former employees, and unsuccessful applicants.

Money—lots of it—has been changing hands. Employers, many of them with archaic discriminatory practices, have been x ·

learning the hard way about employment discrimination law. And they've been footing the bill. Meanwhile, the victims of their employment discrimination—women, blacks, other racial minorities, religious minorities, and older workers—have begun in increasing numbers to assert their rights and thereby reap the benefits of the federal laws enacted years ago for their protection.

Another type of money is involved: that which flows—or doesn't flow—from the federal government in the form of grants and contracts. When the city of Chicago in 1977 had more than $100 million in federal revenue sharing funds withheld from it because of the Chicago Police Department's racially and sexually discriminatory practices, the city quickly implemented a policy of non-discrimination. And when Uniroyal, Inc., the country's third-largest manufacturer of rubber and plastics, found itself in June 1979 barred by the Office of Federal Contract Compliance Programs (OFCCP) from receiving further government contracts—it then had $36 million worth—the company within three months agreed to change its practices and to pay more than $5 million to the women who had charged it with sex discrimination.

Employment discrimination is not a recent phenomenon. But the climate changed dramatically in the 1970s. It was in 1974, in fact, that the Kaiser Aluminum Company agreed through collective bargaining with the United Steelworkers of America to establish a one-to-one, one black for every white, hiring program for its skilled craft positions. This is the affirmative action plan that subsequently was upheld by the Supreme Court in 1979 in the celebrated *Weber* case. Interestingly, this major aluminum company implemented its plan in 1974 not out of beneficence for its black employees but primarily because it wanted to continue to receive federal contracts and also wanted to cut its potential back-pay losses in any future employment discrimination lawsuits filed by black workers. Kaiser, in fact, had recently been investigated by the Office of Federal Contract Compliance Programs. And it had been sued at two of its fifteen plants, with one lawsuit resulting in a back-pay settlement of $225,000, a relatively small sum compared with the $30 million back-pay settlement agreed to in 1974 by leading companies in the steel industry.

As might be expected, the attitudes and actions of the victims of discrimination have changed considerably in recent years. No longer content to sit on their rights, people have begun to assert them. And it's only beginning. In 1977, more than 300,000 charges of discrimination were filed with state and federal equal employment agencies against private, federal, state, and local government employers. Close to twice that number can be expected this year. Many of these charges are settled, but others lead to lawsuits—now more than five thousand each year. As Lloyd Cutler, senior partner of the prestigious Washington, D.C., law firm of Wilmer, Cutler & Pickering, recently remarked, employment discrimination law is a growth field for lawyers: "It is the fastest growing new specialty of them all." And it will continue to "grow like wildfire."

This surge of employment discrimination charges and lawsuits owes its development in part to the law itself. The laws on the books only seventeen years ago weren't worth their weight in paper. But Congress in the 1960s and 1970s defined old rights and added new ones. As a result, women can complain about sexual harassment from male supervisors, older workers can complain about being laid off when younger workers are retained, and minority applicants can complain that they were denied employment through culturally biased aptitude tests. In fact, they do complain. And more often than not, they win their rights.

The explosion of employment discrimination charges also derives from the creation of new federal agencies which have been increasingly required by Congress and the President to enforce the laws prohibiting employment discrimination. Years ago, the only enforcement tool was the private lawsuit. But that too has changed.

• Seventeen years ago, the federal Equal Employment Opportunity Commission [EEOC] did not exist. Today the EEOC annually receives 100,000 charges of discrimination alleging employer violations of the Equal Pay Act, of Title VII of the Civil

Rights Act of 1964, and of the Age Discrimination in Employment Act. If the EEOC cannot resolve the discrimination charges informally, it is empowered to sue the private employers.

• A decade ago, the Office of Federal Contract Compliance Programs (OFCCP) was a moribund agency. Today it actively enforces Executive Order 11246, which prohibits discrimination by the 29,000 employers who contract with the government and requires them to engage in affirmative action employment of minorities and women. Backed by the power to terminate lucrative government contracts, the OFCCP is able to negotiate multimillion-dollar equal employment settlements with such government contractors as AT&T, which agreed in 1973 to a settlement package ultimately totaling nearly $80 million for the benefit of its minority and female employees.

• Five years ago the Office of Revenue Sharing [ORS] allotted billions of dollars in revenue sharing payments to 39,000 local governments without a thought about whether its recipients were engaged in unlawful discrimination. Today, under the strongest civil rights enforcement mandate that exists, the ORS is required to withhold federal funding from those governments which it finds are more likely than not to be engaged in discrimination. Thus, when the ORS in 1979 threatened to terminate San Francisco's $22 million in annual revenue sharing funding, the city quickly agreed to restructure its entire employment system and to engage in affirmative action hiring.

To be sure, active federal enforcement of the laws forbidding employment discrimination has helped to foment the revolution now underway in employment discrimination law. But the primary impetus for change, again, has come from the individual victims themselves. They have realized, at long last, that the law is on their side. They know that not every charge of discrimination will lead to a multimillion-dollar settlement. But they have been learning that it nonetheless is to their advantage to assert their rights.

After *Cynthia DiSalvo* left her $8,200-a-year job as "associate editor" of *Kansas City Magazine,* she was replaced by a man who performed the same job but who was given the title of "communications specialist" and an annual salary of $12,000. Believing that this violated the Equal Pay Act (see Chapter 1) and Title VII of the Civil Rights Act of 1964 (see Chapter 2), she asserted her rights. And won. She didn't want her old job back, but by asserting her rights she obtained more than $13,000 in back pay from her former employer.

*Phillip Houghton,* an experienced test pilot with McDonnell Douglas Corporation, suddenly found himself at age fifty-two demoted to a less prestigious and lower-paying job, and shortly thereafter without a job at all. He asserted his rights under the Age Discrimination in Employment Act (see Chapter 3). As a result, he won back his test-pilot job and also received full back pay.

*Robert Nelson* and *Willie Ford,* black police officers with the 60-member LaGrange, Georgia, Police Department, were suspended without pay in late 1977. Believing the suspensions to be discriminatory, they asserted their rights under the Revenue Sharing Act (see Chapter 4). They filed charges of racial discrimination with the ORS, caused the threatened suspension of $400,-000 in revenue sharing funding, and won reinstatement, back pay, and an expungement of the suspensions from their personnel records.

*Barbara Sabol,* a licensed practical nurse and registered nurse with a master's degree in counseling, guidance, and personnel administration, was denied employment as a Health Occupations Supervisor with a State Board of Education. When she learned that the white male who was given the job was less qualified and hadn't even applied for the job, she asserted her rights to non-discrimination on grounds of race under the Civil Rights Act of 1866 (see Chapter 6) and under the Civil Rights Act of 1871 (see Chapter 7). Although she had found a better job, she nonetheless sought and won $2,500 in back pay and $1,000 in punitive damages.

Obviously, some people know how to obtain their rights. But many others still do not. They don't know that they can win their rightful place in their employer's work force, can win back pay and retroactive seniority for the period they were discriminated against, sometimes can win double back pay and other monetary damages, and, if they have to sue to win, can recover their attorney's fees from their boss.

This book is written for people who have suffered from employment discrimination, and for their lawyers. It fully explains the rights and remedies under the seven major federal laws prohibiting employment discrimination. And it does so, in part, by describing the experiences of many of the people who already have obtained their rights and remedies. Like them, you will learn to:

• Determine for yourself whether the discrimination you encounter actually is unlawful.

• Use all of the seven major federal laws to your best advantage to eliminate that discrimination.

• File proper and timely administrative charges of discrimination with the appropriate federal agencies.

• Win against your boss without hiring a lawyer or going to court.

• Find a lawyer who's right for you if you actually have to sue your boss.

Unfortunately, each of the seven major federal laws forbidding employment discrimination is different from the others. They were enacted at different times and have been amended in a piecemeal fashion. As a result, they vary in the range of employers that are covered, in the types of discrimination prohibited, in the scope of protection provided to individuals, and in the methods of enforcement by federal agencies and by private individuals. The laws also have intricate administrative procedures which *must* be followed before they can be invoked effectively against employers. No law is simple. But employment discrimination law —despite the lucrative settlements and other victories now frequently achieved—unfortunately has come to be viewed by employees and employers alike, and their lawyers, as unduly complicated.

The purpose of this book is to make the law of employment discrimination understandable to everyone. But the primary objective is to make the rights and remedies more widely known and available to persons who may have been, or yet may be, discriminated against on grounds of race, color, national origin, religion, sex, or age.

The first seven chapters of this book provide a detailed explanation of how to use each of the seven major federal laws barring employment discrimination. Each chapter describes how to use one of the laws.

Chapters 1, 2, and 3 review the first modern federal laws: the Equal Pay Act, Title VII of the Civil Rights Act of 1964, and the Age Discrimination in Employment Act. These laws are enforced through the Equal Employment Opportunity Commission, which receives and investigates charges of discrimination and which seeks to resolve these charges. The laws also are enforced through lawsuits filed by the EEOC and by the Department of Justice, and through lawsuits filed by private individuals.

Chapters 4 and 5 review two other modern civil rights laws: the Revenue Sharing Act and Executive Order 11246. They too are enforced through federal administrative agencies—the Office of Revenue Sharing, and the Office of Federal Contract Compliance Programs, respectively—which receive, investigate, and seek to resolve charges of discrimination. But these administrative agencies also have the tremendous power to terminate federal grants and contracts to discriminatory employers. The laws also may be enforced through lawsuits filed by the Department of Justice. And the Revenue Sharing Act additionally can be enforced through lawsuits filed by private individuals.

Chapters 6 and 7 discuss the oldest laws prohibiting discrimination: the 1866 and 1871 Civil Rights Acts. More than a hundred years old, they are not as useful as the modern laws, especially since they are enforced only through lawsuits filed by private individuals. Nonetheless, if you have to sue your boss for intentional discrimination, these old laws should be used in conjunction with the newer ones to increase the monetary remedies available to you.

Each of these seven chapters provides you with information and numerous examples about six specific concerns:

• Who is covered by the law: which employers, employees, and applicants for employment are covered by the law.

• Discriminatory practices which are unlawful: what practices are unlawful and on what grounds.
• Major exceptions: which employees are not covered by the law, and what practices are exempted and hence lawful.
• The federal agency responsible for enforcement: which federal agency, if any, is responsible for resolving administrative charges of discrimination and for enforcing the law.
• Methods of enforcement. What you should do, and when, in order to obtain your rights.
• Remedies: What you can get when your rights have been violated: what types of remedies, such as back pay, double back pay, punitive damages, retroactive seniority, etc., you can receive when you successfully enforce your rights against your boss, your former boss, or your future boss.

As you will learn, the answers to these six concerns are slightly different and sometimes vastly different under the seven major federal laws prohibiting employment discrimination. This leads us into Chapter 8.

Chapter 8 emphasizes that you are entitled to pursue your rights to non-discrimination under any or *all* of the laws reviewed in Chapters 1 through 7 as well as under other laws not extensively addressed in this book. In fact, you are encouraged to pursue your rights under as many laws as are applicable to your particular situation in order to maximize the remedies available to you. But you have to be careful. There are strict time periods which *must* be followed separately under each of the laws. This means that you sometimes will have to choose which laws ultimately will be the best ones to pursue fully. Nonetheless, at the outset, you always should file administrative charges of discrimination with as many of the federal agencies as may be appropriate.

Chapter 9 focuses on the most important step you can take toward winning your rights: the filing of administrative charges of discrimination. It advises you about when and how to file proper and timely charges with such federal agencies as the EEOC, the ORS, and the OFCCP. And it provides you with a list of the regional and district offices of the federal agencies.

Chapter 10 tells you how to find the right lawyer in the event that you actually have to sue your boss. Very often it will not be necessary to bring a lawsuit, such as when your administrative charge of discrimination is resolved satisfactorily, or when the EEOC or Department of Justice sues your boss on your behalf. But in some instances you might have to sue, and then you will need a lawyer.

Since most of the federal laws prohibit more than one type of discrimination, this book is not organized around the type of discrimination, for example sex discrimination, which has been practiced against you. Instead, by exploring separately each of the seven major federal laws, this book provides you with a detailed review of the major legal tools available for winning your rights.

Nonetheless, you may be concerned with only one type of discrimination, and you may want to know which chapters apply to you. This you can easily ascertain by turning to the charts at the end of this book in Appendix A. But a note of caution is necessary. The charts, by their nature, can only summarize general points. They cannot provide you with the specific information you need to know. In order to win your rights, you should carefully review the information and examples provided in each chapter of this book that is relevant to you and your situation.

Once you know the law and know how to obtain your rights and remedies under the seven major federal laws, you will be ready to assert your rights. But before you do so, you must keep in mind several important considerations, the most important of which is that you might be subjected to retaliation and harassment from your employer if you seek to obtain your rights.

Like most discrimination that you may challenge, *retaliation is unlawful.* Nonetheless, retaliation by employers against individuals who assert their rights does occur. Many employers, after all, don't want to be charged with unlawful discrimination any more than they want to alter their discriminatory practices. In response, they sometimes increase their illegal practices by making life difficult for individuals who assert their rights. This retaliation might come in the form of subtle harassment directed against those who file charges of discrimination. Or it might mean loss of your job.

*Sandra Drew,* a claims adjustor who had an excellent employment record with an insurance company in Atlanta, Georgia, was fired for her "poor attitude" the day after her boss learned that she had filed a charge of sex discrimination with the EEOC.

*Jane Mitchell,* a production-line worker for a Kentucky manufacturer of precision springs, filed a charge of sex discrimination with the EEOC and thereafter urged other female employees to do the same. Within a week, she was called into the plant supervisor's office. Handing her a final paycheck, he stated, "You are a good worker, but you're a troublemaker. I'm going to have to let you go."

*Bessie Givhan,* a junior-high-school teacher in Mississippi, who never filed a formal charge but complained privately to her school principal that the school's employment practices were racially discriminatory, suddenly found her teaching contract not renewed.

The risk of retaliation of course is at its highest point if your efforts are directed at your current employer. Nonetheless, especially when it results in loss of a job, retaliation is more than just an inconvenience, for it virtually assures that you will have to sue your boss to stop the retaliation. This, in fact, is precisely what Sandra Drew, Jane Mitchell, and Bessie Givhan had to do to win their jobs back. But whatever your situation, you must evaluate the risk of retaliation versus your courage to seek your federal rights to non-discrimination. If, after a careful assessment, you are willing to take the risk, you then should proceed to assert your rights.

Winning your rights involves a second important consideration. You have to file a *timely* administrative charge of discrimination. In fact, *filing a charge of discrimination is the most important step you will take toward winning your rights.* As we have seen, five of the seven major federal laws prohibiting employment discrimination are enforced initially by federal agencies which are obligated to act on your behalf to resolve unlawful discrimination. In order to initiate federal agency action, you have to file a proper and thorough administrative charge of discrimination with each of the agencies. The charges must be filed very quickly, ordinarily within six months of your employer's discrimination against you. Some of the time periods are longer. But whatever time periods apply to you, those time periods *must* be met. If you file late, after waiting for a union grievance to be resolved or delaying for some other reason, your charges as well as any subsequent lawsuit ordinarily will be dismissed, with the result that you will not be able to obtain your rights no matter how severe the discrimination is against you.

Time periods for filing administrative charges of discrimination with the federal agencies are not the only procedural requirements under the major federal laws. Some of the laws also require that charges of discrimination be filed with state or local administrative agencies. And all of the laws have time periods within which you must file your lawsuit if in fact you intend to or have to sue your boss. Overall, complying with these various procedural requirements is the most difficult aspect of employment discrimination law. Accordingly, each required procedure under each of the seven major federal laws is described in detail in each of the following seven chapters. Additionally, all of Chapter 9 is devoted to the considerations involved in filing proper and timely administrative charges of discrimination.

A final consideration that you have to weigh involves the matter of settlements. Although settlement agreements ordinarily give you less than you might believe you deserve and allow your employer to deny that unlawful discrimination ever occurred, many discrimination disputes are settled informally before formal charges are ever filed. Indeed, most administrative charges of discrimination are settled without ever turning into lawsuits. In fact, the vast majority of the five thousand employment discrimination lawsuits filed each year are settled before trial.

These settlements occur, quite simply, because there are strong incentives for both sides in an employment dispute to get the matter over with, no matter how much you and your adversary share contrary perceptions that the dispute is entirely one-sided. If the employer doesn't settle, it may be confronted with a loss of federal grants or contracts; with a lawsuit filed by the EEOC, by the Department of Justice or by you; and with an administrative or judicial finding of unlawful discrimination resulting in liability to you and others of full back pay, and sometimes double back pay, and occasionally other monetary damages. There also are strong reasons for you to settle. If you don't, you may have to pay a lawyer to sue your boss; you might find yourself involved in year after year of unresolved legal proceedings; you might lose your lawsuit and receive nothing (except bills from your attorney); and if your lawsuit loses badly and is deemed by a court to have been without merit, you even can be ordered under several of the laws to pay your employer's attorney's fees. The prudent course, quite obviously, is one which results in a settlement.

In view of these warnings about retaliation, filing timely charges, and probable settlement, it by now needs to be reemphasized that the seven major federal laws prohibiting employment discrimination are very much in your favor. Quite simply, the laws have developed very fast. They're on your side. They provide you with vast protection. And they're waiting to be used.

In 1977, two stewardesses sued American Airlines, claiming that its policy requiring female flight attendants to take mandatory maternity leaves without pay when they became pregnant was sex discriminatory. As part of the settlement reached two years later, American agreed to withdraw its policy and to pay $9,155 in back wages to Linda Timberlake and $5,321 to Louise Milotes, the women who had filed the suit. American also established a $1.25 million fund to provide similar back pay awards to many of American's other 1,502 flight attendants. Also in 1979, another airline, Eastern Airlines, agreed to pay $280,000 in back wages to eight former flight attendants whom it had involuntarily retired in violation of the Age Discrimination in Employment Act.

In another age discrimination lawsuit settled the same year, the Hartford Insurance Co. agreed to end its alleged age discrimination and to pay $240,000 to seventy-two of its older employees who had claimed that they had been discriminatorily denied promotions, demoted, or fired. Also in 1979, Oklahoma City's Lee Way Motor Freight Inc. agreed to end its discrimination against minority truck drivers, to establish annual long-term goals for hiring and promoting minority employees, and to pay $2.4 million in back pay to eighty-two discriminated-against truck drivers—five of whom received more than $100,000 each.

Scores of similar agreements have been obtained administratively without the need for lawsuits. The EEOC, in fact, annually wins wage settlements for individuals totaling more than $20 million. The Office of Revenue Sharing and the Office of Federal Contract Compliance Programs, with their powers to deny federal monies to discriminatory employers, often obtain broader and more immediate results. In 1978, when the ORS in response to two charges of sex discrimination threatened to withhold $1.6 million in annual revenue sharing funding from the city of Durham, North Carolina, the city quickly rehired Judy McCoy as a police officer and paid her $17,993 in lost wages, promoted C. G. Hargrove within the Recreation Department and provided her with $33,271 in back wage adjustments, and implemented a city-wide affirmative-action training and hiring program. And, when the OFCCP told Hoffman-LaRoche, Inc. that its sex discrimination made it ineligible for a $9 million Department of Defense contract, the large New Jersey pharmaceutical company agreed to end its alleged sex discrimination in job assignments and promotion and provided $1 million in back pay and other job benefits to four hundred of its women workers.

These examples represent only a few of the thousands of people who have won not only their employment rights but substantial justice too by forcing an end to job discrimination and by being awarded thousands of dollars in back pay and other monetary remedies from their discriminatory employers. Yet the changes that have been accomplished and the number of individuals who have benefited to date are relatively insignificant compared with what lies ahead. The laws prohibiting employment discrimination are here to stay. And people like you have only begun to assert and to win their rights.

# PART ONE

## Your Basic Rights under the 1960s Civil Rights Acts

# Winning Equal 1
## Pay for Equal Work

### EQUAL PAY ACT OF 1963, AS AMENDED

#### [SEX]

Historically, women have been paid less than men even when performing the same jobs. By enacting the Equal Pay Act of 1963, the first of the modern laws prohibiting employment discrimination, Congress took an important first step toward eliminating this disparity by outlawing the payment of unequal wages for equal work.

"Congress' purpose in enacting the Equal Pay Act," the Supreme Court recently stated, "was to remedy what was perceived to be a serious and *endemic* problem—the fact that the wage structure of 'many segments of American industry has been based on an ancient but outmoded belief that a man, because of his role in society, should be paid more than a woman even though his duties are the same.' The solution adopted was quite simple in principle: to require that 'equal work will be rewarded by equal wages.' "[1]

Despite the simple principle of equal pay for equal work, thousands of women know that outmoded beliefs do not die easily. And they are continuously learning that the Equal Pay Act, in order to be effective, has to be actively enforced against recalcitrant employers.

Maureen Bullock is one of these women. A young business-

3

woman, Ms. Bullock was hired as a Unit Manager for Pizza Hut of Louisiana. After completing a management-training program, she successfully ran one of the most profitable Pizza Huts in the state. Then she learned that she was being paid less than a male colleague who was performing the same work.

During their training program, Ms. Bullock and her colleague —both had been hired at the same time—were paid a starting salary of $450 per month. But after graduating from the training program, Ms. Bullock's salary was raised only to $600 per month, while the monthly salary of her male colleague was raised to $750. Three months later, when her salary was raised to $720, his was increased to $800.

Maureen Bullock suspected that she was being paid less simply because she was a woman. Knowing that this violated the Equal Pay Act, she decided to assert her rights to equal pay. First she filed a charge of discrimination with the federal Equal Employment Opportunity Commission [EEOC]. When the EEOC failed to resolve her charge, she sued her boss in federal court.

In order to win her rights under the Equal Pay Act, Ms. Bullock had to compare her Unit Manager job with the Unit Manager job held by her male colleague, and she had to show that the jobs required substantially equal skill, effort, and responsibility and were performed under similar working conditions. This she had no trouble proving. But she didn't stop there. She also presented testimony from co-workers showing that the male General Manager believed that a woman should not hold a managerial position and should not make as much money as Ms. Bullock was earning. And she also showed that a Pizza Hut official altered the statistical records which it kept on the race and sex of employees whenever the figures looked unfavorable.

Pizza Hut, despite the strong case against it, nonetheless tried to defend its payment of unequal wages. The company argued that women could be paid less in managerial positions because being female inhibited development of leadership qualities. Rejecting this claim, the court observed that Pizza Hut's "stereotyping . . . is clearly an inappropriate factor under the law."[2] Eliminating such stereotyping in fact is one of the goals of the Equal Pay Act.

Maureen Bullock won her lawsuit and her right to equal pay.

She was awarded the back wages denied to her: a total of somewhat more than $1,000. Because Pizza Hut had willfully denied her equal pay for equal work, the court doubled the back pay award. Lastly, the court ordered Pizza Hut to pay Ms. Bullock's attorney's fees.

The back pay awarded under the Equal Pay Act often is considerably greater than that awarded to Maureen Bullock. And it often is awarded against the federal government itself. On May 20, 1980, for example, a federal court in Washington, D.C., ordered the Government Printing Office to pay $3 million in back wages to twenty-eight women who had been denied equal pay as government bookbinders. Not only did the women receive an average of $100,000 each in back wages, but their current salaries were raised by an average of $10,000 per year to be commensurate with the salaries paid to men performing substantially equal work. By asserting their rights, these women—like so many others—are making employers realize that the principle of equal pay for equal work is a matter of established federal law.

*The Equal Pay Act of 1963 requires that there be no sex discrimination in the payment of wages and other forms of compensation in jobs which are substantially equal. Although the act does not prohibit other forms of employment discrimination, it does require equal pay for equal work. It is a useful complement, and often a more powerful alternative, to the prohibition against sex discrimination found in Title VII of the Civil Rights Act of 1964.*

*The Equal Pay Act was enacted in 1963 as an amendment to the minimum wage law [the Fair Labor Standards Act], and thus became applicable to nearly all private employers and jobs in interstate commerce. In 1974, equal pay protection was extended to nearly all jobs in state and local governments and in the federal government.*

*The Equal Pay Act is enforced through administrative investigation and conciliation by the Equal Employment Opportunity Commission and through lawsuits filed by the EEOC and by individuals.*

*If you succeed in winning your rights under the law, you are entitled to have your pay increased to the pay level of a male colleague who performs work which is substantially equal to your own.* *You also can receive up to two or three years of back wages that were wrongfully denied to you, and in some instances double back wages.*

## WHO IS COVERED BY THE LAW

The Equal Pay Act of 1963,[3] enacted as an amendment to the minimum wage law [the Fair Labor Standards Act],[4] applies to all employers that are covered by the minimum wage law, as well as to other employers and unions that aren't. In general, the Equal Pay Act covers nearly all private employers, the federal government, all state and local governments, and some unions. As a result, *virtually all working women are protected by the Equal Pay Act.*

The specific definitions of who is covered by the Equal Pay Act are somewhat complicated, but not problematical. Unlike the other federal laws discussed in this book, the Equal Pay Act does not list the types of employers and other organizations covered by the Act. This limitation derives from its parent, the minimum wage law. That law, and hence the Equal Pay Act, apply to any "establishment"[5] of an "enterprise"[6] engaged in interstate commerce. This means that both laws apply to any private employer that provides or receives goods or services beyond the boundaries of any single state. The laws also protect any individual employee who is engaged in commerce or engaged in the production of goods for commerce.[7]

The fact of the matter is that nearly all employers and jobs, in some way, are in interstate commerce. For example, in determining the applicability of another civil rights law to establishments engaged in interstate commerce, the Supreme Court held that Ollie's Barbecue, a small, family-owned restaurant employing thirty-six employees, was in interstate commerce because it purchased its hamburger from a local supplier who in turn had procured the meat outside the state.[8] For all practical purposes, most private employers are engaged in interstate commerce and thus are covered by the Equal Pay Act.

The Equal Pay Act also protects virtually all federal civil ser-

vice employees—workers who also are protected by the minimum wage law.[9] Additionally, the Act protects a large group of
public employees not covered by the minimum wage provisions
of the federal minimum wage law: state and local government
employees. The legal explanation for this extended equal pay
protection is complicated and unnecessary to review here.[10] It is
sufficient to know that the Equal Pay Act simply does protect all
employees (except elected and high appointive officials[11]) of any
"public agency,"[12] and that a public agency includes any agency
of a state or local government.[13]

Finally, the Equal Pay Act is broader than the minimum wage
law in two other important ways. First, all of the executive, administrative, and professional jobs which are exempted from
minimum wage coverage are covered by the Equal Pay Act.[14]
And labor organizations, which are not included in the minimum
wage law,[15] are covered by the Equal Pay Act in a limited manner in that they are prohibited from "causing or encouraging" an
employer to violate the Act.[16]

As you can see, nearly all private, federal, state, and local
employees are protected by the Equal Pay Act. If you are doubt-
ful about whether your employer, union, or job is covered by the
Act, you should assume, wherever you work, that you are protected by the Act.

## DISCRIMINATORY PRACTICES WHICH ARE UNLAWFUL

The Equal Pay Act prohibits only that form of sex discrimination which results in unequal pay for equal work. The Act does
not make it unlawful for an employer to refuse to hire women.
But once women are employed, the Equal Pay Act makes it
unlawful for an employer to pay them less than male employees
are paid for performing substantially equal work.

The word "pay" is not limited only to hourly or weekly wages.
Pay means all forms of payment made to or on behalf of an
employee as remuneration for employment[17]—including regular pay, vacation pay, holiday pay, and overtime pay. It also
covers the reasonable cost to the employer of providing an em-

ployee with board, lodging, or other facilities. And it means take-home pay after deductions for pension fund contributions.[18] Under the Equal Pay Act, all of these forms of pay or wages must be equal for females and males where both are performing substantially equal work.

In the words of the Equal Pay Act, it is unlawful for an employer to discriminate on the basis of sex by paying wages to employees of one sex "at a rate less than the rate at which [the employer] pays wages to employees of the opposite sex for equal work on jobs the performance of which requires equal *skill, effort,* and *responsibility,* and which are performed under similar *working conditions.*"[19] Note that this language focuses on "performance." Violations of the law are determined not by looking at an employer's asserted requirements for a job but by looking at actual job performance. The phrase "equal work" also is conveniently defined. There are four components: equal skill, equal effort, equal responsibility, and similar working conditions. This means that in order to determine whether your right to equal pay has been violated, it is necessary to establish that comparable jobs actually require substantially equal skill, effort, and responsibility and are performed under similar working conditions. Each of the four aspects of equal work will be fully discussed later. But first, there are several important rules to keep in mind.

*Equal does not mean identical.* The use of the word "equal" may be scary. But don't be put off. Equal does not mean either identical or precisely equal. In interpreting this word, the courts have uniformly held that "Congress in prescribing 'equal' work did not require that the jobs be identical but only that they be substantially equal."[20] In other words, equal pay must be provided for different jobs which require substantially equal skill, substantially equal effort, and substantially equal responsibility, and are performed under similar working conditions.

*Job titles are irrelevant.* Job titles and job descriptions often do not tell very much about how jobs are actually performed. Since job performance is the focus of the Equal Pay Act, job titles and job descriptions are not particularly important. As one court recently observed: "The Act cannot be avoided because the job titles of employees are not the same, nor is the Act avoided if the official job descriptions of employees specify different duties. 'Actual job requirements and performance are controlling.' "[21] Under this standard, job performance has been proven to be substantially equal, and the payment of equal wages has been required, for jobs which had such different titles as teacher assistant and teacher,[22] stewardess and purser,[23] car marker and police officer,[24] and associate editor and communications specialist.[25]

*The act requires equal pay not only in contemporaneous jobs but also in successive jobs.* Most of the time the Equal Pay Act is applied to jobs which are contemporaneous—jobs performed at the same time. Jobs are compared to see if the actual performance of employees who might work side by side—for example, the teacher assistant and the teacher,[26] or the stewardesses and the pursers[27]—are substantially equal.

The Act also applies to jobs which are successive—jobs that follow one another. These jobs are compared in the same way. For example, in Fargo, North Dakota, female car markers who were hired to replace more highly paid male police officers were found to be entitled to the higher pay because the jobs were substantially equal.[28] Similarly, Cynthia DiSalvo, the woman who had been employed as the associate editor of *Kansas City Magazine,* and who had been replaced by a man given the title of communications specialist and paid a higher salary, was entitled to the higher pay (in back wages) because the jobs were substantially equal.[29]

*Payment of equal wages means increasing the lower pay to the higher pay rate.* The Equal Pay Act requires not just the payment of equal wages but the payment of equal wages at the highest pay rate of comparable jobs. As the Supreme Court observed, quoting from the legislative history of the Equal Pay Act: " 'The objective of equal pay legislation . . . is not to drag down men workers to the wage levels of women, but to raise women to the levels enjoyed by men.' "[30] When you obtain your rights under the Equal Pay Act, you will always win higher wages.

*The Equal Pay Act and Title VII are to be interpreted in a similar manner.* The Equal Pay Act makes it unlawful to pay unequal wages for substantially equal work, but it does not prohibit other forms of sex discrimination. Title VII of the Civil Rights Act of 1964, discussed in Chapter 2, prohibits many forms of sex discrimination including discrimination in compensation,[31] and it specifically incorporates part of the Equal Pay Act.[32] What is important here is that the courts have held, at least with regard to denials of equal pay for equal work, that "the provisions of Title VII regarding sex discrimination in the area of compensation must be construed in harmony with the Equal Pay Act."[33] This means that women who have been denied equal pay and who also have been discriminated against in other ways can and should assert their rights under both the Equal Pay Act and Title VII. This dual course of action is discussed more fully in Chapter 8.

The key to using the Equal Pay Act effectively is understanding the meaning of the words "equal work." As we have seen, equal work means substantially equal work; and it includes four criteria: substantially equal skill, substantially equal effort, substantially equal responsibility, and similar working conditions.

## Substantially Equal Skill

"Skill" means the academic knowledge necessary to perform a job, or the training or learning necessary to perform a job.[34] The focus is on what skills are actually used in and necessary to job performance. If the requisite skills are substantially equal, an employee's possession of additional skills not necessary to perform the job is irrelevant. For example, since most secretarial jobs require the skills of typing and taking shorthand, an employee who possesses a Ph.D. in physics does not possess greater skill for that job for purposes of the Equal Pay Act.

More to the point is Cynthia DiSalvo's case involving the *Kansas City Magazine* editorial job with the Chamber of Commerce of Greater Kansas City. Just as the successive job titles were irrelevant, so too was the fact that the male communications specialist possessed greater editorial, writing, and photographic experience than the female associate editor he replaced. Since they both performed the same job (editing the employer's monthly magazine), and since they both possessed the necessary basic skills to perform that job well, the skills required were held to be substantially equal.[35]

Equal skills often are possessed by employees who work at jobs in different departments. For example, the Miller Brewing Co. in Milwaukee had two separate scientific laboratories, the Analytical Lab and the Materials Quality Control Lab, where laboratory technicians analyzed the chemical and physical characteristics of beer. The women in the Analytical Lab, however, were paid 70 cents an hour less than the men assigned to the Materials Quality Control Lab. In due time, the lower-paid female technicians asserted their rights. Upon examination by a court, the laboratory jobs were found to require equal academic content and nearly identical training. In fact, many of the experienced but lower-paid female technicians actually provided initial training to the more highly paid male technicians. The skills were found to be substantially equal.[36]

In another instance, a Montgomery, Alabama, clothing store argued that its male sales personnel were more highly skilled than its female sales personnel because fitting a man's suit required greater skill than fitting a woman's suit. The employer's argument lost.[37] Slow to learn, Sears, Roebuck & Co. advanced a nearly identical rationale several years later. Its male clothing division managers, Sears argued, were more highly skilled than its female clothing division managers because supervising alterations on men's suits required more skill than supervising alterations on women's suits. Needless to say, Sears also lost.[38]

Remember, skill refers only to those skills actually used in and necessary to perform a job. Any other skills are irrelevant.

## Substantially Equal Effort

The "effort" required to perform a job refers to the physical or mental exertion expended on a job.[39] Jobs which require substantially equal effort do not need to have exactly the same duties. Many jobs which are comparable under the Equal Pay Act will have different or additional duties and assignments, but divergent job elements do not necessarily make the performance effort unequal, especially where the additional duties are performed only occasionally or are not central to the basic requirements of the job.[40]

Several years ago, an Arkansas company that manufactures paper products paid its male night-shift machine operators 20 cents more per hour than it paid its female day-shift machine operators. The men performed an extra task. In addition to operating their machines, the night-shift operators spent up to 7 percent of their time loading their machines with heavy rolls of paper. The female operators had this task performed for them during the day by unskilled maintenance men. The extra task, despite its regularity of performance by the night-shift operators, was found by a court to be too insignificant an extra duty to support the denial of equal pay to the women.[41]

The performance of extra tasks has been frequently asserted by hospitals as the reason for discrepancies in pay between hospital orderlies (usually men) and nurse's aides (usually women). Both the orderlies and the nurse's aides provide patient care, assist with medical treatment, and engage in general housekeeping. But the orderlies sometimes weigh bedridden patients, set up traction devices, and transport oxygen tanks. The nurse's aides sometimes are required to clean bedpans, make beds, and care for infants. Despite these different duties, some of which require greater physical effort by the orderlies, the overall effort by orderlies and nurse's aides has been found by most courts to be substantially equal.[42]

In many instances, of course, different jobs will require substantially different effort. But even in this situation, it is crucial to investigate actual job performance. For example, in one recent Equal Pay Act violation, male janitors concededly had been assigned numerous tasks which were substantially different from those assigned to female janitors. But in court the male janitors admitted that they did not actually perform the assigned tasks. In fact, a few male janitors said that they had never even been told that they were expected to perform the additional tasks. Thus, despite the different assignments, the actual effort of the male and female janitors was the same.[43]

The fact that some men in a higher-paying job classification actually do perform substantially different duties does not necessarily defeat an equal-pay claim where at least a few of the comparable women and men do perform substantially similar duties. For example, Sears, Roebuck & Co. has a history of paying its female division managers less than its male division managers. Sued in court for equal-pay violations, Sears argued that the higher pay for the men was based upon the greater tasks performed by the male division managers. Sears tried to support its argument by parading two male division managers who performed such additional duties as conducting new employee orientation sessions, supervising shoplifting-prevention crews, and interviewing job applicants. These extra tasks concededly were not performed by the female division managers. But the court pierced the ruse. "No other division managers, *male or female*, performed an equivalent amount of extra tasks." Accordingly, this "set these two men apart in terms of Equal Pay Act comparisons." The proper comparison was between the duties performed by the other male division managers and those performed by the female division managers. Since these differences were only "incidental," the court found that Sears had violated the Equal Pay Act.[44]

## Substantially Equal Responsibility

"Responsibility" is more difficult to define and to apply than are the equal-work criteria of substantially equal skill and of substantially equal effort. The problem is that the degree of responsibility in any particular job usually is based upon a subjective judgment. Nonetheless, responsibility generally refers to concepts such as accountability to the employer, importance of the job duties to the employer, and the degree of supervision by others and of others.[45]

Obviously, if one job has substantially more responsibility than another job—financial officer vs. messenger—the jobs are not considered equal for equal pay purposes. Differences in responsibility also exist in very similar jobs. For example, one company which had a large computer operation used its computer operators in very different ways. One set of computer operators, most of whom were women, was responsible for reading complicated computer tapes. Another group, most of whom were men, was responsible for manually editing and checking upon the accuracy of the same tapes. Since the success of the employer's business rested heavily on the accuracy of the computer tapes, the second set of computer operators had jobs with much greater responsibility. Although the computer operators used identical skill and expended equal effort, their responsibility was not substantially equal. Pay differentials in this instance were lawful.[46]

On the other hand, an examination of actual responsibility in on-the-job performance will often show that alleged differences in responsibility do not exist in fact. When a group of stewardesses sued Northwest Airlines under the Equal Pay Act, the company argued that the male pursers were responsible for reporting directly to the company after each flight and for performing overall supervision during the flights—responsibilities not required of stewardesses. The court's review of actual job performance, however, revealed that the accountability existed only on paper, not in practice, and that the stewardesses actually performed more supervisory duties than did the pursers.[47]

## Similar Working Conditions

This fourth aspect of equal work, "similar working conditions," is usually the easiest to establish. There are only two conditions that are relevant: physical surroundings and possible hazards. You usually can determine if the working conditions are similar or different through your own observation.

Women and men with jobs requiring equal skill, effort, and responsibility generally are presumed to be performing under similar working conditions.[48] In this situation, the physical surroundings normally are similar. So, too, are the possible hazards. Inconsequential differences in working conditions are not sufficient to justify a differential in pay.

This does not mean that employers have not tried to justify pay differentials by arguing that similar working conditions are dissimilar. It simply means that for the most part their arguments have failed. For example, in one case a court rejected an employer's argument that the performance of work in different departments inside a company constituted dissimilar working conditions.[49] In another case, the Supreme Court held that working at night instead of during the day is not a different working condition.[50] In almost every instance, working conditions will be found to be similar when the other criteria of equal work are satisfied.

## Proving the Four Elements of Equal Work: Skill, Effort, Responsibility, and Working Conditions

When you decide to obtain your right to equal pay, you simply have to remember each of the four elements of equal work. Under the Equal Pay Act, you have to show that different-paying jobs actually do constitute substantially equal work. Be prepared: your employer probably will argue that the different-paying jobs do *not* constitute substantially equal work.

Sometimes an employer will focus upon only one of the four aspects of equal work set forth above to support its defense that the jobs are not equal. But more often, employers will try to argue that two or more of the four criteria operating together make the jobs unequal. You thus have to be prepared to show that each of the four elements of equal work is present. If you do, you'll be in a good position to win.

Until 1973, the city of Fargo, North Dakota, assigned several male police officers to mark cars for overtime parking and to issue tickets for parking and other non-moving violations. In 1973, the city reassigned the officers to other patrol duties, established a new position entitled "car markers," hired three women for the positions, and paid them half what the male police officers had been paid for the same work. The women accepted the jobs. Then they sued their boss. The city first argued that it had not violated the Equal Pay Act because the men possessed the skills and extensive training of police officers, whereas the women possessed only limited skills and training as car markers. The city's "skills" argument was rejected by the court: "The crucial question under the Equal Pay Act is not whether one sex possesses additional training or skills, but whether the nature of the duties actually performed require or utilize those additional skills. . . . Possession of a skill not needed to meet requirements of the job cannot be considered in making a determination regarding equality of skill." With its first argument rejected, the city next argued that the men expended extra effort and shouldered additional responsibility because they performed the additional duties of providing downtown security and of assisting patrol car units responding to crimes. Upon examination by the court, these "effort" and "responsibility" arguments too were rejected because the extra duties "were very insubstantial. The extra duties performed consumed a minimal amount of time and were essentially incidental to the actually assigned and performed duties of the position." Having lost on the first three elements of equal work, the city chose not to argue that the working conditions were not similar—since the working conditions obviously were identical. The court ruled that the city's pay differential violated the Equal Pay Act, and that the women thus were entitled to the higher pay.[51]

### Retaliation

In addition to prohibiting the payment of unequal wages for equal work, the Equal Pay Act also prohibits retaliation against individuals who assert their rights. Specifically, the Act incorporates a provision from the minimum wage law which makes it unlawful for any employer "to discharge or in any other manner discriminate against any employee" who attempts to secure her rights under the Equal Pay Act.[52]

This prohibition means that, whether or not your employer actually is denying you equal pay for equal work, it is barred from retaliating against you for trying to obtain equal pay. But just as employers deny equal pay for equal work, so too do they sometimes harass employees merely for trying to win their rights. Worse, they sometimes fire employees who assert their rights. Maureen Bullock, for example, was fired after she charged Pizza Hut of Louisiana with denying her equal pay.[53] Since the risk of retaliation is a real one, you must be willing to take that risk when you assert your rights.

## MAJOR EXCEPTIONS

The Equal Pay Act, as reviewed thus far, is quite comprehensive. There are, however, several exceptions to the requirement of equal pay for equal work.

## Exempted Employers and Employment

Employees of some small private employers are not covered by the Equal Pay Act. Specifically, you are not protected by the Act if neither you nor your employer is engaged in commerce or engaged in the production of goods for commerce. But, as we saw at the beginning of this chapter, surprisingly few employers can be considered exempted.

There also are a number of specific statutory exceptions in the Equal Pay Act which deny protection to small groups of employees in isolated situations.[54] For example, exempted from coverage and hence denied protection under the Act are:

• Employees who work for amusement or recreational establishments which are in operation during fewer than eight months per year.
• Employees in the fish industry who catch, cultivate, process, can, or pack fish.
• Employees of relatively small agricultural farms.
• Employees of small newspaper publishers whose regular circulation is less than 4,000 papers.
• Employees who work as switchboard operators for small, independently owned public telephone companies.[55]

These few statutory exceptions obviously are relatively minor. Virtually *all* employees *are protected* by the Act.

## Employment Practices Subject to Statutory Exceptions

Even when you are covered by the Equal Pay Act, and when you prove that you have been paid less for substantially equal work performed under similar working conditions, you still can be denied protection of the Act under four exceptions set forth in the Act itself. These exceptions allow an employer to deny equal pay for equal work where the wage differences are based on a seniority system, on a merit system, on a system which measures earnings by quantity or quality of production, or on any factor other than sex.[56] Don't be discouraged. These exceptions are not as broad as they may seem. Additionally, your employer has to prove the existence of an exception. And an exception can be claimed by your employer *only* if "the factor of sex provides no part of the basis for the wage differential."[57] In other words, these four exceptions are irrelevant if the factor of sex plays any part in an employer's payment of unequal wages.

*Seniority systems.* Under the Equal Pay Act, it is permissible for an employer to deny equal pay for equal work when the unequal payment is based on the provisions of a seniority system. But this first exception, like the others, becomes irrelevant if the factor of sex plays any part in the payment of different wages.

This seniority system exception was argued in a case mentioned earlier, where female day-shift employees were paid less than male night-shift employees. The company claimed that its night-shift differential not only was justified by different working conditions (working at night) but also was based on a seniority system. The Supreme Court disagreed and found the company in violation of the Equal Pay Act because the factor of sex had played a part since, in the past, women had been assigned only to the day shift and men only to the night shift.[58]

*Merit systems.* Unequal pay also may be allowed where an employer can show that the unequal wages are paid because of a merit system—a system where higher quality of work is rewarded with higher pay. If a truly objective merit system is in existence, the pay need not be equal if the pay discrepancies actually are based on that merit system. On the other hand, if the alleged merit system is entirely subjective, it does not meet this merit system exception. Additionally, if sex is at all a factor, the exception, again, does not apply.

A few employers have claimed that use of subjective evaluations by supervisors qualifies as a merit system, thereby allowing unequal pay. Their arguments have lost. As many courts have stated, "Subjective evaluations of the employer cannot stand alone as a basis for salary discrimination."[59]

Other employers have argued that training programs qualify as merit systems, thereby allowing male trainees to be paid higher than female non-trainees. This argument, too, usually is rejected. Since most training programs are male-dominated, they are not free from the use of sex as a factor and they accordingly do not qualify for the exception allowing a wage differential.[60] Similarly, "recognition by management of the ability of [male] employees to 'work their way up the ranks' does not constitute a training program and is immaterial [under the Equal Pay Act]."[61]

*Systems which measure earnings by quantity or quality of production.*  The third exception allows the payment of unequal wages according to a system which measures earnings by quantity or quality of production. This type of system, like a merit system, must be objective. Any system which uses subjective evaluations will not qualify under this exception. And if sex is at all a factor in the measurement system, the exception cannot be invoked.

*Any factor other than sex.*  Lastly, pay differentials are allowed if based upon any factor other than sex. This catch-all exception, like the other exceptions, is narrowed considerably since the factor of sex cannot play any part in the wage differential. Accordingly, the few employers that have tried to invoke this exception have not succeeded.

A Pennsylvania employer, which paid its male barbers $165 more per month than it paid its female beauticians, contended that separate state licensing of barbers and beauticians somehow was a factor other than sex that justified the wage differential. A court found the separate licensing to be irrelevant to job performance. The employer was found to have violated the Act.[62] A classic argument advanced not long ago by a bank in Texas was that since some women will work for less pay than some men will, this is a factor other than sex allowing unequal pay. The argument lost: "The 'market force' theory, i.e., a woman will work for less than a man, is not a valid consideration under the Act."[63] A Missouri employer took this market-force theory even further by arguing that a woman's knowing acceptance of lower pay was a valid factor other than sex. This sexploitation argument too was rejected.[64]

Many other arguments also are irrelevant under the Equal Pay Act. Payment of higher wages to a male "head-of-household" is not a factor other than sex.[65] Similarly, a claimed difference between the average cost of employing women as a group and the average cost of employing men as a group is not a factor other than sex.[66] These claimed factors, like so many other factors, merely "perpetuate and promote the very discrimination at which the Act is directed."[67]

## THE FEDERAL AGENCY RESPONSIBLE FOR ENFORCEMENT

The federal agency responsible for administering and enforcing the Equal Pay Act is the Equal Employment Opportunity Commission.[68] The EEOC has district and area offices throughout the United States. The locations of these offices are listed in Chapter 9. The main office of the EEOC is located in Washington, D.C.:

Equal Employment Opportunity Commission
Columbia Plaza Highrise
2401 E Street, N.W.
Washington, D.C. 20506

202/634-7040

The EEOC enforces the Equal Pay Act by receiving charges of discrimination from individuals like you, by investigating those charges, and by attempting to resolve the charges informally with your boss. More than half of all charges alleging unequal pay for equal work have been successfully resolved in this manner. If a charge of discrimination is not successfully resolved, the EEOC also may enforce the Equal Pay Act by suing your boss.

## ENFORCEMENT: HOW TO OBTAIN YOUR RIGHTS

Many employers, possibly including your employer, continue to discriminate on the basis of sex in the payment of wages.

Ordinarily, these employers will comply with the law only if they are forced to comply. Under the Equal Pay Act, it is up to you to assert your rights. If you are being paid less than a male co-worker who you believe is performing work equal to yours, see if you can prove to yourself that the jobs are substantially equal. Take notes. Talk to friends. Compare the jobs. Then get ready to initiate enforcement against your boss.

If you are being denied equal pay by a private employer or by a state or local government, there are three methods of winning your right to equal pay:

• A charge which you send to the EEOC alleging that your employer has denied you equal pay may be resolved through negotiations undertaken by the EEOC.
• A charge which you send to the EEOC may result in a successful lawsuit brought by the EEOC on your behalf.
• A charge which you send to the EEOC might lead to a successful lawsuit brought by you.

For federal employees, the methods of enforcement are the same[69] except that you cannot expect the EEOC to sue another federal agency on your behalf. In other words, federal employees who are denied equal pay can have the discrimination resolved only through negotiations undertaken by the EEOC or through lawsuits filed by the individuals themselves.[70]

As is obvious, each of these methods of enforcement depends on your taking the formal step of filing a charge of discrimination against your employer. This step, it should be pointed out, is not required under the law. But only by taking this step can you force an end to your employer's discrimination through an EEOC administrative resolution of the charge or through a subsequent lawsuit filed by the EEOC.

## Administrative Resolution of Charges of Discrimination

If you believe that you have been discriminated against in violation of the Equal Pay Act, you should send a letter to the EEOC charging your employer with discrimination. A sample charge is set forth at the end of this chapter. [Note that this charge is different from a formal charge of discrimination filed

with the EEOC under Title VII. This is discussed in Chapter 2.]
In your Equal Pay Act charge, you should:

- Give your name, address, and telephone number and your employer's name and address.
- Describe fully the nature of your work.
- Compare your wages with the wages of a male employee who you contend is performing equal work.
- State how long you have been denied equal pay.
- Charge your employer with violating the Equal Pay Act.

You should send your charge as soon as possible to the closest office of the EEOC or to the EEOC's principal office in Washington, D.C.

Upon receipt of the charge, the EEOC will notify the accused employer or union that a charge has been filed, but it need not and ordinarily does not disclose the name of the person who filed the charge.[71] Later the EEOC will investigate the charge and will attempt to eliminate the discrimination by trying to persuade your employer to pay equal wages now and in the future and to pay some back wages to those persons who have been denied equal pay.

This process will involve you directly. During the investigation stage, representatives from the EEOC will contact you probably both by phone and in person. Since they will want to know all of the facts surrounding your employer's payment of unequal wages, you should save all documents and notes which you think might be relevant to your claim. Resolution of the discrimination also will involve you. In fact, the purpose of the administrative enforcement procedure is to obtain a written agreement in which your employer agrees to pay *you* equal wages in the future and to provide you with back wages. The agreement, which usually will be proposed by the EEOC, must be agreed to by you and by your employer. If you don't find the proposed agreement satisfactory, you don't have to agree. But, as we saw in the introduction, there are strong incentives for both you and your boss to reach a settlement agreement.

If your employer refuses to enter into an informal settlement agreement, or if you find the proposed agreement unsatisfactory, the next step usually is the filing of a lawsuit.

## Lawsuits by the EEOC

The second method of enforcement, a lawsuit by the EEOC, usually will not occur unless you've sent a charge to the EEOC complaining about the payment to you of unequal wages. Unless you complain to the EEOC, there is little chance that the EEOC will know about the discrimination against you. If the EEOC believes from its investigation that you have been unlawfully discriminated against, and if the EEOC has been unable to obtain a written agreement from your employer eliminating that discrimination, then the EEOC might file a lawsuit in federal or state court on your behalf against the accused employer.[72]

The purpose of this lawsuit, of course, is to allow you to obtain your rights by forcing the employer to comply with the law. This lawsuit must be filed by the EEOC, if at all, within two years of the alleged Equal Pay Act violation, or within three years if the lawsuit alleges that the employer's discrimination was willful (meaning that the employer had reason to know that its payment of unequal wages was covered by the Equal Pay Act).[73]

If your employer's payment of unequal wages is not resolved administratively by the EEOC, it is to your advantage to have the EEOC file a lawsuit on your behalf. When this occurs, the power and resources of the federal government will be used against your employer. And you won't have to bear the burden or expense of suing your boss. You thus should stay in contact with the EEOC, urging it to file a lawsuit. But if the EEOC doesn't sue your boss, you have a right to do so yourself.

## Lawsuits by Individuals

The third method of enforcement, a lawsuit filed by you, is very similar to the previous method, where the EEOC files the lawsuit. But you cannot file a lawsuit if you have accepted a written settlement agreement agreed to by your employer.[74] And no such lawsuit may be filed if the EEOC already has filed a lawsuit against your employer to enforce your rights.[75] In other words, you lose your right to sue if the EEOC sues first.

Assuming that you have not accepted a settlement agreement, and assuming that the EEOC has not sued, your lawsuit, similar to a lawsuit by the EEOC, must be filed within two years of the alleged violation, or within three years if you claim that the violation was willful.[76] If the EEOC administrative procedure stretches out for several years—and sometimes it does take that long—you will have to decide finally whether to sue your boss.

Filing a lawsuit is not an easy step. If you want to or have to sue, you should find a lawyer who will represent you in your lawsuit. One of the unique problems which you might encounter in trying to find a lawyer to represent you in an Equal Pay Act lawsuit involves a limitation in the Act on the use of class action lawsuits. In a normal class action lawsuit, you can sue your employer not only on your own behalf but also on behalf of all other persons who also have been discriminated against; if you win, then you and all "unnamed" members of the class who have been discriminated against can receive appropriate remedies, including back pay. Class-action lawsuits of this nature are very common under Title VII of the Civil Rights Act of 1964, as we will see in Chapter 2. Under the Equal Pay Act, however, class action lawsuits on behalf of unidentified employees are *not* permitted. Instead, in order to obtain back pay in a lawsuit filed by you only under the Equal Pay Act, your colleagues must affirmatively join your suit. They either must be among the plaintiffs who initially file the lawsuit or shortly thereafter must file with the court written consents agreeing to be identifiable class members.[77] In other words, in order to receive back pay in a lawsuit filed by you only under the Equal Pay Act, all similarly situated employees must affirmatively come into the lawsuit if they wish to benefit financially. Otherwise only you will win back pay.

One way around this problem, assuming that you want to sue on behalf of your colleagues, is to file your lawsuit not just under the Equal Pay Act but also under Title VII. This procedure of combining the laws to your advantage is discussed in Chapter 8. Nonetheless, because of the greater monetary remedies sometimes available to the individuals who join a lawsuit under the Equal Pay Act, you ordinarily should try to find other employees bold enough to identify themselves in a lawsuit based in part on the Equal Pay Act.

## REMEDIES: WHAT YOU CAN GET WHEN YOUR RIGHTS HAVE BEEN VIOLATED

Finally: the rewards. When you win your rights under the Equal Pay Act, you are entitled to have your employer's denial of equal pay fully remedied. Most basically, you immediately will receive equal wages for equal work. You also are entitled to the payment of back wages along with other fringe benefits which you were wrongfully denied in the preceding two and sometimes three years.

These remedies may be obtained administratively through a written settlement agreement sought and obtained for you by the EEOC.[78] In this situation, your employer normally will not admit to a violation of the Equal Pay Act. But what is important is the provision of a satisfactory remedy. If the settlement agreement gives you equal pay and some back wages, both you and the employer are able to avoid a potentially expensive and time-consuming lawsuit. And with the EEOC acting administratively on your behalf, there usually is no need for you to retain a lawyer.

The same remedies also may be obtained through a lawsuit filed by the EEOC or by you.[79] In fact, in lawsuits under the Equal Pay Act, there is an additional remedy available to you: double back wages—a remedy formally called "liquidated damages." This remedy can be won, however, only if your employer willfully violated the law so as to intentionally and knowingly deprive you of your right to equal pay for equal work.[80] The liquidated damages which are available, over and above back pay, need not relate to specific harm done (that is why they are called liquidated damages), but they are limited under the Equal Pay Act to an amount equal to the award of back wages. In other words, if a court finds that your employer willfully violated the Equal Pay Act, you can obtain double back wages.

In a lawsuit filed and won by you against your employer, you also can recover your attorney's fees. Under the Equal Pay Act, courts are required to award to the successful plaintiff (you) "a reasonable attorney's fee to be paid by the defendant" (your employer).[81] Since there is no comparable authorization for awarding an attorney's fee to a successful defendant, only you and not your employer can obtain fees in a lawsuit.[82]

The remedies available under the Equal Pay Act can be quite rewarding for employees who insist on their rights. For example, the Milwaukee brewery which paid its female laboratory technicians 70 cents per hour less than it paid its male technicians for equal work was sued by three of its female technicians. When the company thereafter lowered the salaries of the male technicians and claimed that it then was paying equal pay for equal work, the federal government also sued the brewery. Both cases were tried together in court, and not surprisingly, the three female technicians and the government won. The company was ordered by the court to pay all female and male technicians the higher wages previously paid only to the male technicians. The three women who brought the initial lawsuit were awarded back pay. And because the company had willfully denied them equal pay, the women also were awarded liquidated damages doubling their back pay award. In total, the three women received a double back pay award of $24,371.20. And because they won their lawsuit, they also received $20,000 from their employer for their attorney's fees.[83]

Back pay awards—even without being doubled as liquidated damages—can be even more costly than this to discriminatory employers. In 1979, a Charleston, West Virginia, department store, The Diamond, settled an Equal Pay Act lawsuit by paying $204,706 in back pay to its female buyers. In Owensboro, Kentucky, several months later, the Owensboro-Daviess County Hospital was ordered by a court to pay to its nurse's aides $336,000 in back wages and an additional $138,700 in interest because of its past equal pay violations. Overall, well over $20 million in back pay is paid every year by employers to remedy their violations of the Equal Pay Act.

* * *

Northwest Airlines, one of the most frequently struck airlines in the country, often has been at odds with its employees. Its most active antagonists have been the various unions which represent its workers. But on occasion, a single employee has challenged the employment policies of this corporate Goliath.

Mary Laffey is such an employee. She began her employment with Northwest in 1958 as a stewardess. For the next decade she worked side by side in flight with male cabin attendants who performed work similar to hers. But the males had different titles. They were classified as pursers, and their salaries ranged from 20 to 55 percent higher than the salaries paid to stewardesses of equivalent seniority. The pursers also had better layover accommodations (pursers were allowed to book single rooms whereas stewardesses were required to share rooms), and they received larger allowances for cleaning their uniforms.

In 1967, Northwest entered into a collective bargaining agreement to open the previously all-male purser position to females. Mary Laffey, with nine years of experience as a stewardess, applied. At first, Northwest continued to hire only men as pursers, despite the fact that they had no relevant flight experience. Finally, in June 1968, Ms. Laffey was hired as a purser. This single step toward equality, however, was not enough to appease Mary Laffey, for it did not change the unequal pay given to stewardesses. As of 1970, Northwest employed 137 male cabin attendants; all were highly paid pursers. Northwest also employed 1,-747 female cabin attendants; all but one were stewardesses. The one exception was Mary Laffey, the sole female purser.

Believing that the purser and stewardess jobs were essentially the same, Mary Laffey and several stewardesses filed administrative charges of discrimination against Northwest with the EEOC. Mary Laffey wanted back pay. The stewardesses wanted equal pay and back pay. When Northwest refused to budge, the women sued Northwest in federal court under the Equal Pay Act (and under Title VII). Thereafter, they were joined by a number of other stewardesses who chose to opt into the lawsuit by filing consents with the court. After years of court proceedings, Mary Laffey and her friends finally won their lawsuit.[84] Since Northwest fought them every inch of the way, arguing that the purser and stewardess positions were not substantially equal, the lawsuit provides a useful example of how the Equal Pay Act actually works.

At the outset of its decision, the court observed that the use of different job titles was irrelevant. Application of the Equal Pay Act, the court said, "is not dependent upon job classifications or titles but depends rather on actual job requirements and performance."

Thereafter, the court examined the jobs with regard to equal skill, equal effort, equal responsibility, and similar working conditions. In each instance, the women proved that the jobs were substantially equal.

*Equal skill.*   First, Ms. Laffey and her friends showed that the jobs required substantially equal skill and training. In fact, they proved that the pursers actually received less training than the stewardesses. And the stewardesses who wanted to be pursers, of course, had flight experience which few of the male applicants had. Overall, it appeared to the court that the pursers actually possessed less skill than the stewardesses.

*Equal effort.*   Northwest strongly contended that the pursers were required to expend greater efforts than were required of the stewardesses. For example, on international flights, pursers were required to administer quarantine procedures for passengers, crew, and cargo. But, the court found, quarantine duties were not required on domestic flights, and in any event, stewardesses performed other minor duties which the pursers did not. Moreover, where the duties with regard to passengers were equal, pursers performed them in the first-class cabin while the stewardesses were mostly serving tourist class. Since there are fewer passengers and fewer duties in first class, the court found that the effort expended by the pursers might actually be less than the effort expended by the stewardesses.

*Equal responsibility.*   Northwest also strongly argued that pursers had greater responsibility, both because they were ultimately accountable for the service provided on a flight and because they had supervisory responsibilities over stewardesses. The court rejected both contentions. Formal accountability to Northwest existed only on paper, and "that difference is derived from status rather than as a function of the job." Supervisory differences too were illusory because actual supervision did not extend beyond that part of the plane to which the cabin attendants were assigned. Pursers were assigned to first class "with the more senior stewardesses, who require little or no supervision." Stewardesses with less seniority were assigned to tourist class with the most junior stewardesses who needed "training as well as normal supervision." Viewed as a whole, "stewardesses' supervisory labors may exceed those of pursers."

*Similar working conditions.* Northwest finally argued that the working conditions were different because pursers, who often were assigned to military charter flights, spent more consecutive days away from home each month than did stewardesses. The court found that this was a distinction without any real difference. "More consecutive days away from home also means more consecutive days at home each month." And most stewardesses, as well as pursers, preferred this schedule to one requiring more frequent, shorter flights.

Because the women successfully proved that the purser and stewardess positions were substantially equal, and because Northwest didn't even try to prove that the wage differential was based on one of the Act's four exceptions, Mary Laffey and the other named individuals won their rights under the Equal Pay Act. Thus, they were entitled to the Act's remedies.

As basic remedies, the court ordered Northwest to increase the pay of all stewardesses to the pay levels of pursers, to provide stewardesses with single rooms on layovers, and to give them the higher cleaning allowances paid to the pursers. The court then awarded Ms. Laffey and the other individuals who had joined the lawsuit two years' back pay and other forms of back compensation. Finding that Northwest's violation of the Equal Pay Act had been willful, the court said that those individuals also should receive a third year of back pay and other back compensation. The court next indicated that liquidated damages doubling the total amount of back pay also should be awarded to Ms. Laffey and to the other identified individuals. And finally, for all their trouble, Ms. Laffey and her friends were awarded their attorney's fees, to be paid by their boss, Northwest Airlines.

As Mary Laffey has taught us, asserting one's rights under the Equal Pay Act can be well worth the effort.

## Sample Letter Charging Discrimination

Charging Party
10000 My Street
My Town, My State 00000
101 234-5678

July 1, 1980

Equal Employment Opportunity Commission
Columbia Plaza Highrise
2401 E Street, N.W.
Washington, D.C. 20506

I believe that I am being paid unequal wages for equal work. I am writing this letter to you because I believe that I am being discriminated against because of my sex in violation of the Equal Pay Act.

I am employed by Insurance, Inc. My employer and my job are in interstate commerce. My job is covered by the minimum wage law. I believe I am protected by the Equal Pay Act.

My employer's main office and the office where I work is as follows:

Insurance, Inc.
100 Commerce Street
My Town, My State 00000

I am employed by Insurance, Inc., as a claims examiner. My job involves reviewing and paying or rejecting claims submitted by our policy holders. Other women in the same job category and I receive $300 per week each, gross pay. The men in a similar job category, who perform the same work as we women perform but who work in a separate office, earn $345 per week gross pay. Because I am a woman I have received unequal pay for equal work ever since I was first employed by Insurance, Inc., on September 1, 1976.

Please investigate this matter and keep me informed of your progress.

Sincerely,

Charging Party

# Implementing 2
## the Bill of Rights
## of Employment Law

### TITLE VII OF THE CIVIL RIGHTS ACT OF 1964, AS AMENDED

[RACE, COLOR, NATIONAL ORIGIN, RELIGION, SEX]

When Willie Griggs sued the Duke Power Company of North Carolina, he never imagined that his case would result in the landmark decision of employment discrimination law.

For many years, Willie Griggs had been employed as a laborer by the Duke Power Company. Like the other blacks at the plant, Mr. Griggs had been assigned to the labor department, the least desirable and lowest paying of the company's many departments. Willie Griggs didn't like it there, but the company didn't employ blacks in other departments.

In the early 1960s, the company finally ended its policy of assigning blacks only to the labor department. And as part of the new policy, it allowed departmental transfers out of the labor department, but only to those employees who possessed a high-school diploma or passed a written aptitude test. Willie Griggs and several of the other blacks in the labor department applied for transfers to the coal handling department. If their transfers were accepted, they would unload, weigh, sample, and transport coal received from the coal mines. And they would double their salaries. They suspected, however, that their efforts to transfer

31

would be futile. They didn't have the required high-school diplomas, and they doubted that they would score high enough on
the aptitude test.

Mr. Griggs and his colleagues felt that they were being unfairly
locked into the low-paying labor department. Many of the white
employees already in the coal handling department and in other
high-paying departments did not have high-school diplomas and
had never been required to pass any tests in order to obtain their
jobs. Additionally, the company conceded that the new requirements had no known relationship to effective job performance in
the higher-paying departments. Believing that they were being
discriminated against, Willie Griggs and several other black
workers filed charges of racial discrimination with the federal
Equal Employment Opportunity Commission. They alleged that
the company's educational and testing requirements were racially discriminatory. When the EEOC failed to resolve the
charges, Willie Griggs and his colleagues filed a class action lawsuit against their employer under Title VII of the Civil Rights Act
of 1964.

Eventually their case made its way to the United States Supreme Court. In the spring of 1971, the Chief Justice of the
Supreme Court, Warren E. Burger, speaking for a unanimous
Court, announced its decision in *Griggs* v. *Duke Power Co.* Employment "practices, procedures, or tests neutral on their face,
and even neutral in terms of intent, cannot be maintained," the
Court held, if they have a discriminatory impact and are "unrelated to measuring job capability."[1]

Under the *Griggs* decision, an employer's good faith or lack
of intent to discriminate is irrelevant. So long as any employment practice—such as a diploma requirement, a written test, a
minimum height standard—is shown to have a discriminatory
impact against minorities or women, and is not shown by the
employer to be directly related to better job performance, then
that practice is unlawful under Title VII. Willie Griggs not only
won his case; he started a revolution in employment discrimination law.

*Title VII of the Civil Rights Act of 1964 is the most comprehen-
sive and most often used of all the federal laws prohibiting*

*employment discrimination. It also is the most specific. It prohibits virtually all forms of discrimination. And it forbids not only practices that are intentionally discriminatory but also practices which have only a discriminatory effect.*

*Title VII was initially enacted in 1964 to prohibit employment discrimination on grounds of race, color, national origin, religion, and sex in private employment. Amended in 1972, Title VII now also prohibits discrimination on the same grounds by state and local governments and by the federal government.*

*Title VII is enforced by the Equal Employment Opportunity Commission through investigation of charges of discrimination and through administrative efforts to obtain voluntary compliance with the law. Title VII also is enforced through lawsuits filed by the EEOC, by the Department of Justice, and by private individuals.*

*When you obtain your rights under Title VII, you are entitled to broad remedies such as hiring, reinstatement, transfer, or promotion—with back pay and retroactive seniority. If you have been discriminated against, you should always seek to win your rights under Title VII.*

## WHO IS COVERED BY THE LAW

Title VII's prohibitions against employment discrimination apply to all medium-size and large employers, to most state and local governments, to labor organizations, and to employment agencies. As the law itself states, Title VII covers:

- All private employers with fifteen or more employees.[2]
- All state and local governments with fifteen or more employees.[3]
- All unions or other labor organizations which maintain a hiring hall or which have fifteen or more members.[4]
- All apprenticeship programs or other training programs.[5]
- All employment agencies which refer persons for potential employment.[6]

By virtue of this broad coverage, all employees, applicants for employment, and other persons who have employment contacts with the above organizations are protected from employment discrimination by Title VII.

Title VII also covers most forms of employment in the *federal government.* In point of fact, it covers all personnel actions affecting employees or applicants for employment in civil service positions in federal executive branch agencies, and in some positions with the legislative and judicial branches of the federal government.[7] The protection provided by Title VII in federal employment, however, is different from the protection provided in other spheres of employment. The difference is that, where Title VII is applicable to federal employment, it is the sole protection available to federal employees and applicants.[8] More will be said about this later.

## DISCRIMINATORY PRACTICES WHICH ARE UNLAWFUL

Title VII broadly prohibits discrimination on grounds of race, color, national origin, religion, or sex.[9]

The scope of the prohibition against sex discrimination, however, was relatively unclear for a number of years because the Supreme Court had difficulty deciding whether discrimination against pregnant women constituted unlawful sex discrimination. In 1978, Congress removed all ambiguities by amending Title VII to make explicit that unlawful sex discrimination includes discrimination "on the basis of pregnancy, childbirth or related medical conditions."[10] In other words, Title VII unquestionably prohibits such sex discriminatory practices as mandatory maternity leaves, loss of seniority during maternity leaves, and exclusion of pregnancy disabilities from disability insurance policies.[11]

Title VII of course prohibits much more than sex discrimination based upon pregnancy. Within Title VII itself, there are a number of *specific provisions* making certain practices discriminatory and unlawful. As we will see, these specific provisions have been widely applied by the federal government and by the courts to prohibit five forms of employment discrimination. But first, let's look at the specific provisions in Title VII itself.

*Specific prohibitions against employment discrimination.* Unlike most other federal laws prohibiting employment discrimination, Title VII enumerates specific practices which are discriminatory and unlawful. Included is nearly every type of discriminatory employment practice you could be faced with. Under the law, an *employer*[12] cannot, on grounds of discrimination:

• Fail or refuse to hire an individual.
• Discharge an individual.
• Limit or classify employees or applicants in any way which would tend to deprive any individual of employment opportunities or otherwise affect his or her status as an employee.
• Otherwise discriminate against any individual with respect to pay or other compensation, or with respect to the terms, conditions, or privileges of employment.

Similarly, a *labor organization*[13] cannot, on grounds of discrimination:

• Exclude or expel individuals from membership.
• Limit, classify, or fail to refer for employment any individual.
• Cause or attempt to cause an employer to discriminate against an individual.

It also is unlawful for an *employer,* a *labor organization,* or any *joint labor-management committee*[14] controlling an apprentice program or other training program to discriminate against any individual in any way in any training program. It is unlawful for an *employment agency,*[15] on grounds of discrimination, to fail or refuse to refer for employment or otherwise discriminate against, any individual. And it is unlawful for an *employer,* a *labor organization,* any *joint labor-management committee,* or any *employment agency*[16] to print or cause to be printed or published any notice or advertisement indicating any preference, limitation, or specifications for individuals of any race, color, national origin, religion, or sex.

Title VII contains an additional prohibition which is of particular importance to those who seek to obtain their rights to nondiscrimination in employment. It is illegal for any *employer, labor organization, joint labor-management committee,* or *employment agency*[17] to:

- Retaliate or otherwise discriminate against any individual who has opposed any unlawful employment practice or who has sought to obtain his or her rights or the rights of others to nondiscrimination in employment.

Under this prohibition, you cannot be denied employment, fired, denied a promotion, or in any other way discriminated against because you seek to eliminate discrimination in your work place. In view of its importance, this prohibition is discussed in some detail later.

## Application of the Prohibitions against Discrimination

Title VII's specific prohibitions have been widely applied against employers and other organizations to stop them from engaging in discriminatory employment practices.

There are, of course, many different types of discriminatory practices. They may be grouped among five categories: overt discrimination, disparate impact discrimination, disparate treatment discrimination, other forms of discrimination, and retaliation. Each of these forms of discrimination, under certain conditions, is illegal. You, however, have to prove the existence of the practices, and you also have to show that they are discriminatory against you. Useful in proving that they are discriminatory are statistics indicating the racially or sexually discriminatory impact of a practice and also work-force statistics showing underrepresentation of women and minorities. In general, proving discrimination is easier than you might think.

## Overt Discrimination

Overt discrimination, when it occurs, is the easiest form of unlawful discrimination to prove. It usually is admitted openly and blatantly. A sign which says NO JEWS, BLACKS, OR WOMEN NEED APPLY needs little explanation.

The enactment of Title VII did not bring an immediate end to overt discrimination. A number of Southern companies continued their overt discrimination by admittedly channeling whites into high-paying job lines while placing blacks in lower-paying job lines.[18] As late as the 1970s, a construction union in New York City refused to accept membership applications from blacks and failed to organize skilled trade shops which employed black workers.[19] These overtly discriminatory practices of course violated Title VII.

Most of the overt discrimination still practiced today is directed against women. An employer in the South which refused to hire women with preschool children but which did hire men with preschool children was found to have violated Title VII.[20] An airline which refused to hire married women but which did hire married men violated Title VII.[21] As recently as 1978, the Chicago Police Department, which refused to assign women to regular patrol sector work, was found to have committed overt discrimination in violation of Title VII.[22]

Fortunately, most forms of overt discrimination are being eliminated. Unfortunately, they often are replaced with other forms of discrimination that are more difficult to prove.

## Disparate Impact Discrimination

The discriminatory practices which adversely affect the largest number of people today are practices which appear to be neutral but which nonetheless have a discriminatory *impact*—usually against minorities and women. Such practices are unlawful unless they are justified by a business necessity. This means that such practices can be used only if they can be shown by the employer to be directly related to producing better job performance and only if no less discriminatory practices are available.[23]

These principles for proving disparate impact discrimination were established by the Supreme Court in *Griggs* v. *Duke Power Co.*,[24] the case in which laborer Willie Griggs proved that his employer's purportedly neutral educational and testing requirements had a discriminatory impact upon blacks. In *Griggs*, the Supreme Court recognized that "Congress directed the thrust of [Title VII] to the consequences of employment practices, not simply the motivation," and thus held that Title VII "proscribes not only overt discrimination but also practices that are fair in form, but discriminatory in operation."[25]

Once an individual like Willie Griggs shows that a practice has a discriminatory impact,[26] that practice is presumed to be illegal. An employer, to repeat, can disprove the presumption and retain the practice only by showing that the practice is a "business necessity" and bears "a manifest relationship to the employment in question" by actually assuring better job performance.[27] In *Griggs*, the Supreme Court held that the employer failed to prove the business necessity of the educational and testing requirements because they were implemented "without a meaningful study of their relationship to job performance ability" and instead were based only on the employer's "judgment that they generally would improve the overall quality of the work force."[28] This was insufficient, said the Supreme Court. Since "neither the high school completion requirement nor the general intelligence test [was] shown to bear a demonstrable relationship to successful performance of the jobs for which it was used," their use violated Title VII.[29]

The standards established by the Supreme Court in *Griggs* have been used to invalidate a wide variety of purportedly neutral employment practices:

• Preferences given to employees' relatives by an employer whose work force was predominantly white have been found to have a disparate impact on blacks and to be non-job-related.[30]

• Minimum height and weight requirements used to disqualify applicants for law enforcement employment have been found to have a disparate impact on women, Chicanos, and Asian Americans and to be non-job-related.[31]

• Denials of employment to applicants with arrest records[32] or with conviction records[33] have been found to have a disparate impact on minorities and to be non-job-related.

• Subjective ratings for promotion made by white supervisors have been found to have a disparate impact on minorities and to be non-job-related.[34]

• Policies requiring the firing of employees who have their wages garnished for non-payment of debts have been found to have a disparate impact on minorities and to be non-job-related.[35]

And, as a direct consequence of *Griggs*, educational[36] and testing[37] requirements have been found in hundreds of cases to have a discriminatory disparate impact and to be non-job-related.

Illustrative of the *Griggs* principle that an employer's good faith is irrelevant in a disparate impact case[38] is a lawsuit won by three black employees against General Motors Corp. several years ago. When they filed their lawsuit, the employees were well aware that General Motors for the previous decade had undertaken an extensive and very successful affirmative action recruitment and hiring program for racial minorities. Nonetheless, the three employees believed that they had been discriminated against by not receiving transfers and promotions to better jobs in the company. The specific practice challenged was the use of word-of-mouth notice from white supervisors about transfer and promotion opportunities plus necessary recommendations from those white supervisors. The court that decided this case recognized the "commendable" results of General Motors' affirmative action recruitment and hiring program. But once blacks were hired, General Motors' responsibility was not over. "Despite efforts and attitudes all should applaud, this Court must look to the actual employment practices of [General Motors] to determine if those practices operate as a barrier against the promotion/transfer of qualified workers."[39] The court looked at those practices, found proof of discriminatory impact, saw they were not defended by the employer as job-related, and held them unlawful under Title VII.

If you are faced with an employment practice which you believe has a discriminatory disparate impact, remember that you have to prove discriminatory impact with statistical evidence. Obtaining the statistics should not be difficult because employers are required to keep them.[40] If you don't obtain the statistics and prove disparate impact, you'll lose.

In one case, a black woman who was denied a job as a data typist sued her potential employer, challenging the employer's tests and oral interview. The employer all but conceded that the tests and interview could not be shown to be job-related. But the unsuccessful applicant failed to show that the practices had a discriminatory impact. "In these circumstances," the court said, "lack of diligence in assembling statistical evidence in support of her case presents us with serious problems." As explained by the court, "nonvalidated tests [tests not shown to be job-related] and subjective hiring procedures are not violative of Title VII *per se.* Title VII comes into play only when such practices result in discrimination."[41] Because this applicant did not show that the practices had a discriminatory impact, she lost her case.

Even if you show that an employment practice has a discriminatory disparate impact, remember that the employer still may retain the practice by proving that use of the practice is a business necessity in that it is directly related to improved job performance and that there are no less discriminatory alternative practices. In order to develop such proof, the employer ordinarily must be prepared to show that the practice has been properly "validated" in accordance with strict federal guidelines and with the standards of the psychological testing profession.[42] This is a very complicated process. Since many employers are not prepared to prove that their practices are "valid" according to these guidelines and standards, nearly all practices which can be shown to have a discriminatory disparate impact will be found to be unlawful.

Once in a while, however, an employer is able to show that a practice with a discriminatory disparate impact is a business necessity and is valid. In one case, a commercial airline successfully defended its policy of hiring only those pilots who had logged 500 hours of flight time.[43] In several other cases employers have demonstrated that their higher-education requirements constituted a business necessity in that they were job-related and there were no alternative selection criteria with a less adverse impact.[44]

These are rather rare examples. Most employers simply cannot show that their discriminatory practices are a business necessity. If you have been the victim of a purportedly neutral practice which has a discriminatory impact, you most likely have been a victim of unlawful discrimination.

## Disparate Treatment Discrimination

Subjective employment practices which are not blatantly discriminatory or which do not necessarily have a statistically disparate impact against a racial group or against women nonetheless may discriminate against you as an individual. If you have been denied a job, rejected for promotion, or fired as the result of a subjective practice which seems to have adversely affected you primarily because of your sex, race, etc., you may be a victim of disparate *treatment* discrimination. As with other discriminatory practices, this form of discrimination usually is unlawful.

Two years after its decision in *Griggs,* the Supreme Court announced the principles which govern disparate treatment discrimination. In *McDonnell Douglas Corp.* v. *Green,* [45] a case involving a company's refusal to rehire a black employee, the Court held that a presumptive case—referred to by lawyers as a "prima facie" case—of discrimination can be established by proving four factors:

• That you are protected by Title VII.
• That you applied and were qualified for a job for which the employer was seeking applicants.
• That despite your qualifications you were rejected.
• That after your rejection the position remained open and the employer continued to seek applications from persons with similar qualifications, or that the position was filled by someone who was not a minority person or a female.

If you are able to establish these four elements (the formula is similar for hiring, firing, promotion, etc.), you then have proved a presumptive case of disparate treatment discrimination. In this situation, the employer's action against you as an individual is unlawful unless the employer can articulate "some legitimate, nondiscriminatory reason" for the disparate treatment. [46] Even if the employer presents such a reason, you still have an opportunity to show that the employer's "stated reason" is "in fact pretext" for discrimination. [47]

Although these principles might appear to be unduly complicated, in practice they are quite simple. In situations where you have been subjected to discriminatory disparate treatment, you can easily establish a prima facie case of discrimination by satisfying the four criteria set forth above. The crucial issue then becomes whether your employer can show that there nonetheless was a "legitimate, nondiscriminatory reason" for its action. In *McDonnell Douglas,* the Court stated that use of purportedly neutral practices such as tests or other criteria which have a discriminatory impact is not a legitimate non-discriminatory reason.[48] This means that the employer's reason must in fact be non-discriminatory.

Illustrative is a case brought by Jeannette Gates, a highly qualified black female accountant who was rejected for an accounting job by an employer in Oregon. Ms. Gates established the four factors: that she was covered by Title VII, that she applied and was qualified, that she was rejected, and that the job remained open. The employer countered by arguing that its refusal was not discriminatory disparate treatment because the company hired accountants under a promotion-from-within policy; since Ms. Gates was not already within the company, she could not be hired. After reviewing the actual operation of the promotion-from-within policy, the court held that the policy could not qualify as a legitimate non-discriminatory reason because there were no blacks in the company's promotion line, and as a result, the promotion-from-within policy had a discriminatory impact. Moreover, since the company at an earlier time had hired a white accountant from outside the company, the "policy" actually was only a pretext for discrimination.[49]

A variation on this theme was encountered by Robert Gilmore, a black man already on the inside who was denied a promotion from within by a railroad in Kansas City. After he had established a presumptive case of discriminatory disparate treatment, the railroad argued that its policy of promoting only those individuals with greater work experience was a legitimate non-discriminatory reason. Not necessarily so, held the court, because the work experience policy itself had a discriminatory impact.[50]

In most disparate treatment situations, employers are unable to justify their actions. Occasionally, however, an employer will have a legitimate non-discriminatory reason. In one case, a black sued the trucking company that discharged him after only ten months of employment as an over-the-road driver. In court, he proved the necessary four elements, thereby establishing a prima facie case of discrimination. The employer, however, insisted that the driver's poor driving record—four preventable accidents in ten months—was a legitimate non-discriminatory reason for the discharge. The driver then contended that this reason was only pretext since the employer's over-the-road work force included 227 whites and only 3 people belonging to minorities. Despite the employer's bad hiring record, the court agreed with the employer that the discharge was based upon the bad driving record and thus was not unlawful disparate treatment discrimination.[51]

## Other Forms of Discrimination

Some forms of discrimination might seem to defy classification. Regardless, so long as the discrimination fits within any of Title VII's specific statutory prohibitions, it usually will be found to be unlawful.

One form which does not fit neatly into any of the above three categories is the sexual harassment imposed upon women by their male supervisors. Where employers knowingly allow such abuse to occur, it violates Title VII's prohibition against discrimination in the terms and conditions of employment.[52] Where a woman resists sexual advances and finds her job abolished[53] or her employment terminated,[54] this too obviously violates Title VII.

Illustrative is the situation of Adrienne Tompkins, a former employee of the Public Service Electric & Gas Co. in Newark, New Jersey. Hired as an office worker in 1971, she was promoted in 1973 to the position of executive secretary under the direction of a male executive. That's when her troubles began. He invited her to lunch to discuss his upcoming evaluation of her work. During lunch he made sexual advances and told her that they would have to have sexual relations if they were to have a satisfactory working relationship. Adrienne Tompkins refused. She attempted to leave the restaurant, but he physically restrained her. He warned her that there would be trouble for her on the job if she complained about his actions to anyone in the company. Undaunted, Adrienne Tompkins immediately complained to his superiors, who promised her a transfer to a comparable position in the company. Instead, she was transferred to an inferior position, and later was threatened with further demotions. In January 1975, Ms. Tompkins was fired. Outraged, she sued. And won. The court held that her supervisor's sexual harassment, ac-

quiesced in and later compounded by the company, violated
Title VII's prohibition against discrimination in the terms and
conditions of employment.[55]

## Retaliation

Adrienne Tompkins's case brings us to a form of discrimination
explicitly prohibited by Title VII: retaliation. Title VII states that
it is unlawful for an *employer*, a *labor organization*, or a *joint
labor-management committee* to discriminate in any way against
any person who "has opposed any practice" made unlawful by
Title VII or who "has made a charge, testified, assisted, or par-
ticipated in any manner in any investigation, proceeding or hearing" to enforce non-discrimination in employment.[56] Under this
prohibition, any retaliation against you is unlawful regardless of
whether the underlying practice being opposed or investigated
in fact is unlawful.[57]

This specific prohibition in Title VII provides you and your
colleagues with at least some protection against possible retaliation. Most employers that have been charged with retaliation
have been found to have violated Title VII. For example, an
insurance company that discharged a woman who filed a charge
of sex discrimination was held to have violated Title VII.[58] A
savings-and-loan association that fired a white male who opposed
his boss's discriminatory practices against women was held to
have violated Title VII.[59] And a bank that gave bad recommendations to other employers about a former employee who had
filed a charge of sex discrimination against the bank was held to
have violated Title VII.[60]

Title VII's protection against retaliation, however, does not
give you license to direct an antidiscrimination campaign on
company time. This lesson was learned the hard way by a female
microbiologist in Massachusetts. After winning an equal-pay lawsuit against her employer, she later charged her boss with sex
discrimination in the terms and conditions of employment. But
she didn't stop there. She disrupted meetings with sex discrimination protests; urged her colleagues to take sides or leave; used
secretarial services, copy-machine services, and her office telephone to campaign against the employer's sex discrimination;

and released confidential employment information to local newspapers. Ultimately, she was fired. Again she sued her boss, this time for retaliation. Her boss conceded that the quality of her scientific research was excellent, but he argued that the discharge was lawful because she went too far in the scope and style of her protests. The court agreed, finding that Title VII does not "grant sanctuary to employees to engage in political activity for women's liberation on company time," and that an "employer remains entitled to loyalty and cooperativeness from employees."[61]

While Title VII's prohibition against retaliation may not protect activist antidiscrimination campaigns on the job, it nonetheless does provide you with some protection when you and your colleagues decide to oppose discriminatory employment practices. To a certain extent, unfortunately, Title VII's protection against retaliation is only a paper protection. Just as many employers still engage in discrimination, they also engage in retaliation. Since fighting for your rights is not always appreciated, you probably should anticipate at least subtle forms of harassment whenever you set forth to win your rights.

## Statistical Proof of Discrimination

Whenever you are adversely affected by an employer's purportedly neutral practice, statistics enable you to show—as you must—that the practice has a discriminatory disparate impact. In other instances, where you have been individually discriminated against and where you have a presumptive case of discriminatory disparate treatment, statistics enable you to show that the employer's alleged non-discriminatory reason in fact has a discriminatory impact and thus is not legitimate.

Other sets of statistics which are not necessary to prove discrimination nonetheless can be very helpful. They include statistics about the composition of your employer's work force, about the surrounding labor force, and about the surrounding population as a whole. These statistics almost always will show severe underemployment of minorities and women in your employer's work force.

Although an employer's work force is not required to mirror

the racial, ethnic, religious, or sexual makeup of the surrounding labor force or of the surrounding population,[62] statistics showing a substantial imbalance are highly useful and sometimes crucial in proving discrimination. As the Supreme Court has stated, "Imbalance is often a telltale sign of . . . discrimination; absent explanation, it is ordinarily to be expected that nondiscriminatory hiring practices will in time result in a work force more or less representative of the racial and ethnic [and religious and sexual] composition of the population in the community from which employees are hired."[63] Where an employer's work force is required to be highly skilled or highly educated in order to perform successfully, the relevant comparative statistics are skilled labor force statistics rather than general population statistics.[64] In either case, the Supreme Court has recognized that proof of statistical imbalance serves an " 'important role' . . . in proving employment discrimination."[65] If you can show that the underrepresentation is especially severe, the statistics alone may be sufficient to prove that the employer has violated Title VII.[66]

But you must be careful here because some statistics can work against you. If, for example, the relevant statistics reveal that your employer's work force is racially and sexually balanced, this may support an employer's argument that you in fact have not been discriminated against.[67] Balanced work forces, however, are quite rare.

A more serious concern is that some employers—especially those with severely imbalanced work forces—will present misleading statistics and computer data tending to show that their work forces are more balanced than they actually are. When this occurs, you have to be prepared to show that their statistical analyses are wrong.

Given the importance of statistics in proving unlawful discrimination under Title VII, and given the fact that minorities and women are almost always severely underrepresented in employers' work forces, particularly at the higher-pay levels, you should always obtain, investigate, and analyze the relevant statistics. Ordinarily this will require the professional help of both a statistician and a lawyer. It's worth it. When your statistical analyses are properly prepared, they invariably will support your claim of unlawful discrimination.

# MAJOR EXCEPTIONS

As you might suspect, Title VII contains several categories of exceptions. Some employers are exempted from Title VII with regard to certain forms of employment. Under a broader category, a number of employment practices which appear to be discriminatory nonetheless are permissible because of specific statutory exceptions. A third category at least arguably works in your favor: affirmative action benefiting women and minorities is not unlawful.

Before we review these exceptions, you should remember that Title VII prohibits discrimination only on grounds of race, color, national origin, religion, and sex. Discrimination on grounds of age is not prohibited. Several other forms of discrimination are subject to finer distinctions.

Title VII's prohibition against discrimination on grounds of national origin does not protect an alien from discrimination against non-citizens.[68] For example, a non-citizen from Mexico can be denied employment by an employer who has a policy against hiring non-citizens. That same company, on the other hand, cannot deny employment to a Chicano who is a citizen on the ground that it refuses to hire persons of Mexican origin.

Title VII's bar against sex discrimination protects men as well as women.[69] It, however, does not bar discrimination against homosexuals or against men who are "effeminate."[70]

The form of discrimination which, in past years, the courts had the most difficulty in defining was sex discrimination involving pregnancy. In 1976, the Supreme Court held that Title VII's prohibition against sex discrimination did not bar discrimination on grounds of pregnancy.[71] Realizing later that discrimination on grounds of pregnancy affects only members of the female sex, the Supreme Court in 1977 backtracked and held that some forms of sex discrimination on the basis of pregnancy were prohibited by Title VII.[72] In 1978, Congress rescued the Supreme Court from its dilemma, overruled the Court's 1976 decision, and prohibited sex discrimination on grounds of pregnancy.[73] Discrimination against women who are pregnant is no longer even a partial exception under Title VII. It is unlawful.

## Exempted Employers and Employment

Title VII, as we saw at the outset of this chapter, describes the employers and other organizations which are covered by the prohibitions against employment discrimination. Those not indicated as covered simply are not covered.

Title VII also has several specific statutory exemptions which allow some employers to discriminate at least in some respects. Bona fide, tax-exempt, private membership clubs are wholly exempted.[74] Religious organizations, including schools, are exempted with respect to the employment of persons who perform work connected with the organizations' religious activities.[75] Businesses on or near Indian reservations are exempted with respect to the use of preferential employment practices which favor Indians.[76] Government employers are exempted with regard to employment in elected positions and in positions within an elected official's personal staff.[77] And all employers in general are exempted with regard to federally recognized "national security" jobs, but only with respect to individuals who do not meet "national security" requirements.[78]

## Employment Practices Subject to Statutory Exceptions

The foregoing exemptions do not seriously alter the basic protection under Title VII against discrimination on grounds of race, color, national origin, religion, or sex. There are, however, five statutory exceptions which have the potential, and in some instances already have been applied, to dilute Title VII's broad protection. First, payment of unequal wages on a sex discriminatory basis is lawful under Title VII to the extent that it is authorized by the Equal Pay Act.[79] Next, practices which are discriminatory on grounds of national origin, religion, or sex are lawful if an employer can show that national origin, religion, or sex is a bona fide occupational qualification necessary for effective job performance.[80] Also, discrimination against a person because of his or her religion is lawful if an employer cannot reasonably accommodate the person's religious practices without undue hardship.[81] And seniority systems, regardless of their discriminatory impact upon minorities and women (especially with regard to last-hired, first-fired layoffs), are lawful so long as they are bona fide seniority systems.[82] Finally, veterans' preference laws, despite their discriminatory impact on women in hiring and promotion in public employment, are not made unlawful under Title VII.[83] The first two exceptions remain quite narrow. The next two were given unduly broad interpretations by the Supreme Court in 1977. The fifth exception, sanctioning veterans' preference laws, poses a severe barrier to equal opportunity for women in public employment.

*Equal Pay Act.* Under the first exception, it is lawful for an employer "to differentiate upon the basis of sex in determining the amount of the wages or compensation paid to the employees of such employer if such differentiation is authorized by" the Equal Pay Act.[84] This exception is virtually harmless because the Equal Pay Act in general does *not authorize* unequal wages based upon sex.[85] To the contrary, it compels employers to pay to women the same wages that are paid to men on jobs which require substantially equal skill, effort, and responsibility and which are performed under similar working conditions. There are, however, four very narrow exceptions to the equal-pay mandate of the Equal Pay Act. It is these narrow exceptions which are incorporated into Title VII.[86]

If you are in a situation where you are being denied equal compensation because of your sex, turn back to Chapter 1, where the coverage and exceptions of the Equal Pay Act are explained in detail. As you will see, the Equal Pay Act's protections have been quite broadly interpreted and applied. For present purposes, it is enough to remember that Title VII's general bar against sex discrimination in the payment of compensation has been "construed in harmony with the Equal Pay Act."[87] As discussed in Chapter 8, some women have wisely used both Title VII and the Equal Pay Act against their employers in order to obtain the benefits of both laws.[88]

*Bona fide occupational qualification.* Another narrow exception to Title VII allows an employer or any other organization to discriminate on the basis of national origin, religion, or sex "in those certain instances" where national origin, religion, or sex "is a bona fide occupational qualification reasonably necessary to the normal operation of that particular business or enterprise."[89] Although this bona fide occupational qualification exception— generally referred to as the "bfoq" exception—arguably could allow some forms of discrimination on grounds of national origin and religion, the exception has been raised by employers only as a defense to their sex discrimination. In nearly every instance, the employers have lost.

Interpreting this exception, the Supreme Court has held that a bona fide occupational qualification cannot be based upon "stereotyped characterizations of the sexes," and "that the bfoq exception was in fact meant to be an extremely narrow exception to the general prohibition of discrimination on the basis of sex."[90] Another court has stated that it is "only when the *essence* of the business operation would be undermined" that the bona fide occupational qualification exception could be applied.[91] Given this narrow interpretation, the exception cannot be used to discriminate on the basis of sex because of assumed turnover rates, or because of co-worker or client preference.[92] Similarly, it cannot be used to deny women the opportunity to apply for manual labor jobs simply because women in general are assumed to be not as strong as men.[93] In fact, the federal guidelines interpreting the exception allow its use only where gender is necessary for authenticity or genuineness, such as in hiring a model.[94]

For fourteen years after the enactment of Title VII, no employer had succeeded in using the bona fide occupational qualification exception as a defense against charges of sex discrimination. In 1978, however, the Supreme Court, despite rhetoric that the exception could not be based upon sexual stereotypes, used it to deny a woman employment as a state prison correctional counselor because the employee's role was "to maintain prison security" in a job that was "a 'contact' position in a maximum security male prison."[95]

As a result of the Supreme Court's reliance on sexual stereotypes, the previously narrow bona fide occupational qualification exception possibly could become broader. But given the somewhat extreme circumstances surrounding the correctional counselor job, the exception can be expected to remain very narrow.

Shortly after the Supreme Court's decision, another court rejected an employer's argument that sex was a bona fide occupational qualification for the position of identification assistant officer in a county jail. The jail, in Mobile, Alabama, housed only male inmates, half of whom were charged with felonies. The job in question required the officer to fingerprint and photograph incoming prisoners in a small room in the basement of the jail. This job was deemed by the court to be much different from the state prison correctional counselor's job, which "was a 'contact' position requiring a great deal of personal physical interaction with the men incarcerated" in a " '*male maximum security* penitentiary.' "[96] Because the "county jail is not a maximum security facility," because the job in question "is, at best, a *minimum* 'contact' position without any real supervisory requirements," and because the job "does not have as its 'essence' the 'maintenance of security,' " the bona fide occupational qualification exception was deemed to be inapplicable.[97]

For the most part, you can assume the bona fide occupational qualification exception is indeed narrow. But you should be aware that some employers have been encouraged by the Supreme Court's decision, and they may try to rely on it to deny women jobs.

*Reasonable accommodation and undue hardship.* Discrimination on the basis of religion has not yet been widely discussed in this chapter. There is a reason for this. It is not because employers do not discriminate on grounds of religion. Rather, it is because Title VII contains an exception which recently was interpreted to be almost as broad as Title VII's prohibition against religious discrimination.

Under the exception, an employer may discriminate against you on grounds of religion if the employer "demonstrates that he is unable to reasonably accommodate to an employee's or prospective employee's religious observance or practice without undue hardship on the conduct of the employer's business."[98] Crucial to this exception is the meaning of "reasonably accommodate" and "undue hardship."

In 1977, the Supreme Court interpreted this language as giving considerable leeway to employers. At issue in the case was whether three forms of accommodation were reasonable or posed an undue hardship on the employer. The employee, a Seventh Day Adventist whose religious observance prohibited him from working on Saturdays, argued that it was reasonable for the employer to allow him to bid for a different work shift contrary to the seniority provisions of the collective-bargaining agreement, to allow him to work a four-day work week, or to allow another employee to work overtime to cover the work on Saturdays. The Supreme Court held that each proffered accommodation would impose an undue hardship on the employer. As to the collective bargaining agreement accommodation, the Court stated: "We do not believe that the duty to accommodate requires [an employer] to take steps inconsistent with the otherwise valid agreement."[99] As to the other two accommodations, the Court stated: "Both of these alternatives would involve cost to [the employer], either in the form of lost efficiency in other jobs or as higher wages. To require [an employer] to bear more than a *de minimus* cost . . . is an undue hardship."[100]

The Supreme Court's decision, however, did not wholly eviscerate Title VII's prohibition against religious discrimination.[101] In several recent cases, employers that fired Seventh Day Adventists who refused to pay union dues on religious grounds were found to have made insufficient efforts at reasonable accommodation and thus were held to have violated Title VII.[102] On the other hand, employer refusals to hire or retain employees who would not work on Saturdays have been deemed lawful.[103]

Unquestionably, the Supreme Court's decision was a major setback to the efforts to prohibit religious discrimination.

*Bona fide seniority systems.* The Supreme Court in 1977 gave another expansive reading, again favoring employers and unions, to another of Title VII's exceptions, an exception which makes it lawful for an employer to apply different compensation, terms, conditions, or privileges of employment "pursuant to a bona fide seniority . . . system . . . provided that such differences are not the result of an intention to discriminate."[104] Until 1977, the unanimous judicial interpretation of this exception was that any seniority system which had a discriminatory impact was not bona fide, and that the exception thus did "not immunize seniority systems that perpetuate the effects of prior discrimination."[105]

Under this interpretation, seniority systems which resulted in disadvantages for minorities and women seeking transfers from low-paying jobs in one department to higher-paying jobs in another department were unlawful.[106] So, too, were seniority systems which worked to the disadvantage of recently hired minorities and women during layoffs.[107]

In 1977, the Supreme Court disagreed with this approach and held that the exception immunized all seniority systems, regardless of their discriminatory impact, unless they were adopted with an intent to discriminate.[108]

The result of this decision is best illustrated through layoffs made on the basis of a seniority system which perpetuated the effects of past discrimination. In New York City, women were not hired as regular police officers until 1973. Before that, a small number of women had been hired, but only as "policewomen." In vastly larger numbers, men had been hired as "patrolmen." In 1973, the city ended its sex discriminatory practice of limiting the job opportunities available to women, and began employing women and men alike as "police officers." Shortly thereafter, as a result of New York City's fiscal crisis, the city had to lay off more than five thousand police officers. Under the seniority system's last-hired, first-fired layoff policy, 74 percent of the women on the force were laid off, while only 24 percent of the men were affected. The recently hired female officers sued, contending that the seniority system was unlawful because it perpetuated past discrimination. Because of the Supreme Court's 1977 decision, they lost.[109]

Although the Supreme Court's 1977 decision means that most seniority systems are lawful regardless of their discriminatory impact, the decision does not affect the right of a person who has been otherwise discriminated against, for example in hiring, to obtain an individual remedy which includes retroactive seniority.[110] This remedy, among others, is discussed later in this chapter.

*Veterans' preference laws.*   The final statutory exception is exceedingly broad in that it allows extensive discrimination against women in public employment. Specifically, Title VII states that it shall not "be construed to repeal or modify any Federal, State, territorial, or local law creating special rights or preference for veterans."[111]

The impact of this exception is substantial. The federal government and most state and local governments give extra points and sometimes an absolute preference to veterans in hiring and promotion. Because of past and present sex discrimination in our armed forces, nearly all veterans are men. Whenever a woman competes with a veteran for a job, the veteran almost always will win. There is no question that this is disparate impact discrimination. Yet, because of the statutory exception in Title VII, such discrimination against women is lawful.

### Affirmative Action Is Not Unlawful

There is one exception which does work in your favor: affirmative action on behalf of minorities and women does not violate Title VII. In fact, the federal guidelines interpreting Title VII encourage employers to implement affirmative-action programs using numerical goals and timetables, and to affirmatively hire and promote more minorities and women.[112] More importantly, the Supreme Court has expressly upheld the voluntary use of numerical ratios, goals, and timetables in private employment as lawful under Title VII.[113]

Although affirmative action is *not required* under Title VII, it can be required of employers that have engaged in extensive discrimination against minorities or women in the past. As we will see later in this chapter, those employers who are successfully charged with discrimination can be ordered to undertake extensive affirmative action to overcome the continuing effects of their past discriminatory practices.

## THE FEDERAL AGENCY RESPONSIBLE FOR ENFORCEMENT

Title VII was enacted with the hope that many instances of discrimination could be resolved informally without the need for individual lawsuits. To accomplish this objective, Congress created a new federal agency, the Equal Employment Opportunity Commission. Unfortunately, Congress did not delegate much power to the new agency. Then, as now, the EEOC was authorized to receive charges of discrimination from individuals, to investigate those charges, and to attempt to resolve the discrimination informally.[114] When informal efforts fail, the EEOC also is empowered to file lawsuits against employers and other covered organizations.

The EEOC has district and area offices in all major cities across the country. The locations of these offices are listed in Chapter 9. The central office of the EEOC is located in Washington, D.C.:

Equal Employment Opportunity Commission
Columbia Plaza Highrise
2401 E Street, N.W.
Washington, D.C. 20506

202/634-7040

The EEOC plays an important role in enforcing Title VII. But the responsibility for initiating that enforcement, as we shall see, remains with those individuals who have been discriminated against.

## ENFORCEMENT: HOW TO OBTAIN YOUR RIGHTS

Winning your rights under Title VII sometimes can seem complicated. In fact, some of the administrative procedures described on the following pages are a bit tricky and cumbersome. But you need to know about them to obtain your rights. Under Title VII, it is up to you, at least initially, to assert and win your rights.

The first step toward obtaining your rights is knowing whether your employer is covered by Title VII and whether the discriminatory practices in fact are unlawful. As a second step, you should gather as much evidence as possible to support your claim: take notes, gather documents and statistics, and talk to colleagues who might be able to testify on your behalf. With this information, you're ready to act.

If you are an employee or an applicant for employment who has been discriminated against by a private employer, state or local government, employment agency or labor union, there are three ways for you to obtain your rights:

• A charge of discrimination which you file with the EEOC may be administratively resolved by the EEOC to your satisfaction.

• A charge of discrimination which you file with the EEOC may result in a successful lawsuit brought by the EEOC or by the Department of Justice on your behalf.

• A charge of discrimination which you file with the EEOC might lead to a successful lawsuit brought by you.

If you are a federal employee or applicant for federal employment, there is a slightly different route to follow to obtain your rights:

• A complaint of discrimination which you file with your discriminatory federal agency and which can be appealed to the EEOC may result in a satisfactory administrative resolution of the discrimination, or may lead to a successful lawsuit brought by you.

All of these methods of enforcement require you to file an administrative charge alleging that your boss has discriminated against you because of your race, color, national origin, religion, or sex. This formal step, and all succeeding steps, are encumbered with strict administrative procedures and short time periods. *These procedures and time periods must be complied with in order for you to obtain your rights. If you do not comply, you will not be able to obtain your rights, no matter how severely you have been discriminated against.*

## Administrative Resolution of Charges of Discrimination

The primary role of the EEOC is to investigate charges of discrimination and to seek to resolve those charges through informal negotiations. Charges may be made by any person claiming discrimination, by another person on behalf of a person who may have been discriminated against, or in rare instances by the EEOC on its own initiative.[115] If you believe that you have been discriminated against in violation of Title VII by a private employer, state or local government, employment agency, or labor union, and if you want to stop that discrimination, you or your representative (a friend or your lawyer) must file an administrative charge with the EEOC.

A charge of discrimination is simply a written complaint outlining the discrimination. There is an official EEOC form (with four carbon copies attached) which the EEOC prefers you to use for making a charge. A copy of this official form is set forth at the end of this chapter. *You don't have to use it.* A thorough letter is sufficient as a charge. In your charge, you should:

• Give your name, address, and phone number.
• State the names and addresses of all the parties (employer, union, etc.) that discriminated against you, and the size of the party (number of employees or members).
• Indicate when the discrimination occurred, and whether you have filed a charge with a state or local agency.
• Describe fully the nature of the discrimination which was practiced against you.

Your charge obviously *must* be in writing. It also *must* be signed, and *must* be sworn to under oath.[116] If these requirements are not met, the EEOC might not be able to investigate or to resolve your charge, and any lawsuit which is subsequently filed by the EEOC, by the Department of Justice, or by you against your boss can be dismissed.[117]

Your charge *must* be filed with the EEOC within 180 days of the discriminatory act. Or, if you are located in an area where there is a state or local human rights agency which is similar to the federal EEOC, and if you file a charge with that agency first, you then *must* file your charge with the EEOC within 300 days of the discriminatory act or within 30 days after that agency notifies you that it has ended its proceedings, whichever occurs first.[118] Don't be confused about the existence of state or local agencies. It usually is best to file first with the EEOC and to forget about any state or local agency, because the EEOC in any event will refer your charge to the appropriate state or local agency for 60 days before assuming jurisdiction.

These time limits for filing charges are strict. They must be observed even if you are pursuing other means of redress, such as filing a union grievance.[119] In very rare circumstances, however, the time limits might be waived if the discrimination against you is a "continuing act," such as a continuing refusal to promote you.[120] But, in general, the 180-day or 300-day time limits *must* be met. If you fail to meet the time limits, the EEOC usually will not be able to help you, and any subsequent lawsuit can be dismissed.[121]

Filing your charge is accomplished by bringing it personally or sending it to the nearest office of the EEOC or to the EEOC's main office in Washington, D.C.

After the EEOC receives your administrative charge of discrimination, it first will refer the charge to an appropriate state or local human rights agency, if there is one, for a period of 60 days, unless the state or local agency terminates its proceedings more quickly.[122] Thereafter, if the administrative charge alleges prohibited discrimination against a non-federal employer or union covered by Title VII, the EEOC will assume jurisdiction of the charge, notify the respondent (employer, union, etc.) of the charge within 10 days, and investigate the alleged discrimination. The investigation may include EEOC requests for documents from you or your employer and testimony from you and your colleagues. Thereafter, the EEOC may make a finding of reasonable cause to believe that the charge is true or of no reasonable cause. If the EEOC makes a finding of reasonable cause, the EEOC is required to attempt to eliminate the unlawful employment practice through "informal methods of conference, conciliation, and persuasion."[123] This means that EEOC officials will try to persuade your employer to stop its discrimination and to remedy past actions by hiring you, reinstating you, promoting you, or providing other relief. If the EEOC is unable to secure an acceptable conciliation agreement, the EEOC may sue your employer if it is a private employer, or the Department of Justice may sue if your employer is a state or local government.[124]

All of these administrative enforcement procedures necessarily will involve you directly. For example, the EEOC prefers that you file your charge in person. If you mail your charge to the EEOC, representatives of the EEOC nonetheless might insist that you rewrite your charge in person at the nearest EEOC office. Once you are there, the EEOC representatives may urge you to limit the scope of your charges. They sometimes try this because they know that it will make both the investigation and the resolution of the charge easier. If the discrimination against you and others has been widespread, you should resist any attempts to narrow your charge. *You are in control. It is your charge, and you can and should charge your bosses with the full extent of the discrimination that has occurred.*

Another procedure which will involve you directly is the EEOC's predetermination settlement conference. Under this recently adopted procedure, the EEOC will try to bring you and your boss together, face to face, to try to resolve the discriminatory employment practice before the EEOC has even investigated your charge. Because of this procedure, you must be ready and willing to confront your boss. And you should be prepared to argue for the remedy which you have decided is appropriate.

The purpose of the informal predetermination settlement conference and of the more formal conciliation procedures which may occur later is to obtain a written agreement in which the employer agrees to stop the discrimination and to provide you with a remedy. The agreement, which usually will be proposed by the EEOC, must be agreed to by you and by your employer in order to be valid. If you don't find the proposed agreement satisfactory, you don't have to agree.

If the employer refuses to enter into a conciliation agreement, or if you find the proposed agreement unsatisfactory, the next step usually is the filing of a lawsuit by the EEOC, by the Department of Justice, or by you.

## Lawsuits by the EEOC or by the Department of Justice

The second method of enforcement involves the filing of a lawsuit on your behalf by the EEOC or by the Department of

Justice. The EEOC is authorized to sue private employers, unions, etc. The Justice Department's authorization permits it to sue state and local government employers, etc. Overall, they are entitled to bring four different types of lawsuits—each of which usually is premised upon your having filed a timely charge of discrimination with the EEOC.

First, when an employer refuses to provide the EEOC with information and documents it requests, the EEOC or the Department of Justice may file a lawsuit against the employer to acquire the desired information and documentation.[125]

Second, if the EEOC concludes on the basis of a preliminary investigation that prompt judicial action is necessary to protect rights guaranteed by Title VII, the EEOC or the Department of Justice may file a lawsuit against the employer and may seek a temporary restraining order and a preliminary injunction to stop the employer's discrimination.[126] For example, if you file a charge of discrimination and your boss retaliates against you by firing you, the EEOC or the Department of Justice may sue immediately to have you reinstated.[127]

Third, if the EEOC has made a finding of reasonable cause against an employer and has been unable to obtain an acceptable conciliation agreement, the EEOC or the Justice Department may file a lawsuit against the employer to eliminate the unlawful employment practices.[128]

Fourth, whenever the EEOC or the Justice Department has reasonable cause to believe that an employer is engaged in a "pattern or practice" of discrimination—discrimination against others besides you—the EEOC or the Department of Justice may file a pattern or practice lawsuit against the employer.[129]

The purpose of these four types of lawsuits of course is to enforce your rights to non-discrimination in employment. It almost always is to your advantage to have the EEOC or the Department of Justice sue your boss on your behalf. When this occurs, the power and resources of the federal government will be used against your employer. You won't have to find a lawyer, and you won't have to bear the burden or expense of suing your boss. And, if you don't like the way the lawsuit is being handled, you can always sue your boss too by "intervening" in the government's lawsuit.[130]

## Lawsuits by Individuals

The third method of enforcement is a lawsuit filed by you. Suing on your own, however, presents certain hurdles, not just opportunities. Suing can be expensive, and it raises the problem of finding a lawyer. It also highlights the importance of following the administrative procedures and time periods. On the other hand, you don't have to proceed alone, for there is always the possibility of your suing not only for yourself but also on behalf of other individuals who similarly have been discriminated against by your boss.

*Finding a lawyer.* If you believe that it ultimately will be necessary for you to sue your boss, you'd better begin to look for a lawyer. Usually you should retain an attorney as early as possible. If your diligent efforts to find an attorney are unsuccessful, you're not out of luck, for Title VII explicitly authorizes the courts to appoint a lawyer for you.[131] In order to obtain a court-appointed lawyer, you have to go to court and make an application for appointment of counsel. In your application, you ordinarily have to show that you have a meritorious case, and that you have tried but have been unable to find a lawyer or are financially unable to hire one.[132] This is the route that was followed by Adrienne Tompkins, who, with her court-appointed counsel, sued her boss for sexual harassment and won.[133]

*Following the administrative prerequisites.* In order to sue your boss, you have to comply with Title VII's administrative procedures. Most important are the procedures governing the timing of your charge and the timing of your lawsuit. Your charge, of course, must be timely. As we have seen, you must have filed a sworn administrative charge of discrimination with the EEOC within 180 days of the discriminatory actions, or within 300 days of the discrimination if you first filed a charge with a state or local human rights agency.[134]

Your lawsuit also must be timely. Timeliness here involves what is known as a "right-to-sue letter"—a letter from the government informing you that the EEOC proceedings have concluded and that you have a right to sue within 90 days. You cannot sue without the letter. You can obtain a right-to-sue letter from the EEOC (if your boss is a private employer) or from the Department of Justice (if your boss is a state or local government) after your charge has been lodged with the EEOC for 180 days, or sometimes sooner. Then you must act quickly. You must file your lawsuit within 90 days after you receive your right-to-sue letter.[135]

Some courts have referred to these requirements as "jurisdictional"[136]—which means that your lawsuit can be dismissed if the requirements have not been met. Individuals who have been only a few days tardy in filing an administrative charge,[137] or in filing a lawsuit,[138] have had their lawsuits dismissed. It cannot be too strongly emphasized that Title VII's administrative prerequisites *must* be complied with.

One important exception to the foregoing requirements, recognized by a few courts,[139] allows you to sue your boss immediately if you are fired for filing a charge of discrimination. If this occurs, and if you can prove that the discharge was unlawful retaliation, the court might order your boss to reinstate you immediately.

In addition to the timing requirements, there are several other possible stumbling blocks. When you sue in court, you can name as defendants (your employer, union, etc.) only those parties whom you named as respondents in your administrative charge.[140] Also, the employment practices which you challenge in court must be the same as, or at least "reasonably related" to, the practices which you complained about in your administrative charge.[141] The lesson here is that the charge you file with the EEOC should be as broad as possible: it should name all the parties which may have contributed to the discrimination against you, it should fully describe all of the practices which may have had an adverse discriminatory impact on you, and it should allege each form of discrimination (race, sex, etc.) that may have been practiced against you.

Once you have met these prerequisites, your lawsuit cannot be dismissed because of the EEOC's failure to perform its duties.[142] Your case *cannot* be dismissed because the EEOC failed to serve a copy of the charge on the named respondents,[143] because the

EEOC did not investigate the charge,[144] because the EEOC never made a finding of reasonable cause,[145] because the EEOC made a finding of no reasonable cause,[146] or because the EEOC never attempted conciliation.[147] Nor can your lawsuit be dismissed even if you refused to conciliate.[148]

*Suing for yourself and on behalf of others similarly situated.*
When you go to court, you may want to sue not only for yourself but also on behalf of other persons who also have been discriminated against by your employer, union, etc. Such a lawsuit is called a class action lawsuit. If you win, you will obtain remedies such as back pay not only for yourself but also for all other persons who were similarly discriminated against.

The procedures involving class actions are too technical to be reviewed in this book.[149] One detail, however, needs to be mentioned. In filing a class action lawsuit under Title VII, only one of the plaintiffs (the persons suing) needs to have complied with Title VII's administrative prerequisites. Other plaintiffs and unidentified members of the class need not even have filed a charge of discrimination with the EEOC.[150] Therefore, even if you have not met the administrative prerequisites but someone else has, you too may join the other person's lawsuit either as a plaintiff or as a member of the class.

There are many considerations relevant to whether you should sue in a class action lawsuit. Some of them are discussed in Chapters 9 and 10. In all candor, however, the best advice is to consult your lawyer.

## Federal Employment: Complaints and Lawsuits by Federal Employees and Applicants

The Title VII enforcement procedures discussed so far apply to individuals who have been subjected to discriminatory practices by employers and organizations which are *not* part of the federal government. The procedures for enforcing Title VII against the federal government are somewhat different from those just discussed. In fact, overall, there are four differences which federal employees and applicants need to know. First, the administrative procedures are stricter and the time periods shorter. Next, only individuals and not the EEOC or Department of Justice are authorized to sue the federal government. Also, the time period within which you must sue your federal employer is shorter. Finally, Title VII provides the only means by which you may obtain your rights to non-discrimination in federal employment. Cumulatively, these differences make Title VII more difficult to enforce against the federal government. Federal employees and applicants thus have to be especially careful about asserting their rights.

*Administrative procedures.* The Title VII administrative procedures required of federal employees and applicants are unnecessarily intricate, and the time periods are too short. Nonetheless, they *must* be complied with.

Within 30 days of the discriminatory act, you *must* bring the matter to the attention of your federal agency's Equal Employment Opportunity Counselor. After informal proceedings with the counselor, and within only 15 days of the "final interview" with the counselor, you *must* file with your agency a formal, written, signed complaint alleging discrimination. Thereafter, the agency itself will investigate the complaint and attempt an administrative "adjustment" of the matter. If an "adjustment" is not reached, and if you desire an agency hearing on the complaint, you immediately *must* request a hearing. With or without the hearing, the agency will reach a "final" agency decision. If you are dissatisfied with the agency decision, you can sue your boss in court, or, alternatively, you can appeal the agency decision to the EEOC.[151] If you appeal and are dissatisfied with the EEOC decision, the only remaining method of enforcement available is to go to court.

Given these short and sometimes confusing time periods, you should be in frequent contact with the agency's Equal Employment Opportunity Counselor. The counselor is there to assist you with every step.

*No lawsuits by the government.* If you are not satisfied with your agency's or the EEOC's administrative decision, you cannot expect the federal government to sue your federal agency. Neither the EEOC, the Department of Justice, nor any other arm of the federal government is authorized to sue your federal agency for employment discrimination.

*Private lawsuit procedures.* If the discrimination is not resolved satisfactorily through the administrative procedures, and if you wish to sue your federal agency, your lawsuit *must* be filed within 30 days of notice of the final agency decision or of the EEOC decision.[152] Obviously, this time period, like the others, is very short. But they all *must* be complied with if you want to be protected at all by Title VII in federal employment. If you fail to meet any of the time requirements, your lawsuit undoubtedly will be dismissed.[153]

Once you get into court, your proof of discrimination need not be limited to the evidence you produced in the administrative hearings. Although discriminatory federal agencies in the past argued that the courts were limited to the administrative record, the Supreme Court disagreed and held that you can supplement that record with additional evidence, documents, and testimony supporting your claim of discrimination.[154] This procedure allows federal employees and applicants to prove discrimination against a federal agency in the same manner that other persons prove discrimination against non-federal employers.[155]

*Title VII is exclusive for federal employees and applicants.* Persons who have been discriminated against by non-federal employers can use any of the applicable laws in this book to stop the discrimination. Federal employees and applicants do not share these options.

When a federal employee or applicant is discriminated against on grounds of race, color, national origin, religion, or sex by a federal agency covered by Title VII, that employee or applicant has only one means to vindicate his or her rights to non-discrimination: through Title VII.[156] In other words, since Title VII is your only hope in federal employment, it is especially important that you comply with Title VII's administrative procedures and short time periods. Otherwise, you won't be able to obtain any remedy for unlawful discrimination.

## REMEDIES: WHAT YOU CAN GET WHEN YOUR RIGHTS HAVE BEEN VIOLATED

Obtaining your rights under Title VII can be well worth the effort. The remedies are considered to be "equitable" remedies, and as the Supreme Court has stated, they are intended to "make persons whole for injuries suffered on account of unlawful employment discrimination."[157] Stated another way, Title VII remedies are designed to situate you in your "rightful place," the place you would be in had the unlawful discrimination never occurred.[158]

The basic remedies available under the "make whole" and "rightful place" objectives of Title VII are: hiring, reinstatement, promotion, etc.; retroactive seniority; and back pay. Additionally, when an employer is found to have engaged in extensive discrimination against minorities or women, affirmative action goals and timetables for hiring or promoting minorities or women can be required in order to overcome the effects of past discrimination. All of these "equitable" remedies, which we will look at more closely in a moment, may be sought and obtained for you by the EEOC as part of an acceptable conciliation agreement, and they also can be sought and won in lawsuits filed by the EEOC, the Department of Justice, or you. And when you sue your boss and prevail, your boss will be ordered to pay your attorney's fees.[159]

Although these remedies are intended to fully compensate you, they will not give you as much as you might want or deserve. Aside from the monetary award of back pay, you are not entitled under Title VII to receive other monetary remedies such as general damages or punitive damages.[160] One consequence of this is that neither you nor your employer is entitled to a jury trial.[161] Instead, Title VII cases are tried only before a judge.

### Hiring, Reinstatement, Promotion, etc.

The rightful-place remedies of Title VII are not limited simply to hiring, reinstatement, or promotion. Instead, they are designed to give you what in fact is your rightful place. For example, if you have been discriminated against because of segregated lines of progression (or career ladders), an appropriate remedy might be a "merger" of previously segregated lines.[162] Another remedy is "red circling," which allows you to transfer to the previously segregated line without loss of pay or seniority.[163] Or if you have long been discriminated against in advancement opportunities, "job skipping" enables you to advance more quickly to obtain your rightful place.[164]

## Retroactive Seniority

As we saw earlier, seniority systems which are not created with an intent to discriminate are lawful under Title VII regardless of their discriminatory last-hired, first-fired impact upon minorities and women.[165] The fact that most seniority systems are lawful, however, has no effect upon your individual right to receive retroactive seniority within an existing seniority system.[166] If you have been discriminated against, retroactive seniority as a remedy helps to assure you of your rightful place and protects you against future layoffs.

Any person who proves that he or she has been unlawfully discriminated against is eligible for retroactive seniority from the date of the discrimination. If you were unlawfully denied a transfer to a more lucrative job for which you were qualified, you are entitled to retroactive seniority on that job.[167] Similarly, if you were unlawfully denied employment or simply deterred from applying for employment, you are entitled to retroactive seniority once you are hired.[168]

## Back Pay

When an employer violates Title VII, an award of back pay for you is presumed—regardless of the employer's good faith or lack of intent to discriminate.[169] And when the EEOC, or a court in a class action lawsuit, finds that an employer has discriminated not only against you but also against a class of persons (for example, through the use of an unvalidated written test which has a discriminatory impact upon many minority applicants), all members of the class are entitled to back pay.[170] Back pay is not limited to straight salary, but also includes overtime pay, shift differentials, vacation pay, pension-plan adjustments, and interest.[171] And despite the words "back pay," it also is possible for you to receive "front pay" to compensate you for future loss of earnings if you are unable to move immediately up the job ladder to your rightful place.[172]

Unfortunately, there are two significant limitations in Title VII which curtail the amount of back pay you can receive. First, back pay is calculated no further back than two years prior to the date upon which your administrative charge of discrimination was filed with the EEOC.[173] Assuming that you have been discriminatorily denied a promotion for ten years by your employer, you are eligible under Title VII to receive back pay only from the two years prior to your filing a charge of discrimination. The back pay period, however, continues to run for the many years that it may take you to obtain your award through the EEOC or through a lawsuit.

Second, the amount of back pay for which you theoretically are eligible is reduced by "interim earnings or amounts earnable with reasonable diligence by the person or persons discriminated against."[174] For example, if you earned $400 a week until January 3, 1980, if you were discriminatorily discharged on that date, if you unreasonably refused to look for any other work until July 3, 1980, and if you thereafter immediately found employment at $250 a week, you then would be able to recover no more than $150 a week back pay for your six months of unemployment as well as thereafter.

Another example of how the reduction of interim earnings from the back pay award actually operates is provided by a sex discrimination case discussed earlier. The case involved the unlawful denial of employment to Rita Jean Manley, a woman who had applied to be a law enforcement officer with responsibility for fingerprinting in a county jail in Alabama.[175] The denial of employment had become effective on January 1, 1976, the date on which two men were hired in place of Ms. Manley. Twenty-three months later, Ms. Manley won her lawsuit. The court ordered that she be employed within thirty days of her written indication that she still wanted the job, and that she be given twenty-three months of back pay. (She also received retroactive seniority and her attorney's fees.) Calculation of the amount of back pay owed her was a bit complicated because she had worked at different jobs with varying salaries, and also had received several months of unemployment compensation.[176] Since Title VII requires that income received must be offset against the salary she would have earned, her back pay award was not overwhelming:

*County jail salary not received*

| | |
|---|---|
| County Jail @ $600.00 per month Jan. 1976 through Oct. 1976 | $6,000.00 |
| County Jail @ $613.00 per month Nov. 1976 through Nov. 1977 | 7,969.00 |
| | $13,969.00 |

*Income received*

| | |
|---|---|
| Employer #1 @ $500.00 per month Jan. 1, 1976 to Feb. 14, 1976 | $750.00 |
| Unemployment Comp. @ $77.50 per week Feb. 15, 1976 to May 9, 1976 | 930.00 |
| Employer #2 @ $475.00 per month May 10, 1976, to Aug. 31, 1976 | 1,741.67 |
| Employer #2 @ $500.00 per month Sept. 1, 1976, to Mar. 31, 1977 | 3,500.00 |
| Employer #2 @ $550.00 per month April 1, 1977, to Nov. 30, 1977 | 4,400.00 |
| | $11,321.67 |

*Back pay*                                                        *$2,647.33*

   The amount of back pay to which an individual is entitled will vary considerably, depending upon the actual loss of pay. For example, in a major class action settlement against the Detroit Edison Company in 1979—where the classwide back pay award for four hundred individuals totaled $4,250,000—most of the individuals received only several thousand dollars, whereas those who had incurred greater losses received more than $50,000 each in back pay.

## Affirmative Action Goals and Timetables

When the EEOC[177] or a court[178] finds that extensive discrimination has been practiced against minorities or women, an affirmative remedy may be imposed requiring hiring, promotion, or admission for minorities or women pursuant to prescribed numerical ratios, goals, and timetables. These remedies usually are imposed when the unlawful discrimination has been particularly egregious. Many employers in this situation have been required to hire prescribed ratios of minorities to compensate for the continuing effects of past discrimination.[179] Similarly, racially discriminatory unions have been required to admit into membership and into apprenticeship programs prescribed ratios of minority workers.[180] These remedies have also been awarded in cases involving sex discrimination.[181]

Illustrative of affirmative action goals and timetables are those imposed by a court upon Steamfitters Local 638, a construction trade union in New York City which was found to have discriminated against black and Hispanic workers. The court, after reviewing labor-force statistics, determined that the union membership goal should be 26 percent minority, the same percentage as in the surrounding labor force. Entering its order in 1975, the court next determined that the goal had to be reached within three years: 18 percent minority membership by July 1, 1975; 23 percent by July 1, 1976; and 26 percent by July 1, 1977. And the court explained that the goals could be reached by admitting skilled minority workers directly into the union, by expanding the union's current apprenticeship program through the admission of 50 percent minorities and 50 percent whites, and by establishing new training programs.[182]

Employers and unions that discriminate unlawfully can anticipate the imposition of similar affirmative remedies when individuals like you successfully charge them with across-the-board, systemic discrimination.

## Attorney's Fees

In any lawsuit which you file to win your rights under Title VII, you finally can recover reasonable attorney's fees whenever you obtain at least some of the benefit sought in bringing your lawsuit.[183] But watch out here, because, if you lose, it is sometimes possible for you to be assessed your boss's fees. Quite simply, Title VII authorizes the courts to award fees to the "prevailing party."[184] This seemingly neutral language, however, is not so neutral, for it has been interpreted by the Supreme Court to contain a dual standard: if you win, you will be awarded fees virtually automatically; while, if you lose, you can be assessed fees only if the court determines that your lawsuit was clearly frivolous, unreasonable, or groundless, or that you continued to litigate after it clearly became so.[185] What this means in practice is that so long as you have a credible case of illegal discrimination, you always will be awarded fees if you win and will not be assessed your boss's fees if you lose. The fee awards in your favor can be substantial even if you are represented free. In the 1979 Detroit Edison settlement, for example, the company agreed to pay $250,000 in fees to lawyers from the American Civil Liberties Union who had represented the plaintiffs without charge. Fee awards such as this, as you can imagine, provide a strong incentive for some employers to settle cases in your favor—and quickly.

\* \* \*

In 1969, Christine Sweeney became an associate professor at Keene State College, a small liberal-arts college which is part of the University of New Hampshire. Obtaining the appointment was no problem: she long before had earned her Ph.D., she was widely published, and she had twenty-five years of teaching experience. Three years later, in 1972, Dr. Sweeney similarly encountered no difficulty obtaining tenure. Her problems began when she sought promotion to full professor.

During the 1973–74 school year, Dr. Sweeney's department recommended her for promotion to full professor. But the responsible faculty committee, whose members were all male, voted unanimously against promotion, and the Dean of the College agreed. Displeased, Dr. Sweeney pursued several faculty appeals, ultimately losing them all. During the 1974–75 school year, Christine Sweeney again was recommended by her department for promotion. A new faculty screening committee, also all male, voted against promotion, and the Dean again concurred. Dr. Sweeney's faculty appeals this time included allegations of sex discrimination. Her appeals were to no avail.

Dr. Sweeney sought promotion for a third time during the 1975–76 school year. Unexpectedly, she succeeded. She became a full professor on July 1, 1976. Pleased but not appeased, Christine Sweeney believed that she would have been made a full professor years earlier had she been male rather than female. In fact, after the first denial of promotion, she had filed charges of sex discrimination with her state commission on human rights and with the EEOC. After obtaining her promotion, she pursued her charges, obtained the necessary right-to-sue letter, and sued her boss.

In her lawsuit, Christine Sweeney alleged that she had been a victim of discriminatory treatment. At trial, she proved the necessary four elements of a discriminatory treatment case: that she was protected by Title VII, that she was qualified for promotion, that she was rejected despite her qualifications, and that the employer continued to consider applicants with qualifications similar to hers.

Keene State College sought to counter her proof of discrimination by alleging—as a legitimate non-discriminatory reason for the denial of promotion—that she was not as qualified as the faculty members who did receive promotions to full professor.

Dr. Sweeney, in turn, argued that the college's allegation was a pretext for sex discrimination. She showed that the college employed few women in high positions: from 1968–69 through 1975–76, the college never employed more than two female full professors, and usually only one, while the number of male full professors increased from seventeen in 1968–69 to thirty-five in 1975–76. Additionally, although the college had always appointed men from outside the college to positions as full professors, it had never appointed a woman from outside. Dr. Sweeney also proved that the faculty screening committees seldom had any female members. This was important because, as the court noted, the "racial or sexual composition of a body which makes subjective evaluations has often been considered a factor in employment discrimination cases."[186] Finally, she proved that although an affirmative action plan was drafted in 1973, it was not adopted until 1976, and even then it did not address salaries or promotion. And the man who served as affirmative action coordinator did virtually nothing to advance the rights of women on campus. In fact, after Christine Sweeney filed her charges of sex discrimination, he not only opposed her but wrote a letter to the president of Smith College asking "for information on how that school had responded to a charge of sex discrimination because he was 'concerned that that form of anarchy may creep north into our virgin territory.' "[187]

On this evidence, the court found that the refusal to promote Dr. Sweeney to full professor in 1974–75 was not based on any legitimate non-discriminatory reason but rather was unlawful sex discrimination, which violated Title VII. Victorious, Dr. Christine Sweeney was awarded back pay, retroactive seniority, and $17,766.67 in attorney's fees.

(PLEASE PRINT OR TYPE)

| APPROVED BY GAO | CHARGE OF DISCRIMINATION | CHARGE NUMBER(S) (AGENCY USE ONLY) |
|---|---|---|

B — 180541 (RO511)
Expires 1-31-81

IMPORTANT: This form is affected by the Privacy Act of 1974; see Privacy Act Statement on reverse before completing it.

☐ STATE/LOCAL AGENCY

☐ EEOC

Equal Employment Opportunity Commission and
(State or Local Agency)

NAME (Indicate Mr., Ms. or Mrs.)                                    HOME TELEPHONE NUMBER (Include area code)

STREET ADDRESS

CITY, STATE, AND ZIP CODE                                          COUNTY

NAMED IS THE EMPLOYER, LABOR ORGANIZATION, EMPLOYMENT AGENCY, APPRENTICESHIP COMMITTEE, STATE OR LOCAL GOVERNMENT AGENCY WHO DISCRIMINATED AGAINST ME. (If more than one list below).

NAME                                                               TELEPHONE NUMBER (Include area code)

STREET ADDRESS                          CITY, STATE, AND ZIP CODE

NAME                                                               TELEPHONE NUMBER (Include area code)

STREET ADDRESS                          CITY, STATE, AND ZIP CODE

CAUSE OF DISCRIMINATION BASED ON MY (Check appropriate box(es))

☐ RACE     ☐ COLOR     ☐ SEX     ☐ RELIGION     ☐ NATIONAL ORIGIN     ☐ OTHER (Specify)

DATE MOST RECENT OR CONTINUING DISCRIMINATION TOOK PLACE (Month, day, and year)

THE PARTICULARS ARE

---

I will advise the agencies if I change my address or telephone number and I will cooperate fully with them in the processing of my charge in accordance with their procedures.

NOTARY — (When necessary to meet State and Local Requirements)

I swear or affirm that I have read the above charge and that it is true to the best of my knowledge, information and belief.

SIGNATURE OF COMPLAINANT

I declare under penalty of perjury that the foregoing is true and correct.

SUBSCRIBED AND SWORN TO BEFORE ME THIS DATE (Day, month, and year)

DATE:                    CHARGING PARTY (Signature)

EEOC FORM 5B MAR. 79     PREVIOUS EDITIONS OF ALL EEOC FORM 5'S ARE OBSOLETE AND MUST NOT BE USED

CHARGE FILE COPY

# Sample Charge of Discrimination

Charging Party
100 My Street
My Town, My State 00000
111/234-5678

July 1, 1980

Equal Employment Opportunity Commission
Columbia Plaza Highrise
2401 E Street, N.W.
Washington, D.C. 20506

Since I am unable to appear personally at an EEOC office, please consider this letter a formal charge of sex discrimination under Title VII of the Civil Rights Act of 1964. I am filing this charge against both my employer and my union:

| | |
|---|---|
| Boss, Inc. | Local Union No. 1000 |
| 10 Main Street | 100 Main Street |
| My Town, My State 00000 | My Town, My State 00000 |
| 111 123-4567 | 111 123-5678 |

Boss, Inc. employs considerably more than 15 employees, and Local Union No. 1000 has considerably more than 15 members. Both are covered by Title VII.

I was hired by Boss, Inc., in September 1979. All of the executives in my department, with one exception, are male. Several of the men have constantly subjected me to sexual harassment of all kinds including guaranteeing me raises and travel in return for my sexual favors. My informal complaints to the personnel department have been laughed at. When I asked our union steward to file a grievance on my behalf, again I was laughed at. Two weeks ago, I received my first unfavorable evaluation. Only last week I was again asked for sexual favors by one of the male executives and also by the only male vice president of our union.

This continuing sexual harassment is directed not only against me but against most of the other women here, and it continues despite our complaints. I sincerely believe that I may lose my job because of my resistance to this unlawful sex discrimination.

I swear under oath that this charge is true.

Sincerely,

Charging Party

Sworn to before me this
1st day of July 1980.

Friend of Charging Party

# Protecting 3
## the Coming of Age

### THE AGE DISCRIMINATION IN EMPLOYMENT
### ACT OF 1967, AS AMENDED

#### [AGE]

Retirement, for many workers, provides a sought-after reward for decades of labor. For others, especially those who cannot easily make ends meet in these years of double-digit inflation, mandatory retirement is a notorious form of age discrimination against older workers.

Kenneth Jones, the Chief of Police in Janesville, Wisconsin, is among those opposed to mandatory retirement. Needless to say, he did not enjoy being involuntarily retired shortly after his fifty-fifth birthday on June 21, 1979. But city policy in Janesville required the termination of his employment when he turned fifty-five.

Believing that the city's mandatory retirement policy violated the federal Age Discrimination in Employment Act of 1967, which prohibits discrimination based on age against persons aged forty through sixty-nine, Chief Jones filed a charge of discrimination with a nearby office of the Equal Employment Opportunity Commission. When the EEOC agreed with Chief Jones that he had been unlawfully discriminated against but was unable to persuade the city to change its policy and rehire Chief Jones, the EEOC sued the city of Janesville in federal court. The EEOC won, and within months of his "retirement," Police Chief Kenneth Jones was back on the job.[1]

Interestingly, Chief Jones could not have benefited from the Age Discrimination in Employment Act of 1967 if he had been involuntarily retired several years earlier. This is because the United States Supreme Court, in 1977, interpreted the Act to allow mandatory retirement.[2] But this interpretation did not last long. Upset by the Supreme Court's decision, a majority in Congress—who thought they had already outlawed mandatory retirement—set out to make the Act's prohibition against mandatory retirement absolutely clear. In fact, only four months after the Supreme Court's 1977 decision, Congress overruled the Court by enacting the Age Discrimination in Employment Act Amendments of 1978. These new amendments, among other things, unequivocally prohibit mandatory retirement.

As a result of the new amendments, most workers, including of course Police Chief Kenneth Jones, are now protected from mandatory retirement prior to age seventy.

*The Age Discrimination in Employment Act protects persons aged forty through sixty-nine from age discrimination in state, local, and private employment. In federal employment, it protects all persons age forty and older.*

*The Age Discrimination in Employment Act initially was enacted in 1967 as an amendment to the federal minimum wage law [the Fair Labor Standards Act] and thus became applicable to most jobs in private employment which affect interstate commerce. In 1974, the Act was extended to cover nearly all jobs in state and local government, and to cover most jobs in the federal government. In 1978 the Act was amended to prohibit mandatory retirement and other forms of discrimination prior to age seventy in most jobs.*

*This comprehensive prohibition against age discrimination is enforced through administrative investigations conducted by the Equal Employment Opportunity Commission, through lawsuits filed by the EEOC, and through lawsuits filed by individuals.*

*When you obtain your rights under the law, you are entitled to such remedies as hiring, reinstatement, and promotion. You also are entitled to back wages for the period of time that employment or full wages were denied. In some instances, you even can receive double back wages.*

## WHO IS COVERED BY THE LAW

The Age Discrimination in Employment Act of 1967, as amended [ADEA], applies to nearly all private employers, state and local government employers, and other organizations.[3] Specifically, the ADEA applies to:

- Private employers with twenty or more employees.
- All state and local governments and their agencies.
- State, local, and private employment agencies.
- Labor unions with twenty-five or more members.

If you are an employee of one of the above-described employers, or if your employment rights have been affected by any of the above-described employers, agencies, or organizations, you are protected by the ADEA if you are at least age forty and not yet age seventy.[4]

The ADEA also applies to most jobs in the federal government.[5] Specifically covered are all jobs in the federal competitive service. Not covered, however, are elective positions and high appointive positions in the federal government. These are few. Most federal government jobs are in the competitive service.

The protection provided by the ADEA is somewhat broader in federal employment than in non-federal employment. If you are at least forty, you are protected by the ADEA. In federal employment, there generally is *no upper age limit* where you can lose the protection of the ADEA. In other words, if you have turned forty, you cannot be discriminated against by the federal government because of your age, regardless of how old you are.[6]

## DISCRIMINATORY PRACTICES WHICH ARE UNLAWFUL

The ADEA, to repeat, protects you against age discrimination in employment only if you belong to certain age groups. In private, state, and local employment, the protected group is comprised of employees and applicants aged forty through sixty-nine. In federal employment, the protected group is comprised of employees and applicants aged forty and older.

Most forms of discrimination which adversely affect older persons protected by the ADEA are unlawful. For example, the ADEA prohibits an employer from preferring applicants younger than forty because such a preference has an adverse impact upon persons in the protected age group. Thus, in one case, where the city of Philadelphia required applicants for the position of security officer to be forty or younger—a policy which was used to deny employment to an applicant aged forty-six—the city was found to have violated the ADEA.[7]

The ADEA also prohibits an employer from giving preference to younger persons in the protected age group because this too adversely affects older persons in the protected group. Thus, for example, the ADEA prohibits an employer from preferring persons in their forties for initial employment, for additional training, or for promotions because this discriminates against protected employees in their fifties and sixties.[8]

As is obvious, the ADEA forbids discrimination against you on the basis of your age. As the law itself states, the purpose of the ADEA is "to promote employment of older persons based on their ability rather than age."[9] On the other hand, the ADEA does not prohibit discrimination based on *necessary* job qualifications or on standards of performance. In other words, a federal employee aged eighty-five can be fired if she or he *cannot* perform the job. But if that employee can perform the job, it is unlawful for the person to be fired because of his or her age.

In point of fact, your employer probably makes a variety of employment decisions about you and your colleagues with your age in mind. Many of these decisions are unlawful. Your employer can violate your rights under the ADEA even if your employer's action was based upon other factors in addition to age. The key is whether age is a *determining factor* in an employment decision which affects you. Thus, a company that reduces its work force as part of a reorganization cannot use age as a determining factor to lay off an older worker. Laying off an older worker in this situation is unlawful, the courts have said, "if one such factor was his age and if in fact it made a difference in determining whether he was to be retained or discharged. This is so even though the need to reduce the employee force generally was also a strong and perhaps even more compelling reason."[10]

The ADEA itself lists a number of forbidden activities. Specifically, an *employer* cannot, on the basis of your age: discharge or fail to hire you[11]; provide you with different compensation, terms, conditions, or privileges of employment[12]; or limit, segregate, or classify you in any way which would tend to deprive you of employment opportunities.[13] Although each of these ADEA prohibitions nominally is directed at separate unlawful activities, sometimes they operate together. A private company in Virginia recently defended the firing of two older employees by arguing that they did not have the same advanced training as did younger employees. The company was found by a court to have violated the ADEA twice—first by denying the older employees training, and then by firing them. Since the discriminated-against older employees took legal action to obtain their rights, they not only won their jobs back but also were entitled to the advanced training.[14]

The ADEA contains other specific prohibitions against age discrimination. It is unlawful for an *employment agency* to fail to refer you for employment or to treat you differently in any way because of your age.[15] And it is unlawful for an *employment agency* or an *employer* to cause to be printed or published any advertisement indicating an age discriminatory preference, limitation, or specification.[16] In fact, this latter prohibition makes it unlawful for an employer to place an advertisement in a newspaper encouraging employment applications from "girl," "boy," or "young" candidates, or from applicants "age 25 to 35."[17] Indeed, an employment agency in North Carolina which published advertisements for "recent college grads" and for persons "one–two years out of college" was found to be in violation of the ADEA.[18]

Finally, the ADEA bars retaliation. Specifically, it is unlawful for an employer or organization covered by the ADEA to retaliate—to take any adverse employment action—against you for opposing an employer's practices as age discriminatory or for participating in any proceeding under the ADEA charging an employer with age discrimination.[19] This means that any person in the protected age group who complains to his or her employer about the discriminatory denial of a promotion or of other job opportunities, or who files a charge of discrimination or otherwise seeks to obtain the protections provided by the ADEA, cannot be fired or otherwise discriminated against for exercising his or her legal rights. This, obviously, is an important protection. But it doesn't guarantee that you won't be retaliated against. Employers who discriminate unlawfully might also break the law by retaliating against a person who challenges the discrimination.

## MAJOR EXCEPTIONS

Despite the extensive coverage of the ADEA, there are two categories of exceptions. A few employers and unions are not covered, and some employees and applicants for employment are not protected. Additionally, some practices are not prohibited.

### Exempted Employers and Employment

As we have seen, private employers with fewer than twenty employees are not covered; nor are labor unions with fewer than twenty-five members.[20] Workers and applicants who are not yet forty are not protected; and except in federal employment, workers and applicants who are seventy or older are not protected.[21]

### Exceptions to Discriminatory Practices

There also are three specific statutory exceptions in the ADEA which allow employers to use employment practices which appear to be discriminatory.

It is lawful for an employer to use age as a factor in an employment decision where age is a bona fide occupational qualification, for an employer to make employment decisions based upon factors other than age, or for an employer to observe a bona fide seniority system or benefit plan. These three exceptions are not as broad as they may seem. And they are seldom invoked, because any employer who tries to use one of the exceptions has the responsibility of proving that the exception actually applies.

*Bona fide occupational qualification.* The ADEA allows discrimination against you when you seek a specified job if the employer can prove that age is a bona fide occupational qualification necessary to the performance of that job.[22] In other words, if successful job performance absolutely requires a younger person in the job, only then can an employer use age as a factor in the employment decision. This is not a broad invitation for employers to discriminate. To the contrary, the federal regulations interpreting this exception state that it is to be "narrowly construed."[23]

Because this exception is intended to be so narrow, few employers have defended their age discriminatory practices by trying to invoke it. Several employers, however, have raised the bona fide occupational qualification exception in court, and have succeeded in making it broader than it is intended to be. For example, two bus companies have been allowed by the courts to retain their policies requiring new bus drivers to be no older than thirty-five, on the grounds that age is a bona fide occupational qualification for that job.[24] On the other hand, another court in a more recent decision refused to give a broad reading to this exception. It held that generalized evidence about physical infirmities does not make age a bona fide occupational qualification, and it thus found that an airplane manufacturer's transfer of a test pilot at age fifty-two to another position was unlawful under the ADEA.[25]

This exception, allowing some forms of age discrimination to be defended as a bona fide occupational qualification, could be troublesome if your employer chooses to make it an issue. As we have seen in Chapter 2, however, a similar exception in Title VII of the Civil Rights Act of 1964 has been interpreted *very* narrowly. This should deter most employers from trying to establish the applicability of this exception.

*Factors other than age.* The second statutory exception is not as complicated. In fact, it is rather obvious. The ADEA does not prohibit an employment decision based on a reasonable factor other than age—at least so long as the factor of age plays no role in the employment decision.[26] In other words, an employer may discharge or discipline an employee for cause. Illustrative is the case of an older employee in Illinois who was repeatedly tardy, who was later fired, and who ultimately sued his boss. The employer invoked this exception by arguing that the discharge was for cause—tardiness—and not because of age discrimination. Since the employer proved the applicability of the exception to the court's satisfaction, the employer won.[27]

Sometimes, however, the "cause" alleged by an employer to support an employment decision is tainted by the factor of age. This is precisely what occurred in Charlotte, North Carolina, when Eastern Air Lines demoted a forty-nine-year-old employee from Supervisor of Departure Services to the position of Air Freight Agent. After the former supervisor sued, Eastern argued that the demotion had occurred in response to complaints of sexual harassment made by three women under his supervision. But the demotion, a court found, was necessarily also based on age, because three other supervisors older than forty had been similarly demoted while younger employees were being promoted. Since age was a factor, the demotion was unlawful.[28]

Employers sometimes assert not just cause but financial or business reasons as reasonable factors other than age to justify the demotion or discharge of older employees. But remember, an employment decision that includes age as a factor is not based on a reasonable factor other than age. In one case, an older sales manager was fired after he had increased his annual sales but had failed to meet the sales objectives of the company. His Georgia employer argued in court that the company's most recent annual deficit of $700,000 constituted a reasonable factor for firing older sales managers and hiring younger, allegedly more energetic ones. Not so, held the court. Since age had been a factor, the financial losses did not justify discharging only the older employees.[29]

A more dramatic and somewhat extravagant business reason advanced by a New York company as a reasonable factor other than age to discharge an older employee was, very simply, liquidation of the company. At first blush, liquidation of a company would appear to be a reasonable factor other than age for discharging anyone. That is precisely what the New York fashion design company wanted its oldest and highest-paid designer, sixty-two-year-old Bertie Feitis, to believe. But Ms. Feitis's investigations uncovered a different story. She learned, after her discharge, that the company had not actually been liquidated. Instead, the primary owner of the company had transferred all of that company's assets to another design company which he had recently and secretly formed. Also transferred from the old company to the new one were the employment contracts of all of the other fashion designers—who were in their twenties and thirties. The only designer not transferred was sixty-two-year-old Bertie Feitis, who had worked for the company for seventeen years, and who was three years away from eligibility for her pension. When these facts were presented in court, the court had little difficulty piercing the ruse. The primary owner of the company, the court held, "never intended to liquidate the company, but rather planned to . . . eliminate the higher salary and pension obligations owing to Feitis."[30] Ms. Feitis's discharge was not based upon a reasonable factor other than age; it was unlawful age discrimination.

*Bona fide seniority systems and benefit plans.* The third statutory exception, the subject of much recent debate, arises in the context of bona fide seniority systems and benefit plans. Prior to the ADEA Amendments of 1978, this exception allowed employers to observe the terms of a bona fide seniority system or benefit plan, and arguably allowed employers to retire employees under any mandatory retirement plan. In other words, some employers used this exception to impose mandatory retirement upon their older workers. When the Supreme Court in 1977 interpreted this exception to permit mandatory retirement,[31] Congress quickly enacted the ADEA Amendments of 1978 to overrule the Court.[32]

The amended exception still allows an employer to observe a bona fide seniority system or benefit plan,[33] but it specifies that no such system or plan can require "the involuntary retirement of any individual . . . because of the age of such individual."[34] This language alone would mean that employees protected by the ADEA could not be mandatorily retired prior to sixty-five. But, because the ADEA Amendments of 1978 also raised the protected age ceiling to seventy in state, local, and private employment, this language actually means that employees in this sector cannot be mandatorily retired prior to seventy.[35] Similarly, because the ADEA Amendments of 1978 eliminated the age ceiling altogether in federal employment, protected federal employees cannot be mandatorily retired at all.[36]

Although Congress acted quickly to forbid mandatory retirement, it did not do so in all categories of employment. Instead, Congress allowed employers some leeway as to three groups of employees.[37] For one group, college professors, Congress allowed mandatory retirement from ages sixty-five through sixty-nine, but only for a few more years. As the law now states, tenured college faculty members can be mandatorily retired at sixty-five or older until July 1, 1982. In other words, any faculty member who has tenure at an institution of higher education may be mandatorily retired at age sixty-five or older until July 1, 1982.[38] After that date, when the increased age ceiling of seventy becomes effective for them, these tenured professors cannot be mandatorily retired prior to age seventy.

The second group, highly paid executives, can be subjected to mandatory retirement for an *unlimited* period of time. Specifically, those persons who have reached sixty-five, who have been employed for the previous two years in executive or high policy-making positions, and who upon retirement are entitled to annual retirement benefits and other forms of compensation totaling $27,000 may be mandatorily retired without violating the ADEA.[39]

The third group is comprised of certain classes of federal employees who also may be mandatorily retired at any age. Alas, the United States Civil Service Commission was granted the unfettered right to establish maximum age limits for selected positions when it determines that age is a bona fide occupational qualification necessary to the performance of the duties of the selected positions.[40] This means that some jobs in federal employment can have a prescribed age for mandatory retirement.

As is evident, the three categories allowing mandatory retirement are quite limited. As a result of the ADEA Amendments of 1978, most employees, undoubtedly including you, are better protected than ever before against mandatory retirement.

## THE FEDERAL AGENCY RESPONSIBLE FOR ENFORCEMENT

The federal agency responsible for administering and enforcing the ADEA is the Equal Employment Opportunity Commission.[41] The EEOC has district and area offices throughout the United States. The locations of these offices are set forth later in Chapter 9. The central office of the EEOC is located in Washington, D.C.

Equal Employment Opportunity Commission
Columbia Plaza Highrise
2401 E Street, N.W.
Washington, D.C. 20506

202/634-7040

## ENFORCEMENT: HOW TO OBTAIN YOUR RIGHTS

Many employers have been egregiously slow in complying with the ADEA. Some have to be forced to comply. Under the ADEA, it is up to you, at least initially, to demand your rights. You usually will be able to obtain your rights only when you take the necessary steps to initiate ADEA enforcement. As you will see, this does not necessarily mean that you have to sue your boss.

For employees and applicants who have been discriminated against on grounds of age by private employers, state and local governments, employment agencies, or labor unions, there are three methods of enforcement through which you may obtain your rights:

• A charge of discrimination which you file with the EEOC may be administratively resolved by the EEOC to your satisfaction.

• A charge of discrimination which you file with the EEOC may result in a successful lawsuit brought by the EEOC on your behalf.

• A charge of discrimination which you file with the EEOC might lead to a successful lawsuit brought by you.

For federal employees and applicants for federal employment, there is a different method of enforcement:

• A notice (described later in this chapter) which you file with the EEOC against a federal agency may result in a satisfactory administrative resolution of the discrimination or may lead to a successful lawsuit brought by you.

All of these methods of enforcement depend upon the initial steps taken by you to obtain your rights. *With each of these steps, there are strict administrative procedures which must be followed, and there are short time periods which also must be followed. If you do not comply, you will not be able to obtain your rights no matter how flagrant the discrimination may be.* Remember, the first step is writing to the EEOC to tell them that your boss has discriminated against you because of your age.

## Administrative Resolution of Charges of Discrimination

If you believe that you have been discriminated against in violation of the ADEA by a private employer, state or local government, employment agency, or labor union, you should file an administrative charge of discrimination with the EEOC. The charge *must* be filed with the EEOC within 180 days of the discrimination against you.[42] There is no prescribed form for a charge of discrimination. A letter is sufficient as a charge. A sample letter is set forth at the end of this chapter. In the letter, you should:

• Provide your name, address, and phone number.
• State your employer's name and address.
• Indicate when the discrimination occurred.
• Describe fully the nature of the discrimination that has been practiced against you.

Your letter to the EEOC should be signed, but it need not be sworn to. Send your letter as soon as possible—no later than 180 days after the discriminatory act—to the closest office of the EEOC or to the EEOC's central office in Washington, D.C.

After receiving your charge, the EEOC will send it to your state fair employment practices agency, if you are in a state which has a state law prohibiting age discrimination and if the state agency is authorized to remedy the discrimination.[43] The EEOC, by law, will defer to that state agency for sixty days before assuming formal jurisdiction over your charge.

Once the EEOC assumes jurisdiction, it must notify your employer and any other named organization that you have charged with discrimination, it must investigate the charge, and it must attempt to eliminate any discriminatory practice by urging voluntary compliance with the law.[44] In undertaking investigations, the EEOC is authorized to issue subpoenas and to hold hearings.[45] Attempts by the EEOC to secure voluntary compliance are to be made "through informal methods of conciliation, conference, and persuasion."[46] This means that representatives from the EEOC will try to persuade your employer to stop its discrimination and to remedy past actions by hiring you, reinstating you, promoting you, or providing other relief.

The investigation undertaken by the EEOC necessarily will involve you directly. Representatives from the EEOC will contact you, probably both by phone and in person. They will want to know all of the facts surrounding the discrimination. You thus should save all documents and notes which you think might be relevant to your charge.

The EEOC conciliation procedures also will involve you directly. The purpose of these procedures is to obtain a written agreement in which your employer agrees to cease and to remedy any alleged discrimination that has been practiced against you. To be effective, it must be agreed to by you and by your employer. You, of course, don't have to agree if you find the proposed agreement unsatisfactory.

In the event that your employer refuses to enter into a conciliation agreement, the next step usually is the filing of a lawsuit.

## Lawsuits by the EEOC

If the EEOC believes that you have been unlawfully discriminated against and has been unable to eliminate that discrimination through its administrative methods of conciliation, conference, and persuasion, then the EEOC *may* file a lawsuit in federal or state court on your behalf against the accused private employer, state or local government, employment agency, or union.[47]

The purpose of an EEOC lawsuit is to allow you to obtain your rights by forcing your employer to comply with the law. This lawsuit must be filed by the EEOC, if at all, within two years of the age discrimination violation alleged in your initial charge of discrimination, or the lawsuit may be filed within three years of the violation if the lawsuit alleges that the employer's discrimination was willful (meaning that the discrimination was purposeful or intentional).[48] These time periods may be extended, but for not longer than an additional year, if the EEOC is continuing to try to resolve the matter administratively.[49] This, of course, is an indication that administrative charges of discrimination sometimes take several years to resolve.

Assuming that your charge of discrimination cannot be administratively resolved, it ordinarily is tremendously helpful to have the EEOC file a lawsuit on your behalf. It's not bad, after all, to have the power and resources of the federal government used against your employer, especially since you won't have to bear the burden or expense of suing your boss yourself. Accordingly, you always should encourage the EEOC to file a lawsuit before you undertake the burden of filing a lawsuit of your own.

## Lawsuits by Individuals

If you believe that you have been discriminated against, if you have filed a charge of discrimination with the EEOC, and if the charge has been properly referred to a state agency for 60 days, you may file a lawsuit in federal or state court against a private employer, state or local government, employment agency, or labor union. You, however, cannot file a lawsuit if you have accepted a conciliation agreement proposed by the EEOC, or if the EEOC already has filed a lawsuit against your employer to enforce your rights. In other words, you lose your right to sue if you agree to a settlement, or if the EEOC sues first.[50]

Assuming that no agreement was accepted and that the EEOC has not sued, your lawsuit must be filed within two years of the discrimination or within three years if the violation is alleged to have been willful.[51] These time periods may be extended, but for no longer than a year, if the EEOC actually is continuing to try to resolve your charge administratively.[52]

Before you go to court, you definitely should find a lawyer. More important, you must have complied with all of the administrative procedures and time limits under the ADEA. Sixty days prior to the filing of your lawsuit, you *must* have filed your charge of discrimination with the EEOC.[53] That charge, the same charge that we've already discussed, *must* have been filed within 180 days after the discriminatory practice occurred—unless a state agency has commenced proceedings pursuant to a state law which prohibits age discrimination.[54] In the latter instance, the charge of discrimination could have been filed with the EEOC within 300 days after the allegedly discriminatory practice occurred, or within 30 days after notice was received that the state proceeding had terminated, whichever is earlier.[55]

There is an additional administrative filing procedure if you are in a state which has a law prohibiting age discrimination and in which there is a state agency authorized to remedy that discrimination. If you are in such a state, a charge of discrimination *must* be filed with the state agency 60 days before you sue your boss.[56] Even if the state agency has a short filing period, which would make your state charge untimely, a charge still has to be filed with the state agency. This may seem like a meaningless step—it often is—but it is mandatory if you intend to file a lawsuit.[57]

These administrative procedures can be quite confusing, especially in a state where there is a state law prohibiting age discrimination in employment. But, rather than worrying about filing two separate charges, one with the EEOC and one with the state agency, there is an easier way. This is simply to file one charge with the EEOC within 180 days of the discrimination. Upon receipt of the charge, the EEOC then will send your charge to the state agency for 60 days if this is necessary.[58] This option allows you to comply with the ADEA's various administrative requirements in only one step.

But remember, your federal charge must be sent to the EEOC within 180 days after the discrimination against you. If you don't meet this requirement, your subsequent lawsuit probably will be dismissed. Although this 180-day requirement is not an absolute requirement,[59] you'd better have a very good reason for not meeting it. In one instance, a court did not dismiss a lawsuit although the individual had filed her federal administrative charge thirty-six days late. The court held that she had a good reason because she was improperly advised of her rights by a federal official responsible for enforcing the ADEA.[60] Most reasons, however, will not be considered good reasons. For example, your lack of knowledge about your rights or about the ADEA time limits will not save your lawsuit from being dismissed. As one court recently said in dismissing an ADEA lawsuit filed by an individual who learned about his rights after the 180 days had already passed: "It is clearly too late in the day to contend that the ADEA is a new statute of which employees are unaware."[61]

Once the administrative procedures have been complied with, you are entitled to file your lawsuit. Under the ADEA, your lawsuit can be filed on your behalf and also on behalf of similarly situated individuals who affirmatively file written consents with the court indicating that each such person desires to be included in your lawsuit. Note that, unlike the use of a class action (a lawsuit filed on behalf of and ultimately benefiting other persons —the "class"—who have been similarly discriminated against) under Title VII, discussed in Chapter 2, an ADEA class action lawsuit can be filed only by or on behalf of individuals who file written consents, and thereby affirmatively "opt into" the class.[62] Because only these identifiable individuals can obtain the remedies provided by the ADEA, you should advise your discriminated-against co-workers of your lawsuit to give them an opportunity to opt into it.

## Federal Employment: Notices and Lawsuits by Federal Employees and Applicants

The methods of enforcement described above do not apply to federal employment. Where there is age discrimination in federal employment, the specific methods of enforcement are different. Although there is some administrative enforcement by the EEOC, and although you have a right to sue your federal employer, the administrative steps are different, and neither the

EEOC nor any other federal agency has the power to sue another federal agency for age discrimination. In other words, you're mostly on your own.

If you are a federal employee or applicant and you believe that you have been discriminated against by a federal employer, you first must file a "notice of an intent to sue" with the EEOC. This notice does *not* mean that you *will* sue your federal employer or even that you necessarily intend to do so. Rather, the notice of an intent to sue is simply the phrase used in the ADEA for a charge of discrimination against a federal employer. There is no prescribed form for the notice. A letter is sufficient. In the letter you should:

- State your name, address, and phone number.
- Provide the name and address of the federal agency or department that has discriminated against you.
- Indicate when the discrimination occurred.
- Describe fully the nature of the discrimination which you have experienced.
- State that you intend to sue if the discrimination is not stopped and remedied.

Your letter to the EEOC should be signed, but it need not be sworn to. It *must* be filed with the EEOC within 180 days of the discriminatory act.[63] Send your letter to the nearest office of the EEOC[64] (the addresses are in Chapter 9) or to the EEOC's central office in Washington, D.C. Upon receipt of the letter, the EEOC will inform your federal employer that a notice has been filed. Thereafter, the EEOC is authorized to "take any appropriate action to assure the elimination of any unlawful practice."[65] This means that the EEOC will try informally to resolve the matter in the same ways as in non-federal employment.

A person who files a notice of an intent to sue does not have to sue. But if you want to sue, you are authorized to file a lawsuit in federal district court at any time after your notice has been filed with the EEOC for 30 days.[66] It usually is best to wait longer than 30 days to see if the EEOC will resolve the discrimination. But if the discrimination is not resolved to your satisfaction, the only remaining method of enforcement is filing a lawsuit yourself against the federal agency.

## REMEDIES: WHAT YOU CAN GET WHEN YOUR RIGHTS HAVE BEEN VIOLATED

Your efforts to obtain your rights under the ADEA can be amply rewarded. The remedies are plentiful.[67]

The basic remedies available under the ADEA are "equitable" remedies designed to give you your "rightful place"—the place you would have been in if no discrimination had occurred. These equitable, rightful place remedies—depending upon your situation—can include hiring, reinstatement, transfer, or promotion; retroactive seniority and fringe benefits; and back pay.

Illustrative of these remedies are those which were awarded to Bertie Feitis, the sixty-two-year-old designer who was discharged unlawfully by a New York fashion design company. After she lost not only her job but also the pension to which she would have been entitled when she reached the age of sixty-five, she sued. By the time she won her lawsuit and the remedies were awarded, she was older than sixty-five and not desirous of reinstatement. But she wanted and won monetary remedies. She received three years of back pay in the amount of $70,200 and a lump sum pension of $57,218.38, for a total monetary award of $127,418.38.[68]

Another person who recently won rightful place remedies is John Cleverly, an engineer who was permanently laid off at fifty-three by a Western Electric Company plant in Missouri after he had worked with the company for twenty-three years. Although the permanent layoff was bad enough, his boss imposed the layoff only six months before Mr. Cleverly's pension rights were to become vested. After asserting and winning his rights, Mr. Cleverly was awarded full back pay, retroactive seniority, and his full pension.[69]

These and other equitable, rightful place remedies may be obtained not only through a lawsuit filed by you or by the EEOC[70] but also administratively through a conciliation agreement sought and obtained for you by the EEOC.[71] In this situation, the employer normally will not admit to a violation of the ADEA. But what is important is whether the employer provides a satisfactory remedy. When this occurs, both you (or the EEOC) and the employer are able to avoid a potentially expensive and time-consuming lawsuit.

In addition to these equitable rightful place remedies, another monetary remedy which may be obtained, but only through a lawsuit, is *double back pay*. This double back pay remedy— referred to in the ADEA as "liquidated damages"—is available when an employer willfully violates the law so as to intentionally and knowingly deprive you, an older person, of your employment rights. The liquidated damages which are available are not related to specific harm done, although they are limited under the ADEA to an amount equal to the award of back wages.[72] In other words, when a court finds that your employer willfully violated the ADEA, you can win double back wages.

Double back pay was awarded in a successful lawsuit filed recently in New Mexico by several laid-off employees. In the lawsuit, the employees challenged two practices: a salary-raise policy which guaranteed automatic annual raises of 5 percent for all younger employees but not for employees in their fifties and sixties, and a reduction-in-force layoff policy which affected older employees almost exclusively. The court found both policies unlawful and awarded the discriminated-against older workers back pay for the periods they had been laid off, and retroactive 5 percent raises. Finding that the unlawful policies had been used willfully to deny employment rights to the older workers, the court doubled the monetary award as liquidated damages.[73]

Because of the availability of this double back pay—liquidated damages—remedy in ADEA lawsuits, both you and your employer have the right to request a jury trial.[74] Since many juries are composed primarily of older persons, you and your lawyer ordinarily should request a jury for the trial of your lawsuit.

Two other remedies that commonly are associated with the right to a jury trial are pain-and-suffering damages—usually called "compensatory damages"—and punitive damages. Although some older persons have tried to recover such damages in their ADEA lawsuits, most courts have held that neither pain-and-suffering damages[75] nor punitive damages[76] are available in ADEA lawsuits.

A final remedy, which *is* available to you in a successful ADEA lawsuit, is a court-ordered award of your attorney's fee. Under the ADEA, courts are required to award to the successful plain-tiff (you) "a reasonable attorney's fee to be paid by the defend-ant" (your employer).[77] Since there is no comparable authoriza-tion for awarding an attorney's fee to a defendant employer, this means that only you and not your employer can obtain fees in a lawsuit.[78] This one-way remedy, of course, provides an incentive to an employer to agree to remedy the discrimination without being sued. The potential award of attorney's fees also will assist you in your efforts to find a lawyer to bring your lawsuit.

The cumulative remedies available to you under the ADEA obviously are worth winning. Earlier in this chapter we referred to a company in Virginia that had denied training to two older employees and then had terminated their employment on the grounds that they lacked adequate training to continue their employment. They responded by asserting their rights under the ADEA. They timely filed the necessary administrative charges, and thereafter timely sued their former employer. The employer was found by the court to have violated the ADEA twice, once by denying them training and a second time by terminating their employment. The remedy ordered by the court required the company to reinstate the individuals and to provide them with back wages "increased by the value of any pension benefits, health insurance, seniority, leave time, or other fringe benefits which [they] would have accrued during the back pay period but for the violation of the Act." The flat back wages for one individ-ual amounted to $21,500, and for the other, $13,000. Although the court did not find the company's violation to be willful, with the result that no liquidated damages were awarded, the court did take the unusual step of awarding pain-and-suffering dam-ages in the amount of $15,000 to each individual because of the emotional distress suffered. Finally, the court awarded to both litigants, who shared one lawyer, $14,700 in attorney's fees. By making the effort to obtain their rights, these two individuals not only were reinstated but together received a total of $79,200, all of which had to be paid to them by their employer.[79]

*     *     *

Charles Schulz devoted twenty-eight years of his life to work-ing for the Hickok Manufacturing Company. Beginning in 1965,

Hickok encountered severe financial problems. By 1969, it was losing a million dollars a year. In 1970, the company changed ownership and cleaned out its top management. Digging more deeply, the company also fired some of its other management employees.

Based in Atlanta, Georgia, Mr. Schulz was one of the company's seven district sales managers. In 1970, the average age of the seven district sales managers was fifty-three. Eighteen months later, the average age had declined to forty. Replaced by younger employees, each of the older district sales managers had been promoted, retired, or fired. Charles Schulz had been fired.

Believing that he had been discriminated against because of his age, Mr. Schulz filed a charge. When the charge was not administratively resolved, Mr. Schulz found a lawyer and sued his boss.

In court, the company contended that the firing of Mr. Schulz was based not on his age but rather on the dire financial status of the company and on the company's need for superstar district sales managers. Essentially, the company argued that Mr. Schulz's discharge was based on two reasonable factors other than age: the company's financial status and the company's determination that Mr. Schulz's work was not sufficiently competent (a "for cause" discharge).

The court analyzed both factors together by closely reviewing Mr. Schulz's job performance. His discharge had not been based on any formal performance evaluation; rather, he had always been advised that his performance was above average. In fact, of the seven district sales managers, Mr. Schulz consistently had produced among the highest annual increases in sales. On the other hand, it was true that the company "clearly had a need for a district manager who could break all previous records," that Mr. Schulz's performance "was not of that caliber," and that these facts made it "a rather close case."[80] Nonetheless, because the company's financial difficulties stemmed from "factors far removed from and far more basic than the performance of a single district manager," and because the company had failed to show "that the discharge was for good cause," the court concluded that the determining factor in Mr. Schulz's discharge was his age.[81] Accordingly, his discharge was unlawful.

As a remedy, the company was ordered to reinstate Mr. Schulz as a district sales manager or to place him in a comparable position. He also was entitled to back pay, minus the severance pay and unemployment compensation he had received, for the two-and-one-quarter years since his discharge. His back pay was calculated as follows:

$49,000   regular pay
−2,308    severance pay
−1,300    unemployment compensation

$45,392   back-pay award

This back pay award, however, was not doubled as liquidated damages because the court determined that Mr. Schulz's unlawful discharge had not been a willful violation of the law. Accordingly, Mr. Schulz received only the $45,392 in straight back pay. But because Mr. Schulz had won his lawsuit, he also was entitled to his attorney's fees. For this he was awarded an additional $5,000.

## Sample Charge of Discrimination

Charging Party
1000 My Street
My Town, My State 00000
111  234-5678

July 1, 1980

Equal Employment Opportunity Commission
Columbia Plaza Highrise
2401 E Street, N.W.
Washington, D.C. 20506

I have been employed by Younger for the past twenty years. During most of those years, I believe I have been treated fairly. Several months ago, however, I believe that I was discriminated against because of my age. I am fifty-five years old. I hereby file this charge of discrimination against Younger under the Age Discrimination in Employment Act.

Younger employs approximately 100 persons. Its main office, the office where I work, is as follows:

Younger
10 Main Street
My Town, My State 00000

Two months ago, on May 1, 1980, my immediate supervisor selected two employees in our twenty-person department for advanced training which undoubtedly will lead to promotions. Each of the selected employees had been with the company only for several years. One is in his late twenties and the other is in her early forties. I believe that I am better qualified for the advanced training than either of them. I applied for the training but was passed over. I believe that I have been discriminated against simply because I am older.

Please investigate this charge and keep me informed of your progress.

Sincerely,

Charging Party

# PART TWO

## The Power to Win Your Rights by Threatening Employers with the Loss of Federal Monies

# Using a Law Designed to Bring **4**
## Discriminatory
# Local Governments to Their Knees

## THE REVENUE SHARING ACT
### [RACE, COLOR, NATIONAL ORIGIN, RELIGION, SEX]

Every local government receives federal revenue sharing funding. The Revenue Sharing Act not only authorizes this funding but also prohibits discrimination by recipients of the funding. Given the current financial condition of our local governments, the threatened or actual suspension of this funding to a discriminatory employer, as mandated by the 1976 amendments to the Revenue Sharing Act, is a powerful method of fighting job discrimination. As a federal judge recently remarked, it "is a device designed to bring [discriminatory employers] quickly to their knees."[1]

Renault Robinson, a Chicago police officer, was among the first to invoke this powerful device. Like other black officers, he believed that the Police Department engaged in extensive discrimination in hiring and promotion against blacks. As president of the Afro-American Patrolmen's League in Chicago, he not only was concerned about that discrimination but decided to do something about it.

In 1970, Renault Robinson and the Afro-American Patrolmen's League, alleging extensive race discrimination in employment by the Chicago Police Department, sued the city of Chicago

103

under the Civil Rights Acts of 1866 and 1871. Several years later, after Title VII of the Civil Rights Act of 1964 was amended to cover public employment, the Department of Justice sued the city of Chicago under Title VII, charging the Police Department with unlawful employment discrimination on grounds of both race and sex.

At approximately the same time that he filed his lawsuit, Officer Robinson also filed an administrative charge of discrimination with the federal Office of Revenue Sharing against the city of Chicago. He had hoped that the Office of Revenue Sharing would find unlawful discrimination under the Revenue Sharing Act and suspend and then terminate the millions of dollars of revenue sharing funding received by the city. In this way, he hoped to force a quick end to the Police Department's discrimination. But the Office of Revenue Sharing did nothing.

In the meantime, the lawsuits filed earlier proceeded to trial. In response to those lawsuits, the federal court in 1974 issued a preliminary ruling finding the entry-level examinations used for hiring police officers to be racially discriminatory and unlawful, finding the background investigations used to hire entry-level police officers to be racially discriminatory and unlawful, finding the promotional examinations used for promotion to the position of sergeant to be racially discriminatory and unlawful, finding the efficiency ratings used to promote officers to the position of sergeant to be racially discriminatory and unlawful, and finding the overt denial of police officer employment to women to be sex discriminatory and unlawful.[2]

Armed with these federal court findings of discrimination, Police Officer Robinson returned to the Office of Revenue Sharing and again urged action. Still nothing happened. He then sued the Office of Revenue Sharing. Something happened. The court ordered the suspension of all revenue sharing funding to the city of Chicago.[3] As a result of the court order, more than $100 million in revenue sharing funding was withheld from Chicago.[4] The city had no alternative. It needed the money. It thus ended its discriminatory practices.

When Renault Robinson won the suspension of revenue sharing funding to the city of Chicago because of the Police Department's discrimination, he invoked a powerful method of civil rights enforcement which had never been used before. It is a weapon which now can be used without a lawsuit. As a result of amendments added to the Revenue Sharing Act in 1976, the suspension of federal funding which Renault Robinson had to obtain in court now is a mandatory administrative procedure. You no longer have to sue the Office of Revenue Sharing or even your boss. All you have to do is file an administrative charge of discrimination with the Office of Revenue Sharing. It should do the rest for you.

*The Revenue Sharing Act of 1972, as amended in 1976, forbids employment discrimination on grounds of race, color, national origin, religion, and sex by all local governments.*

*The Revenue Sharing Act's prohibition against job discrimination, and the remedies available to individuals, are quite similar to those in Title VII. Although the Revenue Sharing Act has not yet been widely used, you should use it whenever you are discriminated against by a local government. All you need to do is file an administrative charge of discrimination against your boss with the Office of Revenue Sharing [ORS].*

*The primary weapon used in enforcing the Revenue Sharing Act against local governments is threatened or actual suspension and termination of revenue sharing funding. This method of enforcement, which ordinarily will bring an immediate end to discrimination, can be invoked administratively by the ORS. Additionally, job discrimination can be stopped and funding terminated through lawsuits filed by the Department of Justice and through lawsuits filed by individuals.*

*Overall, the Revenue Sharing Act provides you with the most powerful method that exists today for obtaining your rights to non-discrimination in local government employment. You should never hesitate to use this powerful law.*

## WHO IS COVERED BY THE LAW

Every local government which receives revenue sharing funding is prohibited from engaging in discrimination by Section 122 of the Revenue Sharing Act [more properly called the State and Local Fiscal Assistance Act of 1972].[5]

Virtually all local governments—39,000 of them—receive revenue sharing funding each year. The amounts of funding are substantial, ranging from hundreds of thousands to millions of dollars. If you have been discriminated against by a county, city, town, or other unit of local government, rest assured that the employer is covered by the Revenue Sharing Act.

Technically, the Revenue Sharing Act prohibits discrimination only in "any program or activity" of a "unit of local government . . . which receives funding made available" from the Office of Revenue Sharing.[6] But the words "program or activity" have been broadly interpreted by the ORS to mean "the operations of the agency or organizational unit of a recipient government," for example "a police department, department of corrections, health department."[7] If there is any discrimination in a major department of a local government, the Revenue Sharing Act simply presumes that the discrimination is being supported by the federal funding; it is up to the local government to prove otherwise.[8]

## DISCRIMINATORY PRACTICES WHICH ARE UNLAWFUL

The Revenue Sharing Act's prohibition against discrimination is straightforward. There is to be no discrimination on grounds of race, color, national origin, religion, or sex.[9] This, of course, includes employment discrimination.

Although the Revenue Sharing Act does not enumerate specific forms of forbidden employment discrimination, the federal regulations interpreting the Act do provide some examples. More importantly, the same types of employment practices that are unlawful under Title VII, discussed in Chapter 2 of this book, also are prohibited by the Revenue Sharing Act.

### Examples of Unlawful Practices

The federal regulations interpreting the Revenue Sharing Act, like the Act itself, broadly mandate that local governments cannot subject any individual to discrimination.[10] Specifically prohibited is the use of employment "criteria or methods of administration which have the effect of . . . subjecting individuals to discrimination [or] perpetuating the results of past discriminatory practices."[11]

Also forbidden is any discriminatory "term, condition, or privilege of employment," a phrase which includes but is not limited to recruiting, advertising, and the processing of applications; hiring, promoting, demoting, firing, and rehiring; setting rates of pay and other forms of compensation; classifying jobs, making job assignments, and providing training; granting sick leave and leaves of absence; and providing fringe benefits.[12] As this long list indicates, all types of employment discrimination are outlawed.

## Practices Which Are Unlawful under Title VII Standards

Employment practices outlawed by Title VII of the Civil Rights Act of 1964 also are unlawful under the Revenue Sharing Act. This is because the federal regulations have incorporated some of the Title VII standards into the Revenue Sharing Act[13] and because the federal courts have agreed that similar practices are prohibited by both laws.[14] Accordingly, any discriminatory practice used by a local government which would violate Title VII also violates the Revenue Sharing Act.

## Overt Discrimination

Overt discrimination—blatant discrimination—unfortunately still exists. For example, Chicago's refusal to allow women to compete for jobs as police officers up through 1977 constituted unlawful overt discrimination in violation not only of Title VII but also of the Revenue Sharing Act.[15] Similarly, the explicit refusal in 1977 to hire women for law enforcement jobs in the Mobile County, Alabama, jail was blatantly unlawful.[16] A different form of overt sex discrimination was practiced—until recently—in Fargo, North Dakota. For decades, the city had assigned several male police officers to the sole duty of marking cars for parking violations and issuing traffic tickets. When it later reassigned those officers to other duties, created new positions titled "car markers," and hired women for those positions at half the pay previously given to men, the city committed unlawful overt discrimination.[17]

Overt racial discrimination recently was practiced by the St. Louis Fire Department. Although at least a few blacks had been hired as firefighters and had been assigned to firehouses throughout the city, they were confronted with segregation in those firehouses. The firehouses, it turned out, had cooking facilities which allowed the firefighters to dine there. In each firehouse, the white firefighters formed a supper club, with one of their number serving as chef. The supper clubs, with the apparent approval of the St. Louis Fire Department, barred admission to the black firefighters. This overt discrimination was found by a court in 1977 to be an unlawful condition of employment.[18]

## Disparate Impact Discrimination

Undoubtedly, the form of discrimination most widely practiced by local governments occurs through their use of purportedly neutral practices which have a discriminatory impact and which cannot be shown by the employer to be a business necessity. As we saw in Chapter 2, these practices violate Title VII. They also are unlawful under the Revenue Sharing Act.[19] As Renault Robinson proved in Chicago, for example, the entry-level examinations, background investigations, promotional examinations, and efficiency ratings used by the Police Department all had a racially discriminatory impact, were not shown to be job-related, and thus were unlawful.[20] Similarly, the supervisory ratings used for promotion by the Chicago Fire Department had a discriminatory impact, were not shown to be job-related, and thus were unlawful.[21]

This is not to say that Chicago should be singled out as the only local government with a history of unlawful disparate impact discrimination. Similar unlawful practices, used by other local governments, include the minimum-height standards, high-school-diploma requirements, and entry-level written tests used by the Buffalo Police and Fire Departments[22]; the minimum-height standards and physical-agility requirements used by the San Francisco Police Department[23]; the apprenticeship graduation and unusually high work experience requirements used by the city of Milwaukee to hire skilled trades workers[24]; and the award of bonus points only to veterans with an honorable discharge used by the Columbus, Ohio, Fire Department.[25] In the Minneapolis Fire Department the unlawful practices included the use of no arrest record and no conviction record requirements, high-school-diploma requirements, and entry-level written tests.[26]

The use of discriminatory written tests seems to be the most common of all unlawful practices. In fact, the discriminatory written examinations used by the Fire Departments in Boston and Baltimore, in St. Louis and St. Paul, and in New York and San Francisco all have been found to be unlawful.[27] Similarly, the written tests used for entry-level police officer positions or for promotions by the Police Departments in Bridgeport, Philadelphia, Cleveland, Toledo, and elsewhere have been unlawful.[28] And not unexpectedly, the written test used by the city of Atlanta to hire golf professionals for the public golf courses was unlawful.[29]

Not all practices which have a discriminatory impact are necessarily unlawful. For even when a practice is shown to be discriminatory, it still can be used if the employer demonstrates that the test or other requirement is a business necessity, meaning that the practice is directly related to performance of the job and that there is no less-discriminatory, equally useful alternative. Most employers, however, cannot satisfy these standards—standards which can be met only through what is called a "validation" study[30]—for the simple reason that employers usually set their job requirements arbitrarily and without any concrete knowledge about whether the requirements actually have anything to do with effective job performance.

Employers who try to prove the business necessity of their discriminatory practices ordinarily fail to satisfy the first standard of showing that the practices are job-related. Occasionally, however, employers arguably show job relatedness but fail to satisfy the second standard of showing that there are no less-discriminatory, equally useful alternatives. The Mobile Police Department, for example, defended its use of promotion procedures which had a racially discriminatory impact by asserting in court in 1978 that its validation study was sufficient to establish the business necessity for the procedures. Not so, held the court. Although the procedures arguably were job-related, the Police Department had not investigated the availability of less-discriminatory, equally valid alternative procedures. Accordingly, use of the discriminatory procedures was unlawful.[31]

## Disparate Treatment Discrimination

Disparate treatment discrimination also is unlawful. If you have been denied a job, denied a promotion, discharged, or otherwise subjected to disparate treatment—treated differently because of your race or sex, etc.—by a local government, you may be able to prove that your boss violated the Revenue Sharing Act. Initially, you can establish a presumptive case (prima facie case) of disparate treatment discrimination by showing that you are protected by the Revenue Sharing Act, that you were qualified for the job, that despite your qualifications you were rejected, and that the position thereafter remained open or was filled by someone with lesser qualifications. Once you establish these factors, your employer can overcome your prima facie case of discrimination only by articulating a legitimate non-discriminatory reason for not hiring you, promoting you, or whatever. If the employer cannot do so, your rights to non-discrimination under the Revenue Sharing Act have been violated.[32]

Several years ago, the Jackson, Mississippi, Police Department fired two black police officers for allegedly accepting bribes. The officers maintained that they were innocent. They also contended that the discharges were racially discriminatory because white officers had not been treated in the same manner. The blacks sued their boss, and proceeded to establish the four elements of a prima facie case of disparate treatment discrimination: they were protected by the law from discrimination; aside from the alleged reason for their dismissal, they were qualified for the jobs from which they were fired; despite their qualifications, they were fired; and their boss did not discharge other employees with similar qualifications. In response to this prima facie case, the Police Department argued that the acceptance of bribes was a legitimate, non-discriminatory reason for the discharges. The department's argument was not persuasive. Its stated reason was merely a pretext for discrimination, since the white officers who had been accused at the same time of accepting bribes were not fired or even investigated.[33]

## Other Forms of Discrimination

Most forms of discrimination fit within one or more of the foregoing three categories. Those that don't may still be unlawful. For example, as is pointed out in Chapter 2, sexual harassment of women on the job is unlawful. If you are a woman and you have been subjected to sexual harassment by your boss, your rights to non-discrimination under the Revenue Sharing Act have been violated.[34]

## Retaliation

The federal regulations interpreting the Revenue Sharing Act prohibit local governments from retaliating against you for any actions you may take to enforce your rights or the rights of others under the Act. Specifically, local governments may not "intimidate, threaten, coerce, or in any way retaliate against" you if you file a charge of discrimination or participate in any proceeding to obtain the non-discrimination rights guaranteed by the Act.[35] This, of course, does not guarantee that you won't be retaliated against. But any local government that violates this prohibition runs the risk of losing all of its revenue sharing funding.

## Statistical Proof of Discrimination

Unlawful discrimination often is proved through the use of statistics. As we saw in Chapter 2, it is necessary for you to obtain statistics showing the discriminatory impact of purportedly neutral practices. Even where you aren't challenging a purportedly neutral practice, it usually is extremely helpful for you to show that minorities or women are severely underrepresented in the job which you seek or in your employer's work force as a whole.

Renault Robinson, in his lawsuit against the Chicago Police Department, used statistics to his advantage. In the early 1960s, when the minority population of the city was 25 percent, minority personnel fluctuated between 22 percent and 26 percent of the sworn police officers. By the early 1970s, however, when minorities were 40 percent of the city's population, they had declined to only 17 percent representation in the Police Department. The statistics on female employment were even more startling. Although women comprised approximately 50 percent of the city's population, their representation among sworn police officers was less than 1 percent.[36]

The minority applicants who sued the Minneapolis Fire Department also used statistics to their advantage by showing that the Fire Department had never in its history employed a minority firefighter.[37] Similarly, the fact that there were no black highway patrol officers in Mississippi, a state with 38 percent black population, was sufficient to establish a prima facie case of hiring discrimination.[38] Identical statistics showing the absence of any black state troopers in Alabama, a state with a 25 percent black population, were found sufficient in and of themselves to prove unlawful hiring discrimination.[39]

In almost every local government work force, especially in the higher-paying jobs, the work force imbalance statistics will work to your advantage. Just as they help you to establish a violation of Title VII, so too will they assist you in proving a violation of the Revenue Sharing Act.

## MAJOR EXCEPTIONS

The Revenue Sharing Act does not prohibit employment discrimination based upon age.[40] Beyond this, there are three categories of exceptions under the Act.

### Exempted Employers

The Act covers only those employers that receive revenue sharing funding. Some units of local government, such as school boards, sometimes do not receive revenue sharing funding. They thus are exempted. As a general rule, however, you can safely assume that nearly all local government agencies do receive revenue sharing funding and are covered by the Revenue Sharing Act.

## Exceptions to Discriminatory Employment Practices

As we have seen, Title VII standards are widely used to determine the types of discrimination prohibited by the Revenue Sharing Act. Title VII, however, contains five statutory exceptions which permit employers to use discriminatory employment practices. Two of these exceptions are applicable to the Revenue Sharing Act.[41]

*Bona fide occupational qualification.* Under Title VII, an employer may discriminate on grounds of national origin, religion, or sex so long as national origin, religion, or sex is a bona fide occupational qualification necessary for job performance. As we saw in Chapter 2, this exception has been raised by employers only in the context of their sex discrimination and it regularly has been construed against them. The Revenue Sharing Act does not contain such an exception, but the federal regulations interpreting the Act do recognize the bona fide occupational qualification exception.[42] Although this regulatory exception may be in conflict with the Revenue Sharing Act's flat ban on discrimination, federal regulations normally are given great deference by the courts.[43] Moreover, since the primary enforcement of the Revenue Sharing Act is undertaken by the federal Office of Revenue Sharing—the agency that issued the federal regulations allowing this exception under the Act—you should assume the applicability of the exception. But remember that a discriminatory local government will have to prove the necessity for the exception, and nearly all such attempts by employers have failed.

*Reasonable accommodation and undue hardship.* This exception is definitely applicable to the Revenue Sharing Act, thereby allowing some discrimination on grounds of religion. As we saw in Chapter 2, there is a statutory exception in Title VII which allows an employer to discriminate on grounds of religion if the employer cannot reasonably accommodate an employee's or an applicant's religious observance without undue hardship.[44] The Revenue Sharing Act incorporates Title VII's prohibition against religious discrimination and specifically adopts "any exemption from such prohibition" in Title VII.[45] In other words, a local government may discriminate against you on religious grounds under the Revenue Sharing Act, in the same manner as under Title VII, but only if it cannot reasonably accommodate your religious observance without undue hardship.

## Affirmative Action Is Not Unlawful

A final exception, pertaining to the use of affirmative action undertaken to increase the representation of minorities and women in an employer's work force, works in your favor. Although few local governments actually engage in affirmative action, the federal regulations interpreting the Revenue Sharing Act expressly authorize it. Specifically, the regulations encourage employers to determine the minority and female underrepresentation in their work forces, to analyze the disparate impact of their employment practices, and to take reasonable steps to correct their underrepresentation and the exclusionary effects of their past practices. The reasonable steps may be race, color, or sex "conscious" and may include the use of "goals and timetables" for hiring and promoting minorities and women.[46]

Beyond the permissibility of voluntary affirmative action, another form of affirmative action may be required. If a local government is found to have discriminated against minorities or women in violation of the Revenue Sharing Act, extensive affirmative action to overcome that past discrimination can be ordered.[47]

## THE FEDERAL AGENCY RESPONSIBLE FOR ENFORCEMENT

When Congress enacted the Revenue Sharing Act of 1972, it created a new federal agency, the Office of Revenue Sharing. The ORS has two primary functions: to channel billions of dollars of revenue sharing funding each year to local governments, and to withhold such funding from any local government which is engaged in discrimination made unlawful by the Act. This civil rights role is performed within the ORS by its Civil Rights Division. Its office is in Washington, D.C.:

Civil Rights Division
Office of Revenue Sharing
Columbia Plaza Highrise
2401 E Street, N.W.
Washington, D.C. 20226

202/634–5157

As Renault Robinson demonstrated through lawsuits against the city of Chicago and against the Office of Revenue Sharing, the ORS in its early years unfortunately was more interested in providing funding to local governments than it was in fulfilling its civil rights enforcement obligations. In response, Congress in 1976 amended Section 122 of the Revenue Sharing Act to make the suspension and termination of revenue sharing funding to discriminatory local governments a mandatory administrative procedure.

*Because of the 1976 amendments, the Revenue Sharing Act provides you with by far the most effective methods that exist today to obtain your rights to non-discrimination in local government employment.* The first and often the only step for you to take is to file an administrative charge with the ORS.

## ENFORCEMENT: HOW TO OBTAIN YOUR RIGHTS

Most local governments are in constant jeopardy of losing their revenue sharing funding because they are not in compliance with the Revenue Sharing Act. You can threaten the loss of that revenue sharing funding, and thereby obtain your rights to non-discrimination, by taking a single administrative step: filing a charge of discrimination with the ORS.

In seeking to win your rights, it is of course helpful to know a little bit about the law. It also is helpful to know as much as you can about your local government's employment practices. This you can find out by talking to your colleagues, to the personnel director, and to the government's equal employment opportunity officer.[48] Whether or not you obtain as much information as you'd like, filing an administrative charge gets the ball rolling.

A discriminatory local government can be required to stop its discrimination against you by any of four procedures. But it's usually up to you to take the first step of filing a charge.

• A charge of discrimination which you file with the ORS may lead to threatened or actual loss of revenue sharing funding and hence to resolution of your charge.

• A holding of discrimination (under another law, such as Title VII), rendered by a federal agency or by a federal or state court, which you send to the ORS, will lead to threatened or actual loss of revenue sharing funding and hence to resolution of the discrimination.

• A charge of discrimination which you file with the ORS may lead to a lawsuit filed on your behalf by the Department of Justice to terminate the revenue sharing funding and to remedy the unlawful discrimination.

• A charge of discrimination which you file with the ORS may lead to a lawsuit filed by you to terminate the revenue sharing funding and to remedy the unlawful discrimination.

These methods of enforcement are incredibly powerful. In contrast to the EEOC, which has to rely primarily on its minimal administrative powers of persuasion to enforce the Equal Pay Act, Title VII, and the Age Discrimination in Employment Act, the ORS is empowered and in fact required to enforce the Revenue Sharing Act's ban on discrimination by suspending and terminating revenue sharing funding to discriminatory local governments.

## Administrative Resolution of Charges of Discrimination

If you believe that you have been discriminated against by a local government, you should send a letter (a charge) to the ORS charging that government with discrimination. There is no prescribed form for the letter. A sample letter is set forth at the end of this chapter. In the letter, you should:

• Give your name, address, and phone number.
• State the government's name and address.
• Indicate when the discrimination occurred.

• Describe fully the nature of the discrimination practiced against you.

• Provide as many comparative work-force statistics as possible to indicate the past discrimination practiced by the employer.

There are no formal requirements which must be met in filing a charge. The charge need not be sworn to by you. In fact, if you fear retaliation, you can withhold your name and have someone else (such as a lawyer or a civil rights organization) file the charge on your behalf.[49] Additionally, the charge need not be very extensive, but the more information you provide, the more likely it is that your charge will be fully investigated. Finally, *there is no time limit for filing a charge,*[50] but in order to ensure a prompt and thorough investigation, you should send your charge to the ORS as soon as possible.

When the ORS receives your administrative charge of discrimination, it is required to investigate quickly. Within 90 days of receiving your charge, the ORS must make a finding of probable non-compliance or compliance—a finding about whether the employer meets the non-discrimination requirements of the Act.[51] The standard for a finding of non-compliance by the ORS is "that it is more likely than not" that the local government has or is engaged in unlawful discrimination.[52] Since this is a relatively easy standard for the ORS to meet, most local governments, including yours, will be found in non-compliance with the Revenue Sharing Act by the ORS.

Once the ORS makes a finding of non-compliance, there are a number of specific steps which the ORS must follow within specific time periods.[53] These steps will lead to compliance by the local government, or to suspension and termination of revenue sharing funding. This can occur quite quickly. In fact, under the steps and time limits, revenue sharing funding can be suspended as early as 30 days after the initial ORS finding of non-compliance.

The various procedures and time limits governing ORS investigations, findings, and suspensions and terminations of revenue sharing funding do not involve you directly. They simply govern the manner and timing of the ORS's relationship with discriminatory local governments and compel the ORS to act quickly. Nonetheless, you should be aware that the ORS ordinarily does not act as quickly as it is required to do. In fact, the ORS regularly takes longer than the required 90 days even to investigate charges. Once the investigation begins, however, you will be directly involved in two ways.

During the ORS investigation of your administrative charge, an investigator from the ORS usually will contact you by phone or in person for additional or supplementary information. You thus should keep your notes and continue to gather as much information as possible about your local government's discriminatory practices. If no one from the ORS contacts you within two months after the filing of your charge, you should write to the ORS to find out the name of the investigator assigned to your charge, and then provide him or her with as much additional information as you have been able to gather. The ORS at all times is required to advise you about the status of your charge.[54]

Whenever the ORS makes a finding of non-compliance, it always will try to negotiate a voluntary compliance agreement with the discriminatory local government. Under law, these negotiations do not have to involve you directly. But, again, you should contact your ORS investigator to indicate what you believe is necessary for voluntary compliance. In other words, you should tell the ORS what you believe is the proper remedy for the discrimination practiced against you and others. Although the ORS must send you a copy of the compliance agreement within 15 days after execution of the agreement,[55] this might be too late if the agreement is unsatisfactory. You thus should be in contact with the ORS as soon and as often as possible. If you don't like the compliance agreement, or if you don't think it does enough for you, be sure to tell the ORS about your objections. Unfortunately, there is no way to insure that a compliance agreement which you find unacceptable also will be found unacceptable by the ORS.

If your best efforts have failed and you do not like the compliance agreement, you can always sue your local government under the Revenue Sharing Act. The administrative procedures undertaken by the ORS have no effect upon your right or the right of the Department of Justice to sue a local government to seek an end to the discrimination through the termination of revenue sharing funding.

## Administrative Responses to Holdings of Discrimination

As we have seen, the customary method of invoking the ORS administrative procedures is through your filing a charge of discrimination with the ORS against a local government. There is, however, a second method of invoking ORS enforcement against discriminatory governments. This method does not involve the filing with the ORS of an administrative charge of discrimination, or even the need for the ORS to make a finding of non-compliance under the Revenue Sharing Act. Instead, this method simply requires the ORS to respond to a holding of discrimination made, after a hearing, by another federal agency or by a federal or state court.

Most individuals who have been discriminated against by local governments are not aware of the Revenue Sharing Act or of the ORS's mandatory enforcement procedures. Rather than filing an administrative charge with the ORS, you instead might have filed a charge with another federal agency such as the EEOC, or filed a lawsuit in federal or state court. If any such agency or court, after a hearing, reaches a "holding"[56]—a ruling—that your local government has engaged in unlawful discrimination, the ORS is required to respond to that holding by initiating its administrative procedures leading to suspension and termination of funding to that discriminatory local government.[57]

This holding of discrimination by another agency or by a court is the equivalent of an ORS finding of non-compliance. Once the ORS receives a copy of that holding, the ORS is required to take the same specific steps within the specified time periods as it is required to take when it finds non-compliance.[58] There is but one difference, and it's in your favor. When the ORS makes its own finding, the local government may present evidence disputing both the finding of discrimination and the presumption that the discrimination occurred in a program or activity supported by revenue sharing funding.[59] But when the ORS instead responds to a holding rendered by a court or by another federal agency, that discrimination holding must be "treated as conclusive" by the ORS, thereby allowing the local government to present evidence only about whether the discrimination occurred in a program or activity supported by revenue sharing funding.[60]

The availability to you of this second ORS enforcement procedure means that even if you don't file a charge with the ORS but you do obtain a holding of discrimination elsewhere—such as by a court under Title VII—the ORS has to react to that holding by threatening and ultimately suspending and terminating its revenue sharing funding. But the ORS can't react to something it doesn't know about. True, all local governments are required to send a copy of any holding to the ORS,[61] but they might overlook that obligation. Obviously, if you learn about a holding of discrimination involving your local government, you should obtain a copy of that holding immediately and send it to the ORS.

## Lawsuits by the Department of Justice

In addition to the administrative procedures which *must* be taken on your behalf by the ORS, there is another method of enforcement which *might* be undertaken on your behalf: the Department of Justice may, under certain circumstances, sue your local government.

The Revenue Sharing Act specifically authorizes the Department of Justice to file "pattern or practice" lawsuits against discriminatory governments.[62] This means that whenever the Department of Justice believes that a local government has engaged or is engaging in more than an isolated instance of discrimination, it may sue that government. When this occurs, you will have the very substantial power and resources of the federal government bearing down on your local government. In such lawsuits, the courts are authorized to enter any orders necessary to stop the unlawful discrimination and to order "the suspension, termination, or repayment" of revenue sharing funding.[63]

It is very helpful, of course, to have the Department of Justice sue your boss on your behalf. Whether or not to sue, however, is a matter of discretion for the Department of Justice. The first step for you, of course, is to file an administrative charge of discrimination with the ORS. It then may refer the matter to the Department of Justice while continuing to invoke its own administrative sanctions.[64] If the Department of Justice for some reason doesn't sue, you still have the right to sue your boss yourself.

## Lawsuits by Individuals

In most situations, ORS administrative enforcement or a Department of Justice lawsuit will provide you with your rights to non-discrimination. There are three instances, however, when you might want to consider filing your own lawsuit against a discriminatory local government. One is when you are not satisfied with the voluntary compliance agreement negotiated by the ORS. An unlikely second instance may arise if the local government refuses to comply voluntarily, choosing instead to lose its revenue sharing funding. The third is when you want to obtain what you believe is a faster remedy. Whatever your reason, the Revenue Sharing Act expressly authorizes you to sue any local government which receives or has received revenue sharing funding and which has discriminated against you.[65]

In order to sue your boss, you have to satisfy only one administrative prerequisite. You simply have to file an administrative charge of discrimination with the ORS, and let it sit there for 90 days. After the 90 days have passed, and assuming that the ORS within those 90 days did not find that the local government was engaged in discrimination, you then are entitled to sue your boss.[66] This means that you don't have to wait the 180 days or usually the 240 days to demand a right-to-sue letter which you need to sue under Title VII. Instead, you can go to court under the Revenue Sharing Act only 90 days after filing an administrative charge.

Once you're in court, the court can enter orders requiring remedies for all of the discrimination or requiring the "suspension, termination or repayment" of revenue sharing funding.[67] But, ordinarily, there will be no need for you to go to court at all. In view of the ORS's mandatory administrative procedures and because of the substantial threat of funding cut-offs, the ORS should be able to remedy all discrimination against you without your having to do anything more than file an administrative charge.

## REMEDIES: WHAT YOU CAN GET WHEN YOUR RIGHTS HAVE BEEN VIOLATED

There are two sets of remedies available to you when you have been discriminated against by a local government. First, you are entitled to compliance remedies to end the discrimination and to place you in the position you would have been in if the discrimination had never occurred. Second, if the compliance remedies are not obtained, the revenue sharing funding to the discriminatory local government can be suspended, terminated, and even ordered to be repaid. These remedies are available to you through the ORS administrative enforcement of the Act and through lawsuits filed by the Department of Justice or by you. Additionally, if you have to sue, and if you win, your boss will have to pay your attorney's fees.[68] If you lose, however, and the court believes that your lawsuit was frivolous, unreasonable, or groundless, you might be ordered to pay your boss's attorney's fees.[69]

### Compliance Remedies

As we have seen, the ORS administrative procedures are directed primarily toward obtaining voluntary compliance from discriminatory governments. Whether obtained by the ORS, or whether ordered by a court in a lawsuit filed by the Department of Justice or by you, numerous compliance remedies, which are considered to be "equitable" remedies, are available for you.[70]

The equitable compliance remedies available under the Revenue Sharing Act are the same as the equitable remedies under Title VII. As discussed in Chapter 2, you are entitled to such remedies as hiring, reinstatement, transfer, or promotion; retroactive seniority; and back pay. If the discrimination has been extensive against minorities or women, the local government can be required to implement affirmative action goals and timetables for hiring minorities or women.[71]

The remedies actually available of course depend upon what is necessary to correct the discrimination. In Durham, North Carolina, for example, where Judy McCoy had been dismissed from the Police Department because of her race and sex, and where C. G. Hargrove had been denied equal pay and then demoted by the Recreation Department because of her sex, the ORS told the city that if it didn't provide full and appropriate remedies it would lose its $1.6 million in annual revenue sharing payments. Ms. McCoy was immediately rehired and given retroactive seniority and $17,993 in lost pay; Ms. Hargrove was promoted to a high-paying job and given $33,271 in back pay; the city implemented a training and upgrading program for current female and minority employees; and the city established affirmative action goals and timetables for hiring and promoting women and minorities at all levels of employment.

## Loss of Revenue Sharing Funding

All local governments—not just New York, Chicago, and Cleveland—are in dire financial condition. They need revenue sharing funding to make ends meet, and like the city of Durham, they are learning that they will lose that funding if they engage in unlawful discrimination or refuse to remedy it.

Administratively, as we have seen, the ORS is required to suspend and then to terminate its funding to local governments that refuse to enter into voluntary compliance. The very real threat of this remedy is so great that the ORS rarely has had to suspend funding. Most governments, when pushed, have chosen to comply with the non-discrimination requirements of the Revenue Sharing Act rather than lose their revenue sharing funding.

Valued revenue sharing funding also is placed in jeopardy the moment a government is sued under the Revenue Sharing Act. During the early stages of the lawsuit, the courts may order the "placing of any further payments [of revenue sharing funding] in escrow pending the outcome of the litigation."[72] Additionally, the courts are authorized to order not only the suspension and termination of funding but also the "repayment" of previous funding.[73] Discrimination can be quite costly indeed.

\* \* \*

La Grange, Georgia, a small Southern town midway between Atlanta, Georgia, and Montgomery, Alabama, is typical of many rural towns across the United States. It uses employment practices which have been unchanged for decades and which are often discriminatory. And it is a recipient of revenue sharing funding. In fact, the more than $400,000 in revenue sharing funds received annually by La Grange constitutes a substantial portion of its municipal budget.

Robert Nelson and Willie Ford are black police officers employed by the 60-member La Grange Police Department. In their view, the Police Department's employment practices were discriminatory. But they felt powerless to do anything about it. Then, in late 1977, they found themselves suspended without pay for alleged insubordination. Angered, they decided to assert their rights.

In February 1978, Officers Nelson and Ford filed charges of discrimination with the Office of Revenue Sharing. In addition to alleging that they had been discriminatorily suspended, Officers Nelson and Ford claimed that black officers were not assigned patrol duties with white partners, that black officers were given more dangerous assignments and ended up with less desirable jobs than the whites, and that many other forms of employment discrimination existed in the Police Department and elsewhere in city government.

The ORS responded to the charges by conducting a thorough investigation. In the process, it turned up so much discrimination that its investigation lasted longer than the 90 days allowed by the Revenue Sharing Act. Finally, in March 1979, the ORS rendered findings of discrimination and offered recommendations about how the discrimination had to be remedied. In the ORS's view, there had been no discrimination in patrol assignments. But the ORS did find that Officers Nelson and Ford had been discriminatorily suspended, and it recommended that this be remedied by an expungement of the incident from their records and by an award of back pay. It found that past racial discrimination contributed to a dearth of blacks in supervisory positions; for this the ORS recommended the adoption of goals and timetables for the promotion of black officers. Significantly, the ORS proceeded beyond the administrative charges and found that the

Police Department also had discriminated against women in hiring; it recommended the adoption of a 45 percent goal for hiring women in order to remedy the past discrimination. Finally, the ORS found that the town jails were racially segregated, for which it recommended desegregation.

The ORS recommendations were accompanied by its powerful enforcement tool. LaGrange was advised that it should prepare to lose its $416,212 in revenue sharing funding if it chose not to comply. Needless to say, LaGrange needed the money. It decided to comply, to implement the ORS recommendations, and thereby to close another chapter on employment discrimination.

## Sample Letter Charging Discrimination

Charging Party
1000 My Street
My Town, Ny State 00000
111 234-5678

July 1, 1980

Civil Rights Division
Office of Revenue Sharing
Columbia Plaza Highrise
2401 E Street, N.W.
Washington, D.C. 20226

I recently was denied employment as a firefighter by the Boss Fire Department. Since I believe that I was discriminated against because of my sex in violation of Section 122 of the Revenue Sharing Act, I hereby file this administrative charge of discrimination against:

Boss Fire Department
10 Main Street
My Town, My State 00000

The Boss Fire Department, in conjunction with the Boss Civil Service Commission, requires applicants for the position of firefighter to pass a written test, a physical agility test, and an oral interview. Applicants who pass the first two tests are allowed to take the oral interview, and thereafter are given a single weighted score on the three criteria. Applicants are ranked and hired on the basis of their composite scores.

In the spring of 1980, after applying and taking the written test, I was told that I had received a passing test grade of 98.5 of a possible 100 points. In June 1980, I took but failed the physical agility test. Accordingly, I was not allowed to continue in the application process.

Nearly all of the other female applicants also failed the physical agility test. I believe that approximately 5 percent of the women passed the test, while 70 percent of the men passed. Current firefighters, of course, do not have to pass the test. I believe that the physical agility test is unrelated to actual job performance and has never been validated.

Prior to 1977, no women had ever been employed as firefighters by the Boss Fire Department. Although women now are allowed to apply, there are only two women who have been hired. The physical agility test keeps most of us out.

Please investigate this charge and keep me informed of your progress.

Sincerely,

Charging Party

# Terminating 5
## Lucrative Federal Contracts
## to Discriminatory Private Employers

### EXECUTIVE ORDER 11246
[RACE, COLOR, NATIONAL ORIGIN, RELIGION, SEX]

Private employers, not just local governments, also are benefi-
ciaries of federal largess. In fact, thousands upon thousands of
private employers receive federal contracts to provide goods and
services to the federal government. The American Telephone
and Telegraph Company and its affiliated operating companies,
for example, provide telephone and other communications services to the United States government. All such government
contractors, including AT&T, are barred from engaging in employment discrimination by Executive Order 11246. If they do
discriminate, the Office of Federal Contract Compliance Programs [OFCCP]—which has enforcement responsibilities over
government contractors—can terminate their lucrative federal
contracts.

During the late 1960s, hundreds of women and minority persons filed charges of systemic discrimination against AT&T, the
largest corporation in the United States. Some of the charges
were filed with the Equal Employment Opportunity Commission under Title VII of the Civil Rights Act of 1964. Other
charges were filed with the Office of Federal Contract Compliance Programs under Executive Order 11246. In 1970, the agen-

cies formally accused AT&T of engaging in systemwide employment discrimination against minorities and women.

In sixty days of government hearings conducted during 1971 and 1972, AT&T was shown to have assigned women to sex-segregated job classifications, and to have assigned women and minorities to low-paying job classifications. There also was compelling evidence that AT&T had systematically denied advancement and promotion to women and minorities, and had hired and promoted only white males to top management positions. During the latter part of the hearings, AT&T began negotiating with the EEOC and with the OFCCP in an effort to settle the discrimination charges. The settlement efforts were overwhelmingly successful because AT&T did not want to lose any of its valuable government contracts. After reaching an agreement in which AT&T denied that it had engaged in discrimination, the government agencies by prearrangement sued AT&T on behalf of discriminated-against women and minorities. On that same day, January 18, 1973, the government and AT&T settled the lawsuit by filing the settlement agreement with the court.

The negotiated settlement—which became a formal court-approved consent decree subject to court supervision—was at the time the most comprehensive affirmative action plan ever obtained on behalf of female and minority employees and applicants. It required AT&T to implement strict numerical goals and timetables for hiring and promoting women and minorities in every job classification in which they were underrepresented. And it awarded $15 million in back pay and $38 million in wage adjustments and training for women and minorities.

AT&T's affirmative action performance under the consent decree was closely monitored by the EEOC and the OFCCP. In 1975, they advised the court that the 1973 and 1974 goals for hiring and promoting women and minorities had not been met. In order to correct these deficiencies, a court-approved supplemental consent decree was agreed to. The supplemental decree not only increased the already huge monetary award by an additional $7 million in back pay and $23 million more for wage adjustments and training but also required that the hiring and promotion goals be met more quickly and without regard to seniority (one result being that in some job classifications only women and minorities could be hired and promoted).

Over the years, telephone industry unions and various white male employees of AT&T challenged the consent decrees in court. They lost,[1] with the result that the AT&T consent decrees have become a model under Executive Order 11246 for the OFCCP to impose upon other companies which provide goods and services under contracts with the federal government.

*Executive Order 11246 prohibits all employers which contract with the federal government for the provision of goods or services valued at more than $10,000 from engaging in employment discrimination on grounds of race, color, national origin, religion, or sex. The Executive Order also requires all large employers with large government contracts to implement affirmative action goals and timetables for minorities and women in jobs where minorities and women are underrepresented. Similar requirements are imposed by the Executive Order upon construction contractors that bid on federally assisted construction contracts.*

*The Executive Order is enforced against government contractors by the Office of Federal Contract Compliance Programs through investigations and administrative efforts to obtain voluntary compliance. Enforcement ultimately leads to an end of discrimination or to a denial of lucrative government contracts to discriminatory contractors. Lawsuits also can be filed against discriminatory contractors by the Department of Justice, but not by individuals.*

*If you have been discriminated against by a private employer, you can initiate enforcement of the Executive Order by filing a charge of "systemic" discrimination with the OFCCP. Under OFCCP enforcement, you are entitled to broad remedies, including back pay.*

*Because of its affirmative action requirements and its powerful threat of lost government contracts, the Executive Order provides you with a significant tool to end discrimination. You should use it along with Title VII whenever possible.*

## WHO IS COVERED BY THE EXECUTIVE ORDER

Executive Order 11246 was issued under presidential authority in 1965[2] to require federal agencies to buy goods and services *only* from employers—"contractors"—that do not discriminate on grounds of race, color, national origin, religion, or sex, and which do engage in affirmative action on behalf of women and minorities. Because the Executive Order requires a non-discrimination and affirmative-action clause to be a part of most government contracts,[3] the Order covers nearly every employer that has a contract or bids on a contract with an agency of the United States government. Overall, the Executive Order applies to more than 29,000 companies, including all major corporations and universities. If you are among the 41 million workers employed by these contractors, or if you are an applicant for employment with one of these contractors, you are protected by the Executive Order.

The Executive Order separately addresses two different types of employers: companies that have or bid for federal contracts or subcontracts,[4] and construction contractors and subcontractors that have or bid for federally assisted construction contracts.[5] These two types of employers are covered by the Executive Order in slightly different ways.

### Employers That Have Federal Government Contracts or Subcontracts

The federal government purchases vast amounts of goods and services from private companies and from some universities. The federal government, at times, also rents or leases its property to others. All of these arrangements are accomplished through formal contracts, and virtually all of them are subject to the Executive Order. Indeed, contracts covered by the Executive Order include "any agreement or modification thereof between any [federal] contracting agency and any person [including a corporation, partnership, or state or local government] for the furnishing of supplies or services or for the use of real or personal property, including lease arrangements."[6]

Companies* that contract with federal agencies are, under two conditions, prohibited from engaging in discrimination and required to undertake affirmative action. All contractors and subcontractors that have contracts in any one year with the federal government totaling more than $10,000 are barred from engaging in *discrimination*. [7] All contractors and subcontractors that employ fifty or more employees and have contracts in any one year with the federal government for more than $50,000 are required to implement *affirmative action* goals and timetables to guarantee that there is no discrimination against women and minorities in hiring and promotion. [8] These requirements cover nearly all government contractors. Remember, the federal government purchases through contracts more than $100 billion in goods and services each year. Most of these contracts far exceed the $10,000 and $50,000 limitations. Pan American World Airways, for example, found itself covered by the Executive Order, not only through its many small contracts, but also through its $229 million, three-year contract with the National Aeronautic and Space Administration to operate and maintain the missile tracking systems at Cape Canaveral, and through its $29 million, one-year contract with the Military Air Command of the Department of Defense to transport troops and equipment. [9]

Many government contracts are not so large, but nearly all government contracts exceed $50,000. Sometimes, the contracting companies are fairly obvious. Utility companies supply gas and electricity to government buildings, transportation companies transport mail throughout the United States, universities perform research for government agencies, insurance companies provide health plans for government employees, and banks hold and transfer government funds. [10] And, of course, paper companies supply federal agencies with writing paper, as well as toilet paper. In fact, all types of supplies and services needed by any company, even the goods and services used by you at home, are bought by the federal government.

*Although government contractors are often referred to in this chapter as "companies" or "private employers," remember that large universities, whether private or public, often are the recipients of research contracts from the federal government and that they too thus are contractors covered by the Executive Order.

The Executive Order not only covers those contractors which provide goods and services to federal agencies but also covers contractors which contract for something from the federal government. For example, under federal law, oil companies can obtain leases from the federal government to develop and market oil and gas deposits beneath the ocean's continental shelf adjacent to the United States. One such company, the Crown Central Petroleum Corp. of Maryland, which held eight leases worth well over $50,000, sued the federal government, contending that it was not subject to the Executive Order. The argument was rejected in court. Just as the Executive Order applies to employers which contract with the government "to supply it with goods, services, and leased property," said the court, so too does it apply to employers who contract with the government "to receive from it goods, services and leased property to be used by the employer."[11]

So, if you are an employee or applicant for employment with a large private company, major university, or bank, you should assume that you are protected by the Executive Order.

## Construction Contractors and Subcontractors with Federally Assisted Construction Contracts

In addition to those employers that contract directly with the federal government, there is another set of contractors covered by the Executive Order: contractors and subcontractors that have or bid for federally assisted construction contracts. For purposes of the Order, a federally assisted construction contract is any "agreement" between two or more people for construction work that is "paid for in whole or in part" with funds obtained through the federal government under any federal program "involving a grant, contract, loan, insurance or guarantee."[12] And a construction contract is any contract for the "construction, rehabilitation, alteration, conversion, extension, or repair of buildings, highways, or other improvements to real property."[13] This language means that virtually every construction contractor is covered by the Executive Order.

But first there is a monetary limitation you should know about.

As we have seen, there are two limitations in the Executive Order as it applies to contractors who contract directly with federal agencies. But, here, only the first of the two limitations in the Executive Order applies to contractors with federally assisted contracts. The Executive Order prohibits *discrimination* by contractors and subcontractors if they have federally assisted contracts or subcontracts in any one year of more than $10,000.[14] The second limitation, which requires affirmative action goals and timetables only of contractors with large contracts, is not applicable to contractors and subcontractors that have federally assisted construction contracts. In the construction field, any contractor or subcontractor with more than $10,000 in federally assisted contracts in any one year is required to engage in *affirmative action.*[15]

What all of this means is that nearly all construction contractors are covered by the Executive Order. The key is *not* whether a contract is made directly with the federal government for the construction of a federal building or highway, or even whether the federal portion of the contract totals $10,000. Instead, the key, as to each contractor or subcontractor, is whether contracts with any federal assistance in them exceed $10,000 in a single year.[16] Most state and local government construction projects, for example, are paid for primarily out of state and local funds. Yet the federal government almost always provides some matching funds for these projects. So long as the contracts themselves exceed $10,000, the contractors working on the projects are covered by the Executive Order, not only on these specific projects, but on all other projects undertaken as well.

Probably the best illustration of the Order's effect on the construction industry is the well-known Philadelphia Plan, the first affirmative action plan imposed on construction contractors and subcontractors. Under the plan, all bidders on federally assisted contracts were required to include affirmative action goals and timetables along with their bids. The opportunity to do so came quickly, for at that time, Pennsylvania was accepting bids for construction of a state dam and water conservation project, which was projected to cost $4 million, with approximately $1 million of the financing being provided by the U.S. Department of Agriculture. Quite simply, all contractors and subcontractors submitting bids on the project were required to have affirmative action goals and timetables.[17]

Plans similar to the Philadelphia Plan are in operation in more than one hundred cities across the country, and they apply to all contractors and subcontractors that bid on federally assisted construction projects. Most workers in all building trades thus are protected by the Executive Order: plumbers and pipe fitters, sheet-metal workers, boilermakers, ironworkers, electricians, steam fitters, elevator constructors, pile drivers, sprinkler fitters, bricklayers, plasterers, roofers, and laborers. Also protected are carpenters, asbestos workers, lathers, operating engineers, painters, glaziers, carpet and linoleum workers, millwrights, riggers, and floor layers.

If you are a worker or applicant for employment in any of the above trades, or in any other construction trade, you cannot be discriminated against by a contractor or subcontractor covered by the Executive Order. In fact, if you are a female or minority craft worker, affirmative action goals and timetables are required on your behalf.

## PRACTICES WHICH ARE UNLAWFUL

Executive Order 11246 does not itself specify employment practices which are unlawful. The Order, however, does require that government contracts and federally assisted contracts include a non-discrimination and affirmative action clause.[18] Included in the clause and specifically required of government contractors are the following eight obligations:[19]

• That the contractor "will not discriminate against any employee or applicant for employment" on grounds of race, color, national origin, religion, or sex.
• That the contractor "will take affirmative action."
• That the contractor will advertise for employees in a non-discriminatory manner.
• That the contractor will advise its labor unions of its obligations under the Order.

- That the contractor will comply with the Order and with federal rules and regulations interpreting and applying the Order.
- That the contractor will permit federal investigations in order to ascertain compliance.
- That the contractor's non-compliance will result in the suspension of current contracts and the loss of future contracts, etc.
- That the contractor will include these contractual provisions in all subcontracts and will make sure that the provisions are satisfied by the subcontractors.

These eight obligations form the heart of the Executive Order contract compliance program. Very neatly, it all is accomplished by contract. Thus, if a contractor refuses to agree to the eight contractual obligations, a lucrative federal contract will be lost at step one. Contractors which do agree—they all do because they all want federal contracts—are contractually obligated to obey the contract.

Of the eight contractual obligations, the most important for present purposes are the first two: the promise not to discriminate and the promise to undertake affirmative action. A third obligation, which requires contractors to comply with all relevant federal regulations, also is significant because the regulations bar all forms of retaliation and intimidation against individuals who assert their rights to non-discrimination.

## The Promise Not to Discriminate

An employer that enters into a contract with the federal government, or that enters into a federally assisted construction contract, obligates itself, through the contract's non-discrimination and affirmative action clause—sometimes also called the "employment opportunity clause"—not to discriminate against employees and applicants on grounds of race, color, national origin, religion, or sex.[20] Although the Executive Order itself does not specify the types of employment practices which are prohibited, federal interpretation of the Executive Order mandates that "practices which violate Title VII are also proscribed by the equal opportunity clause under the Executive Order."[21]

This means that the same discriminatory practices which violate Title VII of the Civil Rights Act of 1964 also violate contractors' obligations under the Executive Order.

In Chapter 2, we reviewed in some detail the five types of discrimination which violate Title VII: overt discrimination, disparate impact discrimination,[22] disparate treatment discrimination, other forms of discrimination such as sexual harassment,[23] and, finally, retaliation. We also reviewed the importance of statistical proof of discrimination. Examples of each of the five types of discrimination and the standards for proving their illegality are provided and explained in Chapter 2 and also in Chapter 4. They are not repeated here. Remember, the same discriminatory practices also are prohibited by Executive Order 11246.[24]

## The Promise to Undertake Affirmative Action

It is not enough for an employer which has or seeks a federal contract or a federally assisted construction contract simply to engage in non-discrimination. Instead, most contractors must adopt and implement affirmative action goals and timetables to employ and advance women and minorities. Under the Executive Order, the affirmative action goals and timetables for contractors with federal contracts are slightly different from the affirmative action goals and timetables prescribed for construction contractors with federally assisted contracts.

*Affirmative action goals and timetables for contractors with federal contracts.* Government contractors or subcontractors that have fifty or more employees and that have federal contracts or subcontracts in any one year totaling $50,000 or more are required to adopt and to implement an affirmative action program. Under the Executive Order, an "affirmative action program is a set of specific and result-oriented procedures to which a contractor commits" itself.[25] That program must include goals and timetables. As the OFCCP regulations state:

> An acceptable affirmative action program must include an analysis of areas within which the contractor is deficient in the utilization of

minority groups and women, and further, goals and timetables to which the contractor's good faith efforts must be directed to correct the deficiencies and, thus to achieve prompt and full utilization of minorities and women at all levels and in all segments of [the contractor's] work force where deficiencies exist.[26]

In plain English, this means that wherever an employer underemploys minorities and women, the employer must establish and implement goals and timetables for the hiring and advancement of minorities and women.

With most employers, the areas where *minorities* usually have been discriminated against and hence where they are underemployed are in the following categories: officials and managers, professionals, technicians, skilled craft workers, sales workers, and office and clerical workers.[27] *Women* usually have been discriminated against and hence are underemployed by most employers in similar jobs, but particularly those in the first four categories: officials and managers, professionals, technicians, and skilled and semi-skilled craft workers.[28] If you are a minority person or a woman, and if you are qualified for employment in any of these areas, remember that affirmative action must be undertaken on your behalf.[29]

There are no specifically prescribed goals and timetables deemed appropriate or necessary for all employers. Instead, each employer is required to set its own goals and timetables through a procedure which is called a "utilization analysis." This procedure requires each contractor to conduct an analysis of its work force and an analysis of the availability of minorities and women in the general labor market. The work-force analysis involves a compilation of every job title, pay level, and job progression line correlated with the total number of females, males, minorities, and non-minorities employed in each category. The availability analysis necessitates a similar compilation correlated with the total number of females and minorities in the surrounding population, surrounding labor market, etc. The separate results are then compared. When the overall comparison shows that the employer has "fewer minorities or women in a particular job group than would reasonably be expected by their availability," then underemployment—or more precisely, "underutilization"—exists, as it always does in a vast number of jobs.[30] The contractor then is required to establish goals and timetables, based upon the availability analysis, to achieve prompt and full employment and advancement of minorities and women.

All of this information must be contained in each contractor's written affirmative action program.[31] Additional facts and data also must be included in the written program,[32] including an "in-depth" review of the contractor's employment practices and the discriminatory impact of those practices.[33] Since contractors are required to keep a copy of the affirmative action programs at each of their offices and to distribute publicly and to publicize their affirmative action programs,[34] you can get a copy of your employer's affirmative action program whenever you want.

*Affirmative action goals and timetables for construction contractors with federally assisted construction contracts.* Construction contractors and subcontractors that have or bid for federally assisted contracts or subcontracts in any one year totaling more than $10,000 are required to follow affirmative action goals and timetables for employing minorities and women.[35] The objectives are the same as with non-construction contracts, but the procedures are a little different.

In the construction trades, a procedure similar to a utilization analysis was conducted and continues to be updated, not by the construction contractors themselves, but rather by the agency which enforces the Executive Order: the Office of Federal Contract Compliance Programs. In the late 1960s and early 1970s, the OFCCP itself, usually in cooperation with construction contractors and trade unions, determined that there was severe underemployment of minority workers everywhere in the construction industry, and it thereby required goals and timetables to be implemented by the contractors in every major city in the United States. The first hometown plan was the Philadelphia Plan.[36] Based upon a utilization analysis procedure, goals and timetables were established for construction contractors in the various building trades in Philadelphia. For example, the goals and timetables set for the employment of minority workers in several trades were as follows:

|                     | 1st Year | 2nd Year | 3rd Year | 4th Year |
|---------------------|----------|----------|----------|----------|
| Electrical Workers  | 4–8%     | 9–13%    | 14–18%   | 19–23%   |
| Ironworkers         | 5–9%     | 11–15%   | 16–20%   | 22–26%   |
| Steamfitters        | 5–8%     | 11–15%   | 15–19%   | 20–24%   |

Similar goals and timetables were established for other trades in Philadelphia. And hometown plans similar to the Philadelphia Plan have been implemented in more than a hundred cities across the country.

Initially, the goals and timetables established in the hometown plans were set only for minority workers and not for female workers. But that no longer is the case. Whether established through hometown plans, imposed solely through the OFCCP, or adopted voluntarily by construction contractors, affirmative action goals and timetables now must be implemented by construction contractors for both minorities *and* women.[37]

## The Protection against Retaliation

Contractors not only are prohibited from engaging in discrimination and required to undertake affirmative action but they also are forbidden to retaliate in any way against an individual who seeks to obtain his or her rights to non-discrimination or affirmative action. In fact, under the Executive Order, contractors must "take all necessary steps" to make sure that there will be no retaliation or intimidation directed against any individual who files a charge of discrimination or who otherwise furnishes information or assists in any investigation under the Executive Order or under any other federal or state law requiring non-discrimination or affirmative action in employment.[38] This is an important protection. But, as we have seen in other chapters, just as many employers still engage in unlawful discrimination, so too do they retaliate against individuals who assert their rights. Retaliation under the Executive Order, however, can be especially costly since any employer that does so stands to lose its valued government contracts.

## MAJOR EXCEPTIONS

Unhappy about the Executive Order, some employers have tried to exempt themselves and all other contractors from its coverage by seeking to invalidate it in court. These employers have argued that since Executive Order 11246 is only a presidential order and is not a federal law enacted by Congress, it is an invalid, unauthorized executive action. The courts have uniformly rejected this employer argument and have held that "the Order has the force and effect of law."[39] Other employers have narrowed their attack by arguing only that the affirmative action goals and timetables requirement is unlawful. This argument, too, has been rejected by the courts.[40]

While frontal attacks on the Executive Order have been unsuccessful, the Executive Order itself and the federal regulations interpreting the Order do contain three sets of exceptions. Some contracts and contractors are not covered. Several employment practices and contracts are specifically exempted. And some employment practices which appear to be discriminatory are not necessarily prohibited.

### Contracts and Contractors Not Covered

The Executive Order, by requiring insertion of the non-discrimination and affirmative action clause in federal contracts, prohibits discrimination and compels affirmative action by most contractors. Some contracts, however, and hence some contractors, are not covered by the Executive Order. As we have seen, any contractor that has less than $10,000 in direct government contracts or in federally assisted contracts in any one year is not covered by the Executive Order.[41] And any non-construction contractor that has fewer than fifty employees and less than $50,000 in direct government contracts is not required by the Executive Order to establish goals and timetables for the employment of minorities and women.[42] These exceptions, as is obvious, exempt very small employers.

## Practices and Contracts Specifically Exempted

Under the Executive Order, there are a few employment practices and types of contracts specifically exempted. Exempted as employers, for example, are religious schools in that they are allowed to hire employees of a particular religion.[43] Contractors on or near an Indian reservation may extend employment preferences to Indians living on or near the reservation.[44] And contracts essential to the national security may be determined to be exempt.[45] These specific exemptions, again, do not undermine the Executive Order but only serve to emphasize its breadth.

## Practices That Appear to Be Discriminatory But Are Not Necessarily Prohibited

The third set of exceptions is a bit more open-ended. As we saw earlier, the Executive Order's prohibition against employment discrimination has been interpreted and applied consistently with the prohibitions against discrimination contained in Title VII of the Civil Rights Act of 1964. Yet Title VII also contains five specific exceptions which permit some discrimination. The Executive Order itself does not contain these exceptions. Nonetheless, two of the exceptions are applicable to the Executive Order and a third might be.

One Title VII exception which is applicable to the Executive Order is the exception to sex discrimination which allows an employer to discriminate if the employer can show that sex is a bona fide occupational qualification for the job. Because the federal regulations on sex discrimination under the Executive Order do recognize the bona fide occupational qualification exception,[46] this very narrow exception is applicable here.

The federal regulations on religious discrimination under the Executive Order also allow an employer to discriminate on the basis of religion if the employer cannot accommodate the employee's or applicant's religious observance without "undue hardship."[47] This Title VII exception is thus also applicable.

An exception which *might* be applicable under the Executive Order is Title VII's exception for bona fide seniority systems regardless of their discriminatory impact on minorities and women. Employers and unions have argued that this exception should apply to the Executive Order. So far there is little legal support for the argument. In fact, since the federal regulations under the Executive Order do not even mention this exception, the OFCCP frequently has sought and obtained the alteration of seniority systems, and the courts have upheld the OFCCP in its efforts.[48]

## THE FEDERAL AGENCY RESPONSIBLE FOR ENFORCEMENT

Enforcement of the Executive Order was expressly delegated to the U.S. Department of Labor,[49] which in turn created a new office responsible for enforcement: the Office of Federal Contract Compliance Programs. The OFCCP is responsible for ensuring that the non-discrimination and affirmative action clause is a part of every federal contract and federally assisted contract. It also is responsible for investigating charges of widespread discrimination, for monitoring compliance by contractors, and for imposing sanctions such as loss of contracts upon non-complying contractors.[50]

The OFCCP has regional offices throughout the United States. The locations of these offices are set forth in Chapter 9. The OFCCP's main office is located in Washington, D.C.:

Office of Federal Contract Compliance Programs
U.S. Department of Labor
200 Constitution Avenue, N.W.
Washington, D.C. 20210

202/523–9475

If you believe that you and others have been discriminated against in violation of the Executive Order, you should send a charge of "systemic" discrimination—widespread discrimination —to the OFCCP. The OFCCP has tremendous power to enforce your rights.

## ENFORCEMENT: HOW TO OBTAIN YOUR RIGHTS

The Executive Order is enforced by the OFCCP primarily through the economic sanctions of suspending payments on government contracts and barring discriminatory contractors from receiving any future contracts. This is a tremendously powerful enforcement tool for the simple reason that most employers, as the OFCCP recognizes, cannot "risk ineligibility for government contracts."[51]

Despite the OFCCP's powerful enforcement tool, many employers covered by the Executive Order do not comply with the non-discrimination and affirmative action clauses in their contracts. This is not only because employers are slow to change their discriminatory ways. It is also because, until recently, there was very little enforcement by the OFCCP against any employers, a posture caused in part by the fact that many people did not know about the Executive Order and thus did not complain about violations. But in the past five years, individuals have begun to assert their rights, and employers are now being forced by the OFCCP to stop their discrimination and to implement affirmative action goals and timetables.

To assert your rights you should learn whether your employer is covered by the Executive Order and you should have a strong suspicion that your employer's practices are unlawful. Then prepare to take action. Ask your employer for a copy of its affirmative action program.[52] Then gather as much evidence as possible to show the breadth of your employer's discriminatory practices: take notes, collect documents and statistics, and urge your colleagues to do the same. When you have obtained as much information as you need, you're ready to act:

• A charge of *systemic* or *broadly based* discrimination which you file with the OFCCP may be administratively resolved by the OFCCP to your satisfaction.

• A charge of *systemic* or *broadly based* discrimination which you file with the OFCCP may result in a successful lawsuit brought on your behalf by the Department of Justice.

These two methods of enforcement, each of which is initiated by your filing a charge of systemic discrimination with the

OFCCP, are more limited than the methods of enforcing the other laws discussed in this book. One difference is that the OFCCP perceives its role as that of investigating and remedying only *systemic* or *broadly based* discrimination. It prefers to take action on its own initiative by conducting what it calls "compliance reviews" of employers that have long histories of not hiring or promoting women or minorities or that do not fulfill their across-the-board affirmative action obligations.[53] Accordingly, the OFCCP has taken the position that it may refer "appropriate" charges of discrimination—non-systemic charges—to the EEOC for investigation and resolution under Title VII of the Civil Rights Act of 1964.[54] In fact, the OFCCP in practice refers to the EEOC all charges "which allege violations of an individual or unsystemic nature."[55] In other words, any charge of discrimination that you file with the OFCCP that is determined to be of an isolated or non-systemic nature simply will be referred to the EEOC, a fact you will learn quickly because the OFCCP must promptly notify you of the referral.[56] *Remember, for the OFCCP to enforce your rights, you must charge systemic or broadly based discrimination.*

Another difference is that you cannot sue your boss under the Executive Order. In almost every instance where individuals like you have filed lawsuits against employers under the Executive Order, the courts have held that individuals have no right to sue.[57] This means that you can obtain your rights under the Executive Order only through administrative enforcement and sometimes through lawsuits filed by the Department of Justice. (Of course, if you really want to sue your boss, you always can do so under Title VII of the Civil Rights Act of 1964, discussed in Chapter 2, and under other laws discussed in this book.)

These two differences limit the methods of enforcing the Executive Order, but they do not alter the vast powers of the OFCCP, nor do they limit the substantial remedies available to you under the Executive Order. In other words, you always should try to avail yourself of these powers and remedies by filing a charge of *systemic* or *broadly based* discrimination against your employer or potential employer with the OFCCP.

## Administrative Resolution of Charges Alleging Systemic Discrimination

The primary role of the OFCCP, as we have seen, is the investigation and resolution of systemic or broadly based discrimination. Such systemic or broadly based discrimination can take the form of an employer's across-the-board pattern of not hiring or not promoting women or minorities in a number of job classifications; an employer's use of a maternity leave policy that requires pregnant employees to take leaves of absence during periods when they or their doctors believe the women are fully qualified to work; an employer's use of hiring criteria, including written tests, that have a discriminatory impact against minority applicants and that are not job-related; or an employer's failure to implement affirmative action goals and timetables for the hiring and promotion of women and minorities in positions where they have been underutilized. Where these and similar systemic practices occur, the OFCCP can force a change by suspending government contracts with non-complying contractors and by barring non-complying contractors from receiving any future contracts.

The OFCCP prefers, as we have seen, to investigate systemic discrimination through its self-initiated compliance reviews of employers.[58] But the OFCCP also responds to charges of systemic discrimination,[59] sometimes by including and resolving charges as part of its compliance review procedures and at other times by investigating and resolving charges independently.[60]

If you believe that you and other individuals have been discriminated against by an employer covered by the Executive Order, you should file a charge of systemic discrimination with the OFCCP. A charge of systemic discrimination is simply a letter alleging that your employer has engaged in extensive discrimination. Although the OFCCP has a prescribed form for making a charge, it need not be used and seldom is. The easiest course is simply to write your own charge on your own paper. A sample charge is set forth at the end of this chapter. So too is the OFCCP charge form. In your charge, you must:

- State your name, address, and telephone number.
- Give the name, address, and phone number of the employer

that is or has engaged in discriminatory practices, and give the name and phone number of an employee who knows about those practices.

• Describe fully the employer's discriminatory practices.

• Indicate, if you know it, the federal agency with which the employer has a contract.

• Provide any other information that you believe will be of assistance to the OFCCP in its investigation.

• Sign your name on the charge.[61]

If you anticipate that filing a charge might result in retaliation against you—or even if you don't—you can have a representative (a friend or your lawyer) file a charge on your behalf. This type of charge—referred to as a "third party" charge—need not identify you so long as your representative states his or her name, address, and telephone number, and signs the charge.[62]

Whichever type of charge is filed, it *must* be filed with the OFCCP within 180 days of the systemic discrimination that affected you, unless the OFCCP decides for unknown reasons that you have shown "good cause" for filing a later charge.[63] Filing the charge is accomplished by sending it to the nearest regional office of the OFCCP or to the main office of the OFCCP in Washington, D.C.

When the OFCCP receives your administrative charge of systemic discrimination, it may investigate the charge.[64] If the OFCCP investigation "indicates a violation" of the employer's non-discrimination and affirmative action obligations, then "reasonable efforts shall be made" by the OFCCP to "secure compliance through conciliation and persuasion."[65] If the employer refuses to stop its discrimination or to remedy its past actions, the OFCCP then may initiate economic sanctions against the employer.[66]

These administrative enforcement procedures necessarily will involve you directly. At the outset, the OFCCP may contact you or your representative by phone or in person and request you to supplement your charge with additional information, and it even may send you its official OFCCP charge form for you to complete.[67] If you fail to return the completed form or fail to provide the requested information to the OFCCP within 60 days, the

OFCCP may dismiss your charge and take no further action on your behalf.[68] In other words, you should be as cooperative as possible with the OFCCP to ensure that your rights will be enforced.

You also may be involved during the administrative resolution stage of the enforcement process. Technically, you do not have a role during this process because it is the OFCCP that acts on your behalf against the employer. Nonetheless, it never hurts to inform the OFCCP during the investigation stage about what you believe would be a proper resolution of your charge. You, after all, will be more familiar with your personal situation than will the OFCCP.

If your employer refuses to stop its discrimination, refuses to implement affirmative action goals or timetables, or refuses to provide an adequate remedy for its past discrimination, then the OFCCP may begin to initiate its economic sanctions against your employer. *These economic sanctions are substantial.*

When an employer refuses to comply with the Executive Order, with the OFCCP interpretation of the Executive Order, or with the non-discrimination and affirmative action clause of the government contract, the OFCCP is authorized to initiate two sets of economic sanctions against the non-complying employer. First, the OFCCP may "cancel, terminate, suspend, or cause to be cancelled, terminated or suspended" any current government contracts, thereby denying the employer continuing payments on the contracts.[69] Additionally, the OFCCP may require all federal agencies to "refrain from entering into contracts" with the non-complying employer until such time as the employer comes into compliance—a sanction called "contract debarment"—thereby giving the employer the option of never receiving another government contract or of coming into compliance.[70] No non-complying contractor can yell "unfair" when these economic sanctions are imposed. As we have seen, all government contracts contain a non-discrimination and affirmative action clause. In part of that clause, the employer agrees that upon a determination of non-compliance, the "contract may be cancelled, terminated, or suspended in whole or in part and the contractor may be declared ineligible for further [federal] contracts."[71]

Nonetheless, the imposition of these sanctions rarely occurs automatically, because in most instances—except where contractors have retaliated against individuals or have refused to provide the OFCCP with compliance information[72]—the OFCCP is required to follow some fairly cumbersome and time-consuming procedures. For example, in order to impose the sanctions, the OFCCP must make a final effort at obtaining voluntary compliance from the contractor.[73] Usually, the OFCCP initiates this step by issuing what is called a "notice to show cause" or a "notice of violations"—notices which require contractors to explain why they will not come into compliance.[74] If a contractor does not come into compliance within 30 days, and sometimes within 15 days, of the OFCCP's issuance of a notice, then the OFCCP can begin formal proceedings against the contractor by issuing an administrative complaint seeking cancellation, termination, or suspension of current contracts and debarment from all future contracts.[75] Before a contractor can be barred from receiving future contracts, the employer is entitled to have a full administrative hearing to determine whether it actually is in non-compliance.[76] If the OFCCP wins the hearing, then the contractor can be debarred.

Debarment, from an employer's perspective, is an extreme sanction. But the OFCCP in the past few years has not been reluctant to invoke it. Three companies, in Virginia, Ohio, and Illinois, which had large contracts providing supplies and services to the Department of Defense have been debarred. In June 1979, Uniroyal, Inc., a plastics and rubber manufacturer with $36 million in federal contracts, was debarred from future contracts. Overall, more than twenty companies have now been debarred. Since these companies, like every other government contractor, cannot afford to be without planned-for government contracts, they ultimately opt for compliance. When they have stopped their discrimination, have provided remedies to individuals like you to compensate for their past discrimination, and have implemented affirmative action programs, the contractors once again are eligible for federal contracts.[77]

## Lawsuits by the Department of Justice

The primary method of enforcing Executive Order 11246, as we have seen, is through the OFCCP imposition of economic sanctions against non-complying contractors. But there is another means of enforcement: a lawsuit by the Department of Justice. Whenever the OFCCP determines that there is a "substantial or material violation" of the non-discrimination and affirmative action clause of an employer's government contract, it may refer the matter to the Department of Justice for the immediate filing of a lawsuit against the employer.[78]

In some situations, the imposition of economic sanctions by the OFCCP against government contractors simply is not feasible. This situation usually arises when the goods or services provided by the contractor are absolutely necessary to the functioning of government and there are no other contractors which can provide such goods or services. For example, federal government agencies in New Orleans purchase a substantial amount of electricity and natural gas from New Orleans Public Service, Inc., a public utility which enjoys a virtual monopoly on electricity and natural gas in the New Orleans area. Because the federal agencies need electricity and gas in order to function, and because the federal agencies in New Orleans "have no alternative source of electric power," the OFCCP is not in the position to be able to suspend current contracts for services or to bar future contracts as a sanction against employment discrimination by New Orleans Public Service, Inc. On the other hand, the OFCCP could refer the contractor's non-compliance to the Department of Justice for a lawsuit, and the Department of Justice could sue the contractor.[79] In fact, in this example, that is precisely what the OFCCP and the Department of Justice did.[80]

The Department of Justice sometimes files lawsuits simply because it would prefer to have a court order in its favor, thereby giving "teeth" to an administrative settlement. For example, the Department of Justice, seeking to enforce the Executive Order on behalf of minorities and women, in 1974 sued the nine largest steel companies and the United Steelworkers of America. Actually, the lawsuit had been preceded by six months of fruitful negotiations with the steel industry. When the Department of

Justice filed its lawsuit, all of the parties several moments later filed settlements which became court-approved consent decrees. The consent decrees altered seniority rights in favor of minorities and women, established numerical goals and timetables for hiring and promoting minorities and women, and required the industry to create a back pay fund in excess of $30 million to be paid to discriminated-against minorities and women.[81]

Although the Department of Justice negotiated with the steel industry in the above example, neither the Department of Justice nor the OFCCP is required to do so under the Executive Order. It is true that, before the OFCCP can initiate its administrative economic sanctions against a contractor, it must make an initial determination of non-compliance and must seek to obtain voluntary compliance from the contractor. But these prerequisites do not apply when Department of Justice lawsuits are involved. In this situation, there "are no procedural prerequisites to a referral to the Department of Justice."[82] Rather than waiting months for voluntary compliance, the OFCCP can quickly refer a contractor's non-compliance to the Department of Justice, and the Department of Justice may sue the contractor immediately.

In any event, the Department of Justice is not likely to file suit unless you send an administrative charge to the OFCCP alleging systemic discrimination against your boss. In fact, the OFCCP and the Department of Justice may never learn about your employer's non-compliance unless you tell them by filing a charge of systemic discrimination.

## REMEDIES: WHAT YOU CAN GET WHEN YOUR RIGHTS HAVE BEEN VIOLATED

When you obtain your rights under the Executive Order, you will find the remedies quite extensive. Whether your rights are enforced administratively by the OFCCP or through the filing of a lawsuit by the Department of Justice, the same remedies are available.[83] And they are the same as the equitable, rightful-place remedies available under Title VII of the Civil Rights Act of 1964. As discussed in Chapter 2, these remedies include hiring, reinstatement, equal terms and conditions of employment, retroactive seniority, back pay, etc.[84] Under the Executive Order, an additional remedy is the required implementation of affirmative action goals and timetables.

The power of the OFCCP to obtain these remedies is not to be taken lightly. Like the ORS in its enforcement of the Revenue Sharing Act, the OFCCP holds the power of the purse. If a non-complying contractor refuses to provide adequate remedies for its past discrimination, the OFCCP has the power to cancel, terminate, or suspend government contracts; and to debar non-complying contractors from all future government contracts.[85] These economic sanctions against employers literally force employers to provide you with your rights.

Because of the OFCCP's considerable enforcement power, and because of its concern with systemic violations of the Executive Order, the back pay remedies often involve enormous sums. This does not mean that you will receive a windfall. But your boss will have to provide some back pay to you and all of your colleagues who were discriminated against. For example, although the training, wage adjustment, and back-pay award in the AT&T consent decree eventually totaled more than $80 million, the award was divided among tens of thousands of employees and applicants, with no one person receiving more than $10,000.[86] The consent decree negotiated with nine steel companies and the United Steelworkers of America contained an award of nearly $31 million, to be divided among 34,000 minority employees and 500 female employees, with no employee receiving more than $1,000.[87] More recently, the OFCCP obtained a voluntary compliance agreement from Gulf Oil in which Gulf agreed to pay approximately $1 million to be divided among 640 discriminated-against employees, with an average award of $1,500 per employee.

In part because of the increasing number of back pay awards, a few employers have argued that while the OFCCP may obtain back pay on your behalf, the Department of Justice may not. You will be pleased to learn that the courts have uniformly rejected this argument, holding that "the government may seek any remedy which will effectuate the purposes of the Order."[88]

\*   \*   \*

On January 31, 1975, Larry Sumner's employment as a sales-person was terminated by his boss, American Cyanamid Company. Larry Sumner is black. He correctly believed that his discharge was racially motivated. He also knew that American Cyanamid employed very few minorities in its sales force in the New York metropolitan area, where he had worked, and he suspected that American Cyanamid probably had an inadequate affirmative action plan if it had one at all.

Larry Sumner didn't want his job back. But he was none too happy about having been fired, and he certainly didn't like the idea of American Cyanamid getting away with racial discrimination. He decided not to sit on his rights. And since he knew that American Cyanamid had large government contracts to provide antibiotics, pharmaceuticals, and other supplies to the Veteran's Administration, he knew the best route to follow.

On July 9, 1975, Mr. Sumner filed a charge of systemic discrimination against his former boss with the OFCCP. His charge was timely because it was sent to the OFCCP within 180 days of the alleged discrimination. In his charge, he alleged that he had been fired because of his race in violation of Executive Order 11246. He also properly alleged that American Cyanamid undoubtedly engaged in systemic discrimination because there were so few minorities in its New York metropolitan area sales force. Because Larry Sumner charged his former boss with systemic discrimination, the OFCCP investigated the charge. The OFCCP also initiated a full-scale compliance review of American Cyanamid's employment practices.

On December 11, 1975, five months after Mr. Sumner had filed his charge and well before completing its full-scale compliance review, the OFCCP rendered findings on the first part of Mr. Sumner's charge. The OFCCP not only found that the company's discharge of Mr. Sumner was a violation of the Executive Order but also recommended that Mr. Sumner be paid $5,000 in back pay and be provided with neutral employment references in the future.[89] American Cyanamid agreed to the OFCCP's proposed remedy. But the matter did not stop there. The OFCCP continued its compliance review, found numerous other violations of the Executive Order, and again forced American Cyanamid to comply with the Order by actually implementing an adequate affirmative action program complete with goals and timetables. As Larry Sumner knew, the OFCCP, backed by its power of the purse, is in a particularly strong position to eliminate forbidden employment discrimination.

OMB Approval No. 044R-1588

**U.S. DEPARTMENT OF LABOR**
EMPLOYMENT STANDARDS ADMINISTRATION
Office of Federal Contract Compliance
Washington, D. C. 20210

**COMPLAINT OF DISCRIMINATION
IN EMPLOYMENT UNDER
GOVERNMENT CONTRACTS**

INSTRUCTIONS: Only complaints of discrimination in employment by companies working under Government contracts are filed on this form. The act of discrimination must be based on RACE, COLOR, RELIGION, SEX, or NATIONAL ORIGIN, and the complaint must be filed within 180 days of the discriminatory act. Other types of discrimination are not handled by this office. Fill in the form, making one copy for yourself and one official copy. The official copy of the form must be typed or printed legibly and signed by you.

YOUR NAME | TELEPHONE NO. | SOCIAL SECURITY NO.

STREET ADDRESS | CITY | STATE | ZIP CODE

**MAIL THIS FORM TO:**

NAME, ADDRESS & ZIP CODE OF THE COMPANY INVOLVED

**U.S. DEPARTMENT OF LABOR
EMPLOYMENT STANDARDS ADMINISTRATION
OFFICE OF FEDERAL CONTRACT COMPLIANCE
WASHINGTON, D. C. 20210**

FOR WHICH GOVERNMENT AGENCY IS THE COMPANY UNDER CONTRACT?

GIVE THE EXACT DATE OF THIS DISCRIMINATION

DISCRIMINATION FOR | WHAT DID IT INVOLVE? (Check only the most apparent factor)

☐ RACE OR COLOR  ☐ RELIGION  ☐ SEX  ☐ NATIONAL ORIGIN

☐ HIRING  ☐ PROMOTION  ☐ DOWNGRADING

☐ LAYOFF OR RECALL  ☐ TRANSFER  ☐ JOB ASSIGNMENT

☐ EMPLOYEE BENEFITS  ☐ WAGES  ☐ SEGREGATED FACILITIES

☐ DISCHARGE  ☐ TRAINING OR APPRENTICESHIP  ☐ OTHER (Explain below)

THE COMPLAINT: | Tell the full story of this act of discrimination. Show all dates, places, and the names and titles of persons involved.

Additional pages may be attached to this form. Please put your name and S.S. No. at the top of each page.

I certify that the information given above is true and correct to the best of my knowledge or belief. (A willful false statement is punishable by law: U.S. Code, Title 18, Sec. 1001)

YOUR SIGNATURE | DATE

**DO NOT WRITE BELOW THIS LINE**

The complainant has reaffirmed this complaint in my presence. This complaint is now the basis of an investigation under EXECUTIVE ORDER 11246 and/or EXECUTIVE ORDER 11375.

NAME OF INVESTIGATOR | TITLE | SIGNATURE

AGENCY OR DEPARTMENT CONDUCTING INVESTIGATION | DATE INVESTIGATION STARTED

GPO 888-156

# Sample Charge of Discrimination

```
                                              Charging Party
                                              1000 My Street
                                              My Town, My State 00000
                                              111 234-5678

                                              July 1, 1980

Office of Federal Contract Compliance Programs
U.S. Department of Labor
200 Constitution Avenue, N.W.
Washington, D.C. 20210

I am filing this charge of discrimination because I believe that Contractor is
engaged in systemic discrimination in violation of Executive Order 11246. This
charge is filed against:

    Contractor
    1 Main Street
    My Town, My State 00000

    111 123-4567

Contractor is a manufacturer of office supplies. It has had, and continues to
have, a number of contracts with the federal government for office supplies.
I believe that Contractor has well over $50,000 worth of federal contracts each
year.

Contractor engages in systemic discrimination. There are few women and minorities
who have been hired or promoted into managerial and professional positions. Con-
tractor maintains a mandatory maternity-leave policy which requires pregnant female
employees to take an unpaid leave of absence at the seventh month of pregnancy.
Pursuant to this policy, I was forced to take a maternity leave this spring
although my doctor advised me and Contractor that I was fully able to continue
working. (Enclosed is a copy of the mandatory maternity-leave policy.)

I asked two Contractor supervisors for a copy of the Contractor affirmative
action program. Each declined to give me a copy. I believe that Contractor has
no affirmative action program.

An official of Contractor who knows about these practices is John Doe. His
telephone extension at the company is 100.

Please investigate this matter and keep me informed of your progress.

                                              Sincerely,


                                              Charging Party
```

# PART THREE

## Additional Rights If You Have to Sue Your Boss

# Increasing the Monetary 6
## Remedies Available
## to Blacks and Other Racial
## Minorities

### THE CIVIL RIGHTS ACT OF 1866—SECTION 1981

[RACE, COLOR, NATIONAL ORIGIN]

The modern laws reviewed to this point provide substantial protection against most forms of employment discrimination. The century-old civil rights laws—the Civil Rights Acts of 1866 and 1871—offer less protection but greater monetary remedies. An individual who sues and wins under the 1866 Act can win, for example, money damages for mental anguish, a remedy not authorized by the modern laws. For those who have to sue to win their rights to non-discrimination on grounds of race, color, and national origin, the 1866 Act should always be used in conjunction with the modern laws.

John Garner in the early 1970s was a police officer with the New Orleans Police Department assigned to the elite K–9 Corps. The only black officer in that unit, he was subjected to occasional but serious harassment, such as when sugar was poured in his gas tank. The fact that he didn't overreact to this harassment only increased the anger of his white colleagues, who wanted him transferred to another unit. Ultimately, the white officers prevailed by forcing their supervisor to recommend a transfer.

When John Garner objected, the Superintendent of Police stepped in and not only ordered his transfer to patrol duty in a high-crime area but also ordered Officer Garner to undergo psychological evaluation. After the humiliating evaluation was completed, John Garner began his patrol duty—without an assigned partner—in high-crime neighborhoods. Then, late one night, near the end of a twelve-hour shift, Officer Garner made a mistake: he disobeyed a direct order given by his radio dispatcher to investigate a probable crime. For refusing to obey an order, he was suspended and ultimately fired.

John Garner sued the New Orleans Police Department under Title VII of the Civil Rights Act of 1964, and also sued the Superintendent of Police for damages under the Civil Rights Act of 1866. To his dismay, he lost his discharge claim, for the court found that the discharge had resulted from his refusal to obey an order rather than from racial discrimination. Accordingly, he was not entitled to reinstatement or back pay. But the court nevertheless found that his transfer from the K–9 Corps and his enforced psychological evaluation had been racially discriminatory. Because of the "mental anguish and humiliation" he had endured as a result of these actions, he was awarded $5,000 in compensatory damages—a remedy not permitted under Title VII but available under the 1866 Act.[1]

Although Officer Garner didn't win his primary claim, if he hadn't sued under the 1866 Act in addition to Title VII, he would not have won even the $5,000.

*The Civil Rights Act of 1866, which was enacted shortly after the adoption of the Thirteenth Amendment, prohibits employment discrimination on grounds of race, color, and national origin. It bars discrimination in state and local government employment and in private employment.*

*The 1866 Act has two limitations. First, the scope of its prohibitions still remains somewhat in doubt a century after its enactment. Second, it is enforced only through the filing of lawsuits by individuals. Nonetheless, if you obtain a court ruling that your rights under the 1866 Act have been violated, you can win substantial monetary remedies that are not available under the modern federal laws.*

*Because of the two limitations, the 1866 Act is rarely invoked as a sole protection against discrimination. It is best used in conjunction with a lawsuit filed under Title VII of the Civil Rights Act of 1964. If you decide to sue your boss for race discrimination under Title VII, or under other laws discussed in this book, you should also always sue under the 1866 Act.*

## WHO IS COVERED BY THE LAW

The part of the 1866 Civil Rights Act applicable to employment—a provision known as "Section 1981"[2]—is nearly universal in its coverage of employers. In a nutshell, it applies to private employers, large and small, and to state and local government employers, large and small.

For more than one hundred years, the 1866 Act was assumed to apply only to state and local government employers. In 1968, however, the Supreme Court implied that the 1866 Act might also cover private employers,[3] an implication made certain in 1975.[4] As a result, the 1866 Act now covers all state, local, and private employers.[5] In fact, the Act applies not just to state and local governments but also to their officials,[6] and it covers not only companies but also their directors, officers, and managers.[7] Unions also are covered by the Act.[8]

The one major exception to the 1866 Act's otherwise broad coverage is that it does not apply to the federal government— at least to the extent that federal agencies are covered by Title VII of the Civil Rights Act of 1964.[9] For most practical purposes, the 1866 Act simply cannot be used against the federal government.[10]

## DISCRIMINATORY PRACTICES WHICH ARE UNLAWFUL

The pertinent part of the 1866 Act, Section 1981, is a one-sentence law which simply guarantees all persons "the same right . . . to make and enforce contracts . . . as is enjoyed by white citizens."[11] Given the race-based nature of this law, the 1866 Act prohibits discrimination only on grounds of race, color, and national origin.[12] It does not prohibit discrimination on grounds of sex, age, religion, or on any other non-racial grounds.

The 1866 Act does not list specific employment practices which are unlawful. Rather, it merely guarantees the right to contract for employment, a right which has been interpreted to guarantee equal terms and conditions of employment.[13]

The absence of any definition within the 1866 Act of the specific types of racially discriminatory employment practices which are unlawful has led to considerable disagreement in the past few years about whether the Act prohibits only intentionally discriminatory practices or also practices which merely have a discriminatory impact. This debate has not yet been resolved by the courts, primarily because the 1866 Act rarely is asserted as a sole prohibition against discrimination. Usually, the 1866 Act has been used in conjunction with Title VII to challenge racial discrimination in state, local, and private employment, with the result that the courts have based their decisions on the more-often-used Title VII. On occasion the 1866 Act has been used in conjunction with the 1871 Act to challenge racial discrimination in state and local employment, and here too the courts have based their decisions on the more-often-used 1871 Act. Accordingly, we know much more about Title VII and the 1871 Act than we do about the 1866 Act.

Nonetheless, even when the 1866 Act is asserted as a sole prohibition, it can be safely argued that it does prohibit two of the major forms of racial discrimination: overt discrimination and disparate treatment discrimination. It may or may not forbid disparate impact discrimination and other forms of discrimination. Regardless, statistics of racial imbalance always are useful to proving violations of the 1866 Act.

## Overt Discrimination

Overt discrimination is blatant, obvious discrimination. When an employer denies employment, transfer, or promotion to a person simply because that person is black, that is overt discrimination. It is outlawed by the 1866 Act.

Illustrative of this prohibition is the successful lawsuit brought several years ago by Marvin Brown, a black welder from North Carolina. Despite his welding qualifications, Mr. Brown was denied employment as a welder by the Gaston County Dyeing Machine Co. because, in the company's view, it was premature to hire a black as a highly paid welder. After Mr. Brown was hired by the company—into an unskilled, low-paying position—he sued his boss to obtain the more highly paid position of welder. He won.[14] His employer had committed overt discrimination.

## Disparate Treatment Discrimination

Disparate treatment discrimination is more subtle simply because the employer will deny discriminatory conduct and usually will have covered its tracks somewhat better. Subtlety, however, does not make discriminatory treatment lawful.

In order to establish a prima facie case of disparate treatment discrimination in hiring, you have to prove four factors: that you are protected by the law, that you applied and were qualified for a job for which the employer was seeking applicants, that despite your qualifications you were rejected, and that, after your rejection the position remained open and the employer continued to seek applications from persons with similar qualifications. Once you establish these four elements, the employer's action will be found unlawful unless the employer can articulate some legitimate, non-discriminatory reason for the disparate treatment. Even if the employer establishes such a reason, you still have an opportunity to show that the employer's stated reason is simply a pretext for discrimination.[15]

These principles are illustrated by a successful case filed under the 1866 Act by a black financial analyst in Washington, D.C., who had been denied employment as a securities seller. He proved that he was protected by the law, that he applied and was qualified for a securities sales position; that despite his qualifications he was rejected; and that, after his rejection, the employer continued to seek applications from other persons with similar qualifications. Faced with this presumptive case of unlawful discrimination, the company asserted two non-discriminatory reasons for the disparate treatment. First, the company contended that the black applicant had not scored high enough on certain pre-employment criteria. Finding that the same criteria had not been applied to all of the white applicants, the court held that "such nonuniform and unequal application of criteria by an employer constitutes an unfair [unlawful] employment practice."[16] Second, the company argued that it had instituted a moratorium on hiring just before the black man applied. To this the court responded that the "avowed moratorium on hiring served as a pretext to exclude [the black applicant] who otherwise was qualified for the position sought."[17] Accordingly, the employer's disparate treatment constituted unlawful discrimination.

## Disparate Impact Discrimination

Disparate impact discrimination occurs when an employer who does not necessarily intend to discriminate nonetheless uses an employment practice which has a racially discriminatory impact upon minority persons generally. The most common example of disparate impact discrimination is the use of a standardized written aptitude test which may appear to be neutral on its face but which has a discriminatory impact against minority applicants. Unfortunately, it is not yet conclusively known whether this form of discrimination is forbidden by the 1866 Act.

As we have seen, Title VII and several other laws in this book unequivocally prohibit practices which have a discriminatory impact regardless of an employer's intent to discriminate.[18] On the other hand, the 1871 Civil Rights Act prohibits only intentionally discriminatory practices, and evidence of disparate impact is insufficient to prove intentional discrimination.[19] In the middle of this dichotomy sits the 1866 Act. Some courts have held that the 1866 Act prohibits employment practices which have a discriminatory impact regardless of intent.[20] In one case, for example, a court held that the written tests and the minimum-height requirements used by the County of Los Angeles to hire police officers were unlawful under the 1866 Act solely because of their discriminatory impact.[21] Other courts have disagreed with this approach and have held that the 1866 Act forbids only intentionally discriminatory practices.[22] A third group of courts has recognized the issue but has expressed no views.[23]

Among the latter group is the Supreme Court, which considered this issue in the Los Angeles case in 1979 but declined to resolve it.[24] Until the Supreme Court decides whether intent to discriminate must be shown under the Civil Rights Act of 1866, the interim result simply will depend upon which court you're in.[25]

## Statistical Proof of Discrimination

Under the 1866 Act, as under the other federal laws forbidding employment discrimination, statistics comparing the representation of minorities in an employer's work force with the representation of minorities in the surrounding population or labor market can be very useful in proving unlawful discrimination. This is so regardless of whether the 1866 Act ultimately is determined to bar only intentional discrimination, for, as the Supreme Court observed several years ago, racial imbalance in an employer's work force "is often a telltale sign of purposeful discrimination; absent explanation, it is ordinarily to be expected that nondiscriminatory hiring practices will in time result in a work force more or less representative of the racial and ethnic composition in the community from which employees are hired."[26] In other words, if an employer's work force is not racially balanced, you should use the comparative statistics as evidence of unlawful discrimination under the 1866 Act.[27]

## MAJOR EXCEPTIONS

The 1866 Act, as we have seen, protects you in private employment and in state and local government employment from discrimination on grounds of race, color, and national origin. However, it does not apply to the federal government, and it does not protect you if you have been discriminated against on the basis of sex or on other non-racial grounds.

Most of the other federal laws contain statutory exceptions which legitimatize some discriminatory employment practices such as the use of bona fide seniority systems regardless of their discriminatory impact. The 1866 Act, in contrast, has no such exceptions.[28]

There is, nonetheless, one exception which works in your favor. Affirmative-action programs, including those which include numerical goals and timetables, are presumed permissible in view of the race-conscious nature of the 1866 Act.[29] And affirmative action of course can be required of an employer that has engaged in past discrimination.[30]

## THE FEDERAL AGENCY RESPONSIBLE FOR ENFORCEMENT

There is no federal agency responsible for enforcing the Civil Rights Act of 1866. This means that there is no federal agency with which you need to file an administrative charge of discrimination, no federal agency to negotiate with your employer on your behalf, and no federal agency to sue your boss. The responsibility for enforcing the 1866 Act rests entirely upon individuals like you.

## ENFORCEMENT: HOW TO OBTAIN YOUR RIGHTS

There are no alternative methods of enforcement under the Civil Rights Act of 1866. The only way to obtain your rights under the 1866 Act is to sue your boss.

If you decide to sue, you should not sue only under the 1866 Act if at all possible. As we have seen, the legal interpretation of the Act is still quite uncertain. You thus should also sue under Title VII and under any other laws that apply to your situation. And, again, because of the uncertainty surrounding the Act's interpretation, you also should find a lawyer. When you have retained a lawyer and are ready to sue, you should file your lawsuit in the federal district court or in a state court located in the area where the discrimination occurred.

There are no administrative prerequisites to the filing of a lawsuit under the 1866 Act. You need not have filed an administrative charge of discrimination with the EEOC[31] or with any state or local agency.[32] Even if you do, that has no effect on your right to sue under the 1866 Act.[33] You can go directly to court as soon as you are ready.

Alas, there is one procedural hitch. Similar to a lawsuit under the Civil Rights Act of 1871, any lawsuit filed under the 1866 Act must be timely. Although the 1866 Act itself has no time limitations, state statutes—called "statutes of limitations"—limit the number of years within which a lawsuit may be filed subsequent to the conduct which you claim is unlawful. Your lawsuit must be filed within the time allowed by the state statute where you file your lawsuit.[34] What this means in practice is that the federal or state court in the state in which you file your lawsuit will apply to any claim under the 1866 Act (or under the 1871 Act discussed in Chapter 7) one of the many statutes of limitations of that state which is most appropriate to the characterization of your lawsuit. There is some confusion here, because any single state has a variety of statutes of limitations and there is little uniformity among the states. For example, the statute which the courts have deemed applicable to a 1866 Act claim in Tennessee is a one-year statute governing civil rights lawsuits[35]; in Texas it is a two-year statute governing back pay claims[36]; in New York it is a three-year statute governing liabilities created by statute[37]; in Illinois it is a five-year statute governing civil lawsuits not otherwise provided for.[38] Some courts within a single state have been unable to decide upon the state statute applicable to claims under the 1866 Act. In Louisiana, for example, the courts initially applied a ten-year statute governing contract lawsuits,[39] but later applied a one-year statute simply governing lawsuits seeking to remedy "offenses."[40] Whatever the time period may be in the state you are in, your lawsuit will be dismissed if it is not filed within the allowable period. And any administrative charges of discrimination you may file have no effect whatsoever upon the continuous running of the applicable time to file your 1866 Act lawsuit.[41]

The confusion about the appropriate time period for filing your 1866 Act lawsuit contains two lessons. First, you should find a lawyer to research this issue for you. Second, you must prepare your lawsuit as quickly as possible after you have been discriminated against.

## REMEDIES: WHAT YOU CAN GET WHEN YOUR RIGHTS HAVE BEEN VIOLATED

When you win in your lawsuit under the 1866 Act, you can receive a variety of court-ordered remedies from your boss. In describing the remedies available, the Supreme Court has stated that a person who wins under the 1866 Act "is entitled to equitable and legal relief, including compensatory and, under certain circumstances, punitive damages."[42]

The "equitable" remedies that are available are the same rightful-place remedies—hiring, reinstatement, promotion, back pay, retroactive seniority, etc.—that are available under Title VII. There is one exception, which usually works in your favor. Under Title VII, back pay liability accrues only from two years prior to the filing of a charge of discrimination with the EEOC. Under the 1866 Act, there is no such limitation. This means that if you sue under the 1866 Act, you may receive back pay for the entire time you were discriminated against,[43] or at least as far back as the state statute of limitations allows.

The provision for "legal" remedies under the 1866 Act means that you can win monetary remedies in addition to back pay and that you can obtain a jury trial if you want one.[44] The monetary remedies available include actual damages, compensatory damages, and punitive damages. In order to obtain these damages, you must prove that you in fact are entitled to them; they are not automatic simply because the 1866 Act has been violated.[45]

The phrase "actual damages" is redundant of back pay because it includes lost wages.[46] But it also encompasses other actual damages, such as the costs of looking for another job and any increased transportation costs incurred in commuting to a new job.[47] If you prove that you lost money because of the discrimination, you are entitled to recover what you lost as actual damages.

Included under "compensatory damages" is financial compensation for any psychological pain or humiliation that you may have suffered as a victim of discrimination. John Garner, remember, was awarded $5,000 in compensatory damages "for the mental anguish and humiliation he endured during the course of his employment"[48]

An award of "punitive damages" is used to punish an employer that has willfully violated the law. In order to recover punitive damages, you have to prove that you suffered actual harm and that your boss discriminated against you not only intentionally but also with malice. Although this is a high standard of proof, punitive damages often have been awarded under the 1866 Act.[49]

In addition to the "equitable" and "legal" remedies available to you under the 1866 Act when you win your lawsuit, you also are entitled to your attorney's fees. Under the 1866 Act, the "prevailing party" in a lawsuit is entitled to attorney's fees.[50] If you win, you are the prevailing party and you thus are entitled to fees automatically.[51] When your employer is the prevailing party, the employer is not necessarily entitled to fees; instead, an employer can recover fees from you only if your lawsuit was brought in bad faith in that it was frivolous or primarily for purposes of harassment.[52] Assuming you have a fairly reasonable lawsuit, this dual standard allows you to recover your fees if you win and not be assessed your boss's fees if you lose.

The availability of these cumulative remedies usually means that the steps you take to obtain your rights under the 1866 Act will be well worth the effort. Illustrative are the efforts made by twenty-seven black railroad workers in Louisiana who sued their boss, the Illinois Central Railroad. In their lawsuit under the 1866 Act, they contended that their employer had discriminated against them in assignments, promotions, and layoffs by assigning whites to positions of carman apprentices and later promoting them to carmen, by assigning blacks to the lower-paying positions of carman helpers with no prospects of promotion, and by laying off in an economic crunch all of the carman helpers. The court agreed that these practices were unlawful. As a remedy, the court ordered the employer to rehire and promote the twenty-seven black workers to positions of carmen, to provide them with back pay and retroactive seniority, to give them $50,-000 in punitive damages, and to pay their attorney's fees.[53]

\* \* \*

Topeka, the state capital of Kansas, established its location on the civil rights map in 1954, when the Supreme Court, in *Brown* v. *Board of Education of Topeka,* upheld Linda Brown's claim that "[s]eparate educational facilities are inherently unequal."[54]

Years later, another black woman from Topeka, Barbara Sabol, encountered another form of discrimination: employment discrimination. Ms. Sabol was licensed as both a practical nurse and a registered nurse. She had a master's degree in counseling, guidance, and personnel administration. And she had a commendable employment record as a nurse, personnel manager, and teacher. Despite her credentials, it was not always easy for her to obtain employment.

In the spring of 1970, Ms. Sabol learned from a friend that the position of Health Occupations Supervisor for the Kansas State Board of Education would become available in July. Her friend, the current occupant of the position, recommended her highly. Her application for the job was timely. When she spoke to the Assistant Commissioner of Education, the man who was to do the hiring, he indicated that he wanted the person hired to be a nurse and to have a health occupations background. Ms. Sabol met and exceeded all the necessary qualifications. Moreover, at the time that the application period closed, she was the only well-qualified applicant for the job. Everything was perfect. Except that she wasn't hired.

Several weeks after the application period had closed, George Bridges, a white male, applied for a different, also vacant supervisory position with the Kansas State Board of Education. Mr. Bridges had some experience as a school administrator but no experience as a nurse and little experience in the health field. His qualifications did not fit the position of Health Occupations Supervisor. But he got the job that Barbara Sabol had applied for, rather than the one he had sought.

Barbara Sabol believed that she had been discriminated against on grounds of race. She found a lawyer, and sued the Assistant Commissioner and Commissioner of Education of the State of Kansas. She based her lawsuit, in part, on the Civil Rights Act of 1866.

In court, Barbara Sabol proved that she had been subjected to discriminatory disparate treatment. She did this by proving the four elements of a disparate treatment case: that she was protected by the law, that she was qualified for the job, that she was rejected despite her qualifications, and that the job remained open thereafter or was filled by a non-minority person. The sued administrators tried to counter her presumptive case of unlawful discrimination by advancing, as an alleged non-discriminatory reason, that George Bridges simply was better qualified. This allegation, according to the court, fell "far below what could constitute a 'defense' and thus cannot be the articulation of a legitimate, nondiscriminatory reason for the employer's rejection."[55]

Barbara Sabol won her lawsuit, with the court basing its decision solely on the 1866 Act. Having won, she was entitled to the job and to damages. She no longer wanted the job. But she did need the money. The court thus ordered that she be paid $2,475 in actual damages (mostly lost pay), $1,000 in punitive damages, and her attorney's fees.

# Obtaining Further Remedies 7
## from State and Local Governments

## THE CIVIL RIGHTS ACT OF 1871—SECTION 1983

### [RACE, COLOR, NATIONAL ORIGIN, RELIGION, SEX, AGE]

Another century-old statute, the Civil Rights Act of 1871, is the most complicated of all of the civil rights laws. And it is unique in that it prohibits nothing but simply allows for the enforcement of such rights as the constitutional guarantee of equal protection of the laws. Nonetheless, the 1871 Act is important to employment discrimination law because it permits individuals to win substantial monetary remedies above and beyond back pay. In fact, because of the availability of such monetary remedies as actual damages, compensatory damages, and punitive damages, the 1871 Act often is used in conjunction with other laws to increase the overall remedies available to victims of intentional discrimination.

Mary Alice Hill, a Ph.D. candidate and an internationally known track and field athlete, was recruited in 1972 by Colorado State University to head its women's athletics program. At that time, women's athletics at the university were based in the Physical Education Department. The men's athletics program, by contrast, was run by the Athletic Department, where all of the administrators and coaches were male. Although the university wanted to expand its women's program, the position offered to Ms. Hill remained in the Physical Education Department. This meant not only that she would be head of the women's athletics program and a coach but that she—unlike the men in the Athletics Department—also would have teaching responsibilities. Nonetheless, aware of the limited professional opportunities for women in 1972, she accepted the job.

After joining the Colorado State faculty that fall, Mary Alice Hill began to realize that the university's commitment to women's athletics was considerably less than she'd anticipated. She also learned that her aggressive advocacy of *intercollegiate* athletic competition for women was viewed throughout the university as a threat to the funding of the men's teams. So powerful was this perceived threat that Ms. Hill, after three years of highly regarded employment, was not offered a renewal of her contract.

Convinced that she had been intentionally discriminated against because of her sex and her strong advocacy of women's athletics, Ms. Hill sued the university under Title VII of the Civil Rights Act of 1964 *and* also sued several of the university's top officials under the Civil Rights Act of 1871. And she won.[1] Her victory under Title VII entitled her to $20,000 in back pay for the one year she'd been unemployed before finding a better job. Under the 1871 Act, she won an additional $30,000 in compensatory damages and $15,000 in punitive damages, remedies she could not have won under Title VII, for the law does not authorize them. Mary Alice Hill quite wisely sued not only under Title VII but also under the 1871 Act.

*The Civil Rights Act of 1871 was enacted in part to enforce various constitutional rights, including the Fourteenth Amendment's constitutional guarantee of "equal protection of the laws." That guarantee, among others, bars discrimination on all grounds, including race, color, national origin, religion, sex, and age, in state and local government employment.*

*The 1871 Act, alas, is accompanied by three limitations. First, it can be used to stop only intentionally discriminatory practices and not practices which merely have a discriminatory impact. Also, it allows employers to retain some forms of sex discrimination and most forms of age discrimination. Finally, it is enforced only through lawsuits filed by individuals. Nonetheless, individuals who win their lawsuits often can obtain broad monetary remedies well beyond back pay.*

*Because of the limitations on the 1871 Act and also because it is a very complicated law, the 1871 Act is seldom used as the sole basis to challenge employment discrimination. Nonetheless, if you decide to sue a state or local government and its officials for intentional discrimination under Title VII of the Civil Rights Act of 1964, or under any other law, you also should sue under the 1871 Act so as to increase the monetary remedies available to you.*

## WHO IS COVERED BY THE LAW

The Civil Rights Act of 1871 can be enforced through its major provision—known as "Section 1983"—against any "person" whose actions are taken "under color of" any state statute, regulation, or other authority.[2] The word "person" includes not only state, county, and municipal government officials but also the governments themselves. In other words, all state and local governments and their officials are "persons" covered by the 1871 Act so long as their actions are official actions. While the Civil Rights Act of 1871 thus does apply to state and local governments, it does not cover the federal government[3] or private employers.[4]

There are no limitations in the 1871 Act about which individuals are protected by the law. *All persons are protected.* Whether you are an applicant, employee, or former employee, you are protected through the Civil Rights Act of 1871 from most forms of intentional discrimination based upon race, color, national origin, religion, sex, or age practiced by state and local employers. But, as we shall see, the scope of the protection varies tremendously, depending upon the type of discrimination practiced against you.

## DISCRIMINATORY PRACTICES WHICH ARE UNLAWFUL

The central part of the 1871 Act, Section 1983, actually does not prohibit anything.[5] Instead, this one-sentence law merely makes every "person" who acts under color of state law to deprive any other person of any *rights secured by the Constitution* "liable to the party injured in an action at law [or] suit in equity."[6] This rather stilted language simply means that you are entitled to sue state and local governments and their officials under the 1871 Act when your constitutional rights are violated.[7]

Among the rights secured by the Constitution are Fourteenth Amendment rights to equal protection of the laws and to due process, and First Amendment rights to free speech and to free exercise of religion. All of these rights, which are enforced against state and local governments and their officials through the 1871 Act, are important to this chapter, but most significant is the right to equal protection of the laws.[8]

The guarantee of "equal protection"—it seems so straightforward—might appear to bar all discrimination by state and local governments. But it does not mean that. In fact, for nearly seventy years, the courts held that equal protection of the laws allowed government-enforced racial segregation, a proposition approved by the Supreme Court in 1896 and not overruled until 1954.[9] The courts have come a long way since 1954, but even now equal protection does not yet forbid all discrimination. There are two reasons for this. First, the Supreme Court has held that the guarantee of equal protection is violated only by intentional discrimination. Second—and this can get complicated— the Supreme Court has deferred to the decision-making of state and local governments by applying three different "standards of review" to different forms of discrimination, standards which allow virtually no intentional discrimination on grounds of race, color, national origin, and religion; arguably allow some sex discrimination; and widely allow most age discrimination. What this all means, as we shall see through an analysis of intentional discrimination and of the variable standards of review, is that not all discrimination is prohibited. On the other hand, retaliation against individuals who seek non-discrimination in employment is strictly forbidden.

### Intentional Discrimination

The scope of discrimination forbidden under the 1871 Act was unclear until 1976.[10] The Supreme Court that year, in a case involving alleged discrimination by a police department, announced that the guarantee of equal protection of the laws prohibits only that discrimination which is intentional.[11] Many employment practices of course are intentionally discriminatory, such as those which cause *overt discrimination* and *disparate treatment discrimination.* These forms of discrimination, which have been presumed by the Supreme Court to constitute intentional discrimination,[12] *continue to be forbidden by the guarantee of equal protection of the laws.* Other employment practices, however, such as those which only result in disparate *impact* discrimination, ordinarily do not constitute intentional discrimination and they accordingly are not barred by the equal protection clause.

As we saw in Chapter 2 and elsewhere, Title VII and other modern laws prohibit the use of employment practices which have a discriminatory disparate impact and are not related to job performance, regardless of the intent or purpose for using the practices. Although this continues to be the law under Title VII, it is not the law under the 1871 Act. In point of fact, the employment practice challenged in the 1976 Supreme Court case was the entry-level written test used by the District of Columbia Metropolitan Police Department, a test which had an undeniably discriminatory impact upon minority applicants and which had a dubious relationship to job performance. Despite the undisputed discriminatory impact of its test, the Police Department arguably had not engaged in intentional discrimination, because at the same time that it had used the test it also had implemented a fairly successful affirmative action program. Announcing that only intentional discrimination was prohibited under the 1871 Act and that the discriminatory impact of a practice alone is not sufficient to prove intentional discrimination, the Supreme Court upheld the use of the written test as lawful.[13]

Another practice which has a discriminatory disparate impact is the allowance under veterans' preference laws of additional points to veterans in the competition for state and local government jobs. The effect of these laws is severly sex discriminatory since nearly all veterans are men—a fact of life flowing from past and present discrimination in the armed services. Despite the discriminatory impact of veterans' preference laws, the Supreme

Court in 1979 effectively barred sex discrimination challenges to such laws under the 1871 Act. It did so by holding that the Massachusetts veterans' preference laws—which accorded an absolute preference to veterans in a state where 98 percent of all veterans were men—was not intentionally sex discriminatory.[14]

In spite of these recent Supreme Court rulings, some disparate impact discrimination still can be considered to be intentionally discriminatory. In order to show intentional discrimination, you need not "prove that the challenged action rested solely on . . . discriminatory purposes," but only "that a discriminatory purpose has been *a* motivating factor."[15] In order to determine whether discriminatory purpose is *a* motivating factor behind a practice, there are six elements to be considered: the discriminatory impact of the practice, the historical background of the practice and of other actions, the sequence of events leading to use of the practice, procedural departures from use of the practice, substantive departures from use of the practice, and the administrative history behind adoption of the practice.[16] When discrimination appears more often than not among these factors, it is likely that the discrimination has been intentional.

In all situations, there is another factor which always is relevant to establishing intentional discrimination: statistics showing a racial, sexual, etc., imbalance in the employer's work force. According to the Supreme Court, "such imbalance is often a telltale sign of purposeful discrimination; absent explanation, it is ordinarily to be expected that nondiscriminatory hiring practices will in time result in a work force more or less representative of the racial and ethnic [etc.] composition of the population in the community from which employees are hired."[17] If your employer's statistics show such an imbalance, you are in a good position to show intentional discrimination. But remember, you have to prove more than just imbalance.

Overall, it is not easy to know without a thorough investigation of all the facts and statistics whether a particular employment practice is sufficiently intentionally discriminatory to be barred under the 1871 Act. Even if your investigation reveals that a practice should be considered to be intentional discrimination, proving it as a fact remains fairly difficult. But it is not impossible. Indeed, as we will see at the end of this chapter, the purportedly neutral discharge practices of the public schools in Sweeny, Texas, have been held to constitute intentional discrimination.[18]

## Standards for Reviewing Discrimination

Once you prove that you have been subjected to intentional discrimination, you have completed only the first step toward a determination that the practice is unlawful. The second step allows the employer to show that the discrimination is legally justifiable. Whether or not the employer's justification is sufficient to make the discrimination lawful usually depends upon the "standard of review" used by the courts to evaluate the legality of different forms of discrimination. Over the years, the Supreme Court has developed three separate standards of review: one for discrimination based on race, color, national origin, or religion; another for sex discrimination; and yet a third for age discrimination.

*Race, color, national origin, and religious discrimination.* Intentional discrimination on grounds of race, color, national origin,[19] or religion is forbidden under the 1871 Act unless the discrimination somehow can be justified by a compelling or overriding purpose. In the words of the Supreme Court, a government employer has a "heavy burden of justification" to demonstrate that an intentionally discriminatory practice is "necessary to promote a compelling government interest"; additionally, whatever government interest is asserted, it "will be closely scrutinized in light of its asserted purposes."[20]

This "strict" standard of review was developed by the Supreme Court decades ago to give particular protection from discrimination to racial minorities—members of groups that have been "saddled with such disabilities, or subjected to such a history of purposeful unequal treatment, or relegated to such a position of political powerlessness as to command extraordinary protection from the majoritarian political process."[21] The strict standard also applies to discrimination which infringes upon religious practices, because the free exercise of religion is a fundamental right protected by the First Amendment.[22]

In practice, this strict standard of review has meant that nearly all intentional discrimination on grounds of race, color, national origin, or religion is unlawful because there ordinarily can be no compelling government interest to justify such discrimination.[23] Illustrative is a case involving not employment discrimination but unemployment discrimination. Some years ago, Adell Sherbert was discharged by her private employer because she refused to work on Saturdays, the Sabbath day of her religion. For the same reason that she was discharged, she also was unable to obtain other employment. Consequently, she applied to the state of South Carolina for her unemployment compensation. This too was denied her. By not being able to work on Saturdays, she was not able to satisfy one of the state's unemployment compensation eligibility requirements, that she be available to work. Adell Sherbert believed that her free exercise of religion had been interfered with both by the private employer's discharge and by the state's denial of unemployment compensation. She couldn't sue the *private* employer under the 1871 Act, but she could sue the state. She did and she won. The Supreme Court held that the state could not in any way justify its infringement on Ms. Sherbert's religious rights.[24]

In the past few years, the Supreme Court has created one narrow exception to this rigid standard of review, an exception which involves national origin discrimination against non-citizens or aliens. Specifically, the exclusion of non-citizens from "important" executive, legislative, and judicial positions designed for persons "who participate directly in the formulation, execution or review of broad public policy" need not be justified by a compelling government interest.[25] Applying this exception in 1978, the Supreme Court held that police officers fell within this category, that a state law prohibiting non-citizens from obtaining employment as state police officers did not need to be justified by a compelling interest, and that, accordingly, the discrimination was lawful.[26] And in 1979, the Supreme Court similarly held that a state law prohibiting non-citizens from teaching in the public schools did not need to be justified by a compelling interest, and hence the discrimination was upheld as lawful.[27] Because of these rulings, other important state and local government jobs involving the formulation, execution, or review of "broad public policy" similarly can be expected to be denied to non-citizens—lawfully. But most discrimination against non-citizens does not fit within the "broad public policy" exception. Ordinarily, non-citizens are discriminated against by state laws and practices requiring citizenship for extensive categories of jobs or for jobs having nothing to do with government policy. This type of discrimination must be justified by a compelling interest, cannot be so justified, and thus is unlawful. The Supreme Court, for example, has struck down a New York law which required citizenship for nearly all civil service jobs,[28] a Connecticut law which required citizenship in order to be licensed as a lawyer,[29] and a law in Puerto Rico which required United States citizenship in order to be licensed as an architect, engineer, or surveyor.[30] Other laws and practices which discriminate against non-citizens—except with regard to broad public policy positions—are similarly unlawful.

*Sex discrimination.* The standard of review for sex discrimination is less rigid than the strict standard applicable to discrimination on grounds of race, color, national origin, and religion. In 1973, the Supreme Court nearly adopted the strict standard as applicable to sex discrimination. Four of the nine Justices voted to do so.[31] But the necessary fifth vote has never been cast.

One vote short, the Supreme Court has settled on an "intermediate" standard of review: any practice that discriminates on grounds of sex "must serve important governmental objectives and must be substantially related to achievement of those objectives."[32] This standard, although formulated more leniently than the compelling state interest standard, is still fairly difficult for an employer to satisfy. In fact, since 1973, the Supreme Court has held to be unlawful nearly every form of intentional sex discrimination which has come before it.[33] Illustrative is a 1973 case in which a woman challenged a statute which allowed men greater fringe benefits than were available to women. Under the statute, all men were automatically able to claim their spouses as dependents in order to obtain higher medical and dental benefits, but women could claim their spouses only if they demonstrated that they in fact provided more than half their spouses' support. In an attempt to rationalize this discrimination, which denied women benefits for their husbands, the government offered no justification other than administrative convenience. The Supreme Court held that administrative convenience was not a sufficient reason to justify the sex discrimination, and the statute was struck down as unlawful.[34]

The intermediate standard of review applicable to sex discrimination may be sufficient to make most forms of intentional discrimination unlawful under the Civil Rights Act of 1871. This generalization, however, does not hold up in one important area of sex discrimination: discrimination against women who are pregnant. The problem here actually arises not from the standard of review but from the Supreme Court's refusal to treat this form of discrimination as sex discrimination under the 1871 Act.[35] In contrast, this form of discrimination of course is forbidden by Title VII of the Civil Rights Act of 1964.[36]

*Age discrimination.* The 1871 Act provides virtually no protection from discrimination based upon age, because the standard of review is very low. The standard, often referred to as the "rational basis" standard, allows any discrimination which might be considered "reasonable, not arbitrary."[37] In fact, discrimination is permitted so long as "any state of facts reasonably may be conceived to justify it"; conversely, the discrimination is unlawful only if it "rests on grounds wholly irrelevant to the achievement of [a governmental] objective."[38]

In other words, a state or local government can successfully defend intentional discrimination based upon age merely by asserting that there is some arguably reasonable justification for the discrimination. Since most state and local governments will argue that their discrimination has some rationale, this lenient standard of review allows virtually all forms of age discrimination. Illustrative is a lawsuit under the 1871 Act challenging a Massachusetts law which required mandatory retirement of all police officers at age fifty. The challenger, Robert Murgia, whose state-awarded fiftieth birthday present was mandatory retirement, contended that he was as fit as ever and that the state law unreasonably discriminated against him on grounds of age by retiring all officers at the arbitrarily set age of fifty. The Supreme Court agreed that Bob Murgia's "excellent physical and mental health still rendered him capable of performing the duties of a uniformed officer," but the Court nonetheless held that mandatory retirement at fifty "clearly is rationally related to the state's overall objective" of "protect[ing] the public by assuring physical preparedness of its uniformed police."[39]

Deference to the rationales offered by state and local governments is not limited to allowing age discrimination only against police officers. Instead, this lenient standard of review applies across the board. For example, under the rational basis standard of review, the courts have upheld most forms of age discrimination, including the mandatory retirement of civil service employees,[40] of schoolteachers,[41] and of state judges.[42]

Because the rational basis standard of review under the Civil Rights Act of 1871 permits almost any form of discrimination on grounds of age, the 1871 Act no longer is very widely used as a vehicle to challenge age discrimination. Since much broader protection against age discrimination, including protection against mandatory retirement, is provided by the Age Discrimination in Employment Act, its rights and remedies are now pursued as the best means of effectively challenging age discrimination.[43]

## Retaliation

The complications surrounding those employment practices which are forbidden and those which might be permitted under the 1871 Act are notably absent with regard to one type of practice. Retaliation is strictly forbidden. The protection against retaliation derives not from the right to equal protection of the laws guaranteed by the Fourteenth Amendment but from the right to free speech guaranteed by the First Amendment. Very simply, a state or local government cannot lawfully retaliate against you for opposing discrimination or for seeking non-discrimination. This, however, does not mean that illegal retaliation has disappeared. Bessie Givhan, a junior-high-school teacher in Mississippi who complained to her principal that the school's employment practices were racially discriminatory, was fired for being too forthright. Ms. Givhan sued her boss under the 1871 Act and won, in 1979, when the Supreme Court held that her free speech rights had been violated.[44] And, as we have seen, Mary Alice Hill also sued and won after she was retaliated against for her aggressive advocacy of women's athletics.[45]

## MAJOR EXCEPTIONS

The Civil Rights Act of 1871 applies exclusively to state and local governments and their officials. It does not cover the federal government and private employers.

The protection of the 1871 Act against discrimination on grounds of race, color, national origin, religion, sex, and age, as we have seen, is not as sweeping as its promise. Practices which are not infected with a discriminatory purpose are allowed under the 1871 Act. And the varying standards of review make some forms of sex discrimination and nearly all forms of age discrimination lawful under the 1871 Act.

A final exception which is not yet conclusively established under the 1871 Act allows state and local governments to engage in affirmative action, including the use of numerical goals and timetables.[46] Such affirmative action unquestionably may be undertaken by or required of government employers that have engaged in past discrimination.[47]

## THE FEDERAL AGENCY RESPONSIBLE FOR ENFORCEMENT

There is no federal agency responsible for enforcing the Civil Rights Act of 1871. This means that there is no federal agency with which you need to file an administrative charge of discrimination, no federal agency to negotiate with your employer on your behalf, and no federal agency to sue your boss.

## ENFORCEMENT: HOW TO OBTAIN YOUR RIGHTS

There is only one way to obtain your rights under the Civil Rights Act of 1871. You have to sue.

Before you do so, you must decide whether you have convincing evidence of intentional discrimination. If you don't, forget about suing under the 1871 Act. On the other hand, if you're certain you can prove intentional discrimination, then you should try to anticipate the reasons the employer might advance to justify the discrimination. Pretend you are a judge required to follow the law. Ask yourself: Are the potential justifications compelling? important? reasonable? Even if you remain convinced that you have a great case, you still should sue primarily under Title VII, the Revenue Sharing Act, and any other laws that are helpful to your situation, and then add a claim under the 1871 Act. It's easier to win under the modern laws, but if you also win under the 1871 Act, you'll find the availability of the Act's monetary remedies quite attractive.

If you are considering suing, you should find a lawyer quickly, a step that is a virtual necessity in view of the Act's many complications. After you have retained a lawyer, you should file your lawsuit in a federal district court or in a state court located in the area where the discrimination occurred. There are no administrative prerequisites if you sue only under the 1871 Act. You need not have filed a charge of discrimination under Title VII with the EEOC,[48] and in fact, you need not have filed any administrative papers anywhere.[49] Under the 1871 Act, you are entitled to go directly to court as soon as you wish, but not as late as you might, for your claim—similar to a claim under the 1866 Act—*must* be filed within the time allowed by the appropriate state statute governing the filing of a lawsuit like yours.[50] State statutes of this nature—called "statutes of limitations"—limit the number of years within which a lawsuit may be filed subsequent to the conduct which you claim is unlawful. The purpose of these statutes is to prevent the filing of stale cases that are many years old. The appropriate state statutes vary from state to state. Many of the appropriate statutes, however, require that an employment discrimination lawsuit under the 1871 Act must be filed no later than one or two years after the discrimination occurred. If you file too late, your claim under the 1871 Act will be dismissed.[51]

When your lawsuit is timely, when you prove that you have been subjected to intentional employment discrimination, and when the discrimination cannot be justified, you then are in a position to recover everything you've lost, and more.

## REMEDIES: WHAT YOU CAN GET WHEN YOUR RIGHTS HAVE BEEN VIOLATED

Winning your lawsuit under the 1871 Act means that you can win more court-ordered remedies from your employer than is possible under any other single law. There are two basic categories of remedies: "equitable" remedies and "legal" damage remedies. Both sets of remedies are available to you in a lawsuit under the 1871 Act.

The availability of "equitable" remedies in employment discrimination lawsuits means, first and foremost, that you are entitled to have the discrimination declared unlawful and terminated. Additionally, you are entitled to your *rightful place*—the place you would have been in if there had been no discrimination against you. The equitable rightful place remedies available under the 1871 Act are the same as the equitable remedies available under Title VII discussed in Chapter 2. There is only one difference. Under Title VII, back pay availability runs from two years prior to the filing of a charge of discrimination with the EEOC. Under the 1871 Act, there is no such limitation. If you win under the 1871 Act, you may receive back pay for as far back as you were discriminated against,[52] or for at least as far back as the state statute of limitations allows.[53]

The availability of "legal" remedies under the 1871 Act means that you can win monetary remedies in addition to back pay and that you, like Mary Alice Hill, can obtain a jury trial if you want one.[54] The monetary remedies available include actual damages, compensatory damages, and punitive damages. In order to obtain these damages you must prove that you are entitled to them. Their availability is not presumed simply because your rights have been violated.[55]

The phrase "actual damages" means what it says. It is redundant of back pay because it includes lost wages.[56] But it also includes other remuneration, such as the costs of looking for another job. If you prove that you lost money because of the discrimination, you can recover whatever you lost as actual damages.

"Compensatory damages" are similar to actual damages but more comprehensive. Included under compensatory damages

are damages for the psychological pain, suffering, and humiliation that you incur as a victim of discrimination. In one recent
case under the 1871 Act, an individual won $80,000 in compen-
satory damages because of the humiliation he had suffered.[57]

An award of "punitive damages" need not be related at all to
any harm actually suffered by you, except that there must be
some actual harm. As the phrase implies, these damages are used
to punish an employer that has violated the law not only intentionally but with malice. Although this is a high level of proof,
punitive damages definitely are available under the 1871 Act.[58]
Mary Alice Hill in fact won $15,000 in punitive damages for
herself.[59]

There is one major limitation upon the availability of the
foregoing monetary remedies. You cannot recover either back
pay or damages in lawsuits under the 1871 Act filed only against
*states* or *state agencies*. This limitation arises because of the
Eleventh Amendment's grant of immunity from monetary liability to states and state agencies—a grant of immunity which the
Supreme Court has interpreted as barring awards of back pay
and damages against unconsenting states and state agencies.[60]
This limitation is not as serious as it may seem, because you still
can win back pay and damages from any *individual officials* you
sue when you show that they knew or should have known that
they were violating your rights.[61]

A final remedy which is available to you when you win your
lawsuit under the 1871 Act—the same as under the 1866 Act—
is an award of your attorney's fees. Under the 1871 Act, the
"prevailing party" in a lawsuit is entitled to attorney's fees.[62] If
you win, you are the prevailing party, and you thus are entitled
to attorney's fees automatically.[63] You can obtain these fees even
in a successful lawsuit against a state or state agency.[64] There is,
however, another side to this coin. State and local government
defendants can recover fees from you if your lawsuit is ultimately
found by the court to have been brought in bad faith in that it
was frivolous or primarily for purposes of harassment.[65] Nonetheless, so long as you have a fairly reasonable lawsuit, this dual
standard allows you to recover your fees if you win and not be
assessed your boss's fees if you lose.

\*   \*   \*

The Sweeny Independent School District, a small school system in southeastern Texas not far from Galveston, began in the late 1960s to desegregate its schools. In the course of this process, which involved closing several all-black schools, the School District's top administrators decided that fewer teachers would be needed in the integrated schools than had been employed in the segregated schools. In order to determine which teachers would be fired, the white administrators went through a three-step teacher evaluation process. First, they made written evaluations of all of the black teachers. Then they compared the black teachers to each other. Finally, they evaluated all the teachers, black and white, on a standardized evaluation form. Announcing that they had used only the standardized evaluation, the school officials discharged seventeen teachers. All were black. A year later, the School District hired seventeen new teachers, all of whom were white.

Led by one of the outraged teachers, Mildred Harkless, the black teachers sued the Sweeny Independent School District under the Civil Rights Act of 1871. They firmly believed that they could show that they had been intentionally discriminated against. Proving this was not as easy as it might appear, for Sweeny steadfastly maintained that the discharges had been caused merely by a neutral evaluation—conducted through the use of a standardized evaluation form—which had an unfortunate and unintended discriminatory impact. Nonetheless, after extensive court hearings held over many years, Mildred Harkless and her colleagues finally won.

Reaching a decision on the case in 1977, the court carefully reviewed all of the facts, including the background of the discharges to see if intentional discrimination had been involved. Although the discriminatory effect of a practice by itself is not enough to establish intentional discrimination, the court observed that the "impact of the action was particularly devastating." As to the initial evaluation of only the black teachers, the court noted that this written evaluation included "disparaging racial comments and its sole focus upon black teachers was" strong "evidence of the intent behind the employment decisions." Also highly relevant was the second evaluation, in which the "black teachers were the only teachers ranked against one another." Further, the court could not avoid the fact that seventeen white teachers "replaced the discharged black teachers." Given all of these facts, the court held that the School District's purportedly neutral, standardized evaluation process to which the black and white teachers all were subjected "was only a pretext for denying [the black teachers] their jobs on the basis of race." In sum, there "was intentional racial discrimination in the nonrenewal of the contract."[66]

Determining the back pay to be awarded to the individual teachers was not an easy task, for the simple reason that most of the teachers, during the lengthy course of their lawsuit, ultimately found better-paying jobs or left teaching altogether. Mildred Harkless, for example, had earned almost as much money in the first two years after her discharge by working in Houston as a substitute teacher. Thereafter, she moved to San Francisco, obtained an M.A. in Business Administration, and began an altogether different professional career. Nonetheless, the back pay awards were computed and general damages were assessed for a total monetary recovery against the School District of $375,-000. Additionally, the Sweeny Independent School District had to pay more than $250,000 in attorney's fees to the teachers' lawyers, who, ironically, had represented Mildred Harkless and her colleagues for free.[67]

# PART FOUR
## How to Obtain Your Rights under All the Laws

# Combining the Laws to **8**
## Win Your Rights and
## the Broadest Remedies Possible

Some victims of discrimination, as we have seen, have wisely asserted their rights and won significant remedies under more than just one of the laws forbidding employment discrimination. Like them, you should keep in mind that there are seven major federal laws. This is not just a mental exercise, for, in order to win the broadest remedies possible, you *always* should assert your rights in a proper and timely fashion under as many of the laws as are applicable to your situation.

As easy as this may appear, it sometimes can be more difficult in practice, because each of the seven federal laws differs in various ways from the other laws. Among those differences, and of primary importance here, are the different procedures for obtaining your rights under each of the laws, and the different remedies available to you under each of the laws. The procedures for obtaining your rights are crucial because they usually involve strict time periods both for the filing of administrative charges of discrimination and for the filing of lawsuits. What makes the different procedures especially critical is that the procedures under each law are separate and independent from those you must follow under each of the other laws. Before you can take advantage of and win the remedies of more than one of the laws, you must comply with the separate procedures of each such law.[1]

The different remedies available under the seven laws are obviously significant because, when combined, they can increase the overall remedies available to you and your colleagues, and because their combination often can facilitate a faster resolution to the discrimination practiced against you. For example, the enforcement device under the Revenue Sharing Act and under Executive Order 11246 of terminating federal monetary assistance to discriminatory employers is an extremely powerful weapon that should always be used. But in order to invoke this threat, as well as to obtain the remedial advantages of all the laws,[2] you again have to comply with the procedures of each of the laws.

Ordinarily there will be more than just one law applicable to your situation. If, for example, you have been intentionally denied equal pay on grounds of sex by a local government, you are protected by four of the laws: the Equal Pay Act, Title VII of the Civil Rights Act of 1964, the Revenue Sharing Act, and the Civil Rights Act of 1871. In this situation—indeed whenever you have more than one legal option—you *always* should assert your rights under as many of the laws as are available.

Not only should you be aware of and pursue all of your options, but you also must realize that bias rarely comes neatly packaged as only one form of discrimination. If you are discriminated against as a woman, you may be a victim of sex discrimination; or, if you also are over forty, of age discrimination; or, if you are also black, of race discrimination. But the chances are that you in fact are the victim of sex, age, *and* race discrimination. There is no need to try to figure out which form of discrimination has been practiced against you, and there is no reason to give your employer the benefit of any doubt. Instead, assume the worst. And protect your rights by proceeding under all of the laws that might possibly apply to your situation.

And remember, the *procedures* under each of the laws are *separate and independent* from each other. Once you've complied with the procedures of several laws, their *remedies* then can be *combined* to your advantage.

# THE INDEPENDENT PROCEDURES FOR OBTAINING YOUR RIGHTS

Since you want to enhance your options under as many of the seven major federal laws as possible, you have to comply with each law's procedures and time limits. Quite simply, you lose the protection of any law that you don't comply with. In this context, remember that not only are the procedures of each of the seven major federal laws distinct from each other but they also are independent from other laws and procedures not discussed in this book. Many people, for example, have wrongly decided to pursue their rights to non-discrimination exclusively under union grievance procedures or under state fair employment laws. Sometimes they have won. More often, by not complying with the independent timing requirements of the federal laws, they have lost their option of pursuing their rights to non-discrimination under the applicable federal laws.[3]

Joan Rudolph's tardy pursuit of her Title VII rights is illustrative. Fired by her Missouri employer, Wagner Electric Corp., Ms. Rudolph filed a union grievance alleging that she had been dismissed other than for cause, contrary to the provisions in her union's collective bargaining agreement. Her union, the International Union of Electrical, Radio and Machine Workers, AFL–CIO, pursued her grievance through arbitration. Several months after losing in arbitration and more than a year after her discharge, Ms. Rudolph filed an administrative charge of sex discrimination with the EEOC alleging that her employer had discriminated against her in violation of Title VII. But her charge, filed with the EEOC more than 180 days after her discharge, was too late. Since an independent pursuit of union grievance procedures does not obviate the necessity of filing an administrative charge under Title VII within 180 days of the discrimination,[4] her charge and her subsequent lawsuit were of no use.[5]

Similarly, Charles Everson sought to remedy his discharge by his Michigan employer by filing a union grievance and by filing a charge of discrimination with the Michigan Civil Rights Commission. Much later, when these routes failed to provide him with a remedy, he filed a formal administrative charge of race discrimination with the EEOC. But his charge and his subsequent lawsuit under Title VII ultimately were dismissed because his EEOC charge had been untimely.[6]

The requirement for filing a timely charge is not the only time period which must be met under Title VII. As indicated in Chapter 2, another Title VII requirement necessitates the filing of a lawsuit within 90 days of receipt of a right-to-sue letter.[7] Failure to act within this time period also can result in dismissal of a lawsuit filed under Title VII. This is precisely what happened to Franklin Prophet, a black steelworker who had been fired from his job by his Texas employer on grounds that he believed were racially discriminatory. His Title VII lawsuit was dismissed as untimely because, although he had filed a timely EEOC charge, he did not file his lawsuit within 90 days of receipt of the right-to-sue letter. He filed it on the ninety-second day, two days late.[8]

Franklin Prophet, in his lawsuit, could have sued his boss also under the Civil Rights Act of 1866. In fact, he did. But, unfortunately, he waited too long under the 1866 Act as well. The Texas statute of limitations applicable to Mr. Prophet's 1866 Act claim required that it be filed within two years of his dismissal from employment. Since he filed his Title VII/1866 Act lawsuit nearly two-and-a-half years after his dismissal, the 1866 Act claim in his lawsuit also was dismissed.[9]

The independence of the laws' differing procedures becomes especially clear from Willie Johnson's Title VII/1866 Act lawsuit. Like Franklin Prophet's Title VII claim, Willie Johnson's Title VII claim was dismissed because he had filed his lawsuit too late. As to his claim under the 1866 Act, Mr. Johnson argued that the one-year Tennessee statute of limitations applicable to that claim had been satisfied by his filing an EEOC charge within one year from his racially discriminatory discharge. This argument was strong enough for the United States Supreme Court to agree to hear his case. But the Supreme Court in 1975 rejected his argument and held that regardless of an individual's pursuit of administrative remedies under Title VII, any claim under the 1866 Act must be filed *in court* within the period allowed by the state statute of limitations.[10]

Despite the untimely pursuit of their rights, Willie Johnson and Franklin Prophet at least were aware that they had more than one option under the seven federal laws. Too many individuals improperly limit themselves to only one course of action. Most of the time, the only option pursued—shortsightedly—is Title VII of the Civil Rights Act of 1964. Under Title VII, as you are aware, a person ordinarily must file an administrative charge of discrimination with the EEOC within 180 days.[11] Failure to meet this requirement means that even a very strong case will lose, simply because it is untimely. But even if you are late under Title VII, you do have other alternatives available.

Several years ago, the Nashville Police Department disciplined a female police officer and a male police officer for socializing with each other in violation of the Police Department's unwritten policy forbidding male and female socializing. Not only was the policy itself probably unlawful, but the Police Department applied it in a classic example of unlawful disparate treatment discrimination. The male officer was merely suspended for ten days, while the female officer, Lorraine Krzyzewski, was fired on the spot, effective that day, August 15, although she remained on the payroll until August 29. Approximately six months later, on February 18, Lorraine Krzyzewski filed with the EEOC an administrative charge alleging sex discrimination against the Nashville Police Department. When the EEOC was unable to resolve the employer's discrimination, Ms. Krzyzewski sued her former boss under Title VII. Despite her very strong case of sex discrimination against the Police Department, she didn't win. In fact, she didn't even have an opportunity to prove her case. After the case was filed, the Nashville Police Department moved to dismiss her Title VII lawsuit on the grounds that she had not filed her administrative charge of discrimination within 180 days of the discriminatory act—her discharge. The court counted the days from her August 15 discharge and concluded that the 180th day fell on February 12. Lorraine Krzyzewski had not filed her charge with the EEOC until February 18, six days later. Nonetheless, Ms. Krzyzewski argued that the 180 days should have run from August 29, the last day she was on the payroll. The court was unpersuaded. Finding that the 180-day administrative filing period runs from the date on which the discriminatory action actually occurs, the court held that Ms. Krzyzewski's charge had been untimely. Her lawsuit was dismissed.[12]

Unfortunately, Ms. Krzyzewski filed her administrative charge and sued *only* under Title VII. What she apparently didn't know is that the Revenue Sharing Act, which prohibits discrimination by local governments including law enforcement agencies, has no time limitation on the filing of administrative charges.[13] Instead of limiting herself to filing an administrative charge only with the EEOC under Title VII, she should have filed an additional charge at the same time, or later for that matter, with the ORS under the Revenue Sharing Act. In view of the considerable enforcement power of the ORS, her charge probably would have been resolved favorably without her even having to sue. And if she wanted to sue, she still could have sued the Nashville Police Department directly under the Revenue Sharing Act. Since her administrative charge would have been timely, her lawsuit would not have been dismissed on procedural grounds. And given the circumstances of her discharge, she undoubtedly would have won her lawsuit.

Title VII may be the most familiar and most often used of the seven major laws prohibiting employment discrimination. But don't limit yourself to Title VII. Now that you know about the other laws, avail yourself of their protection by complying with their procedural and timing requirements.

## THE COMBINED REMEDIES AVAILABLE TO YOU

When you comply with the independent procedures under the federal laws applicable to your situation and prove that you have been unlawfully discriminated against, you are eligible for the cumulative remedies available under any and all of those laws.

Unfortunately—this needs to be stressed again—countless victims of discrimination have asserted and won their rights under only one of the laws, thereby depriving themselves and their colleagues of the greater remedies available through pursuit of their rights under all of the applicable federal laws. Many other individuals have obtained their rights and remedies only after initiating lengthy and expensive lawsuits which may not have been necessary had the individuals filed administrative charges of discrimination with the ORS and the OFCCP, which hold the purse strings of many employers. Again, the simple answer is that you *always* should pursue your rights under as many of the federal laws as are applicable. And, if you have to sue, you should sue under as many of the federal laws as are applicable. When you win, you might be able to obtain remedies under all of the laws.

As suggested earlier, women who have been discriminated against on grounds of sex by a local government agency always should file administrative charges of discrimination with the ORS under the Revenue Sharing Act. They also should pursue their rights under Title VII and, if the discrimination is intentional, under the Civil Rights Act of 1871. Two women who forgot about the Revenue Sharing Act but pursued the latter two laws are Nancy Bradshaw and Mary Alice Hill. Nancy Bradshaw applied for but was denied the position of education director with the San Diego Zoo. When she learned that a male with fewer qualifications was awarded the job, she filed a timely administrative charge of discrimination under Title VII with the EEOC. When the EEOC failed to resolve her charge, she filed a lawsuit under Title VII seeking the job and back pay, and under the 1871 Act seeking compensatory and punitive damages. Over the zoo's objections, the court held that Nancy Bradshaw could combine her remedies.[14]

A similar tactic was followed by Mary Alice Hill. As we saw in Chapter 7, Ms. Hill was discharged by Colorado State University because of her aggressive advocacy of intercollegiate athletics for women. Suing her boss under two laws paid off. She won $20,000 in back pay under Title VII, and $30,000 in compensatory damages and $15,000 in punitive damages under the 1871 Act.[15] If Mary Alice Hill had sued only under Title VII, she would have denied herself the broader remedies she ultimately won. Instead, Ms. Hill, like Nancy Bradshaw, used more than one law to her considerable advantage.

Black employees who have been discriminated against by a union ordinarily have only two of the major federal laws available: Title VII and the Civil Rights Act of 1866.[16] Both of these laws were used recently by fifteen black transit workers in St. Louis who successfully sued their union, Amalgamated Transit Union Local 788, for retroactive seniority, back pay, and other benefits guaranteed to them by various collective-bargaining agreements. The background of their case is somewhat complicated. Essentially, St. Louis in one year witnessed the merger of a dozen transit companies into one metropolitan transit company. Concurrent with the merger, the Transit Union conducted a membership campaign to attract all of the transit workers to Local 788 membership. As part of that campaign, Local 788 agreed to waive the normal $100 initiation fee and to give full seniority credit for past transit employment. After the metropolitan transit company recognized the union without an election, the union's promises were incorporated into the collective bargaining agreements. Two years later, the transit company purchased one of the few remaining independent transit companies —one that employed a predominantly black work force. The black workers joined Local 788, but much to the company's dismay, the union refused to waive the initiation fee and refused to allow them seniority credit. Two of the black transit workers filed timely administrative charges of discrimination with the EEOC. When the charges were not resolved, the two transit workers and thirteen of their black co-workers sued the union under Title VII, and also under the 1866 Act in order to increase the monetary remedies available to them. After winning their lawsuit, they were awarded retroactive seniority, back pay, the $100 initiation fees that they had unlawfully been required to pay, and their attorney's fees—all under Title VII. Finding that the union had willfully discriminated against the black transit workers, the court also awarded each of them $1,000 in punitive damages—a remedy not available under Title VII but proper under the 1866 Act.[17]

The availability of punitive damages, as well as other general damages, has made the 1866 Act a convenient companion to Title VII in race cases. Not only does the Act enhance the overall remedies, but it sometimes can allow a remedy even when the Title VII claim fails. John Garner (see Chapter 6) lost his Title VII discharge claim against the New Orleans Police Department, but he nonetheless won $5,000 for "mental anguish and humiliation," a remedy not available under Title VII but nonetheless available to compensate for other discrimination that violated the 1866 Act.[18]

Combining the applicable federal laws is especially useful to women challenging denials of equal pay. As we have seen, the Equal Pay Act prohibits only the denial of equal pay for equal work, while Title VII forbids many other forms of sex discrimination beyond discrimination in compensation. If you have been denied equal pay or other forms of compensation on the basis of sex, you can secure your rights under the Equal Pay Act or under Title VII. But you *should* seek to obtain your rights under *both laws*. As one court recently stated, "The same set of facts may form the basis for redress under both Title VII and the Equal Pay Act if the requirements of each are separately satisfied and the claimant (employee) does not reap overlapping relief for the same wrong."[19]

Despite these similar prohibitions against denials of equal pay on grounds of sex, the Equal Pay Act and Title VII provide remedies which differ in five ways. Three of the differences favor the use of Title VII, the fourth is seemingly neutral, and the fifth favors the use of the Equal Pay Act.

• Denials of equal pay can be challenged either under the Equal Pay Act or under Title VII. But other sex discriminatory practices, which often are related to denials of equal pay, can be challenged only under Title VII. Obviously, sex discrimination claims can be much broader under Title VII than under the Equal Pay Act.

• Claims of discrimination under the Equal Pay Act usually can be directed only at a single "establishment" maintained by your employer. The focus of Title VII, however, is not upon any single establishment but on the "employer." Accordingly, any equal pay claim can have a broader impact against an employer under Title VII than under the Equal Pay Act.

• The back pay which is available in a lawsuit under the Equal Pay Act can be obtained only by the individuals who sue or who file written consents with the court indicating that they want to be a part of the lawsuit. Under Title VII, on the other hand, back pay may be awarded not only to those individuals who filed or joined the lawsuit but also in a class action lawsuit to all unidentified persons who have been similarly discriminated against. This means that in a class action lawsuit, you can obtain broader back pay remedies for your colleagues under Title VII than are available under the Equal Pay Act.

• The fourth difference between the two laws also concerns back pay. Whether the Equal Pay Act or Title VII is more advantageous depends upon your situation. Under the Equal Pay Act, back pay runs from two years prior to the dates on which the lawsuit was filed and the other individuals opted into the lawsuit; where the violation is willful, back pay is available for a third year. Under Title VII, back pay availability runs from two years prior to the filing of the first administrative charge of discrimination with the EEOC. These differences mean that the amounts of back pay available will vary depending when you formally assert your rights.

• The fifth difference concerns an additional monetary remedy that can be obtained only under the Equal Pay Act. When an employer's denial of equal pay is willful, a person proceeding under the Equal Pay Act can recover double back pay, a remedy referred to as "liquidated damages." The availability of this remedy means that you often can recover a greater monetary remedy under the Equal Pay Act than you can under Title VII.

These differences, at first blush, may seem confusing. But in practice they simply provide you with options for winning the broadest remedies possible. In any event, you always should seek to remedy equal pay violations under both the Equal Pay Act and Title VII.

The interrelationship between the Equal Pay Act and Title VII is exemplified by the sex discrimination lawsuit filed in Pittsburgh by Sandra Wetzel and Mari Ross against the Liberty Mutual Insurance Company. Ms. Wetzel and Ms. Ross were employed in the Claims Department in one of Liberty Mutual's 130 branch offices. Each Claims Department had a similar line of progression with two classifications, Claims Adjuster and Claims Representative, at the bottom of the line. Although Claims Adjusters and Claims Representatives performed essentially identical jobs, there were three major differences between the two classifications. One was that only Claims Adjusters were eligible for promotion to the top jobs. Also, Claims Adjusters were paid $2,700 a year more than Claims Representatives. Finally (if you haven't guessed it already), nearly all Claims Adjusters were men while all Claims Representatives were women. An honest characterization of these two classifications would have read: "Claims Adjuster (male)" and "Claims Representative (female)."

Claims Representatives Sandra Wetzel and Mari Ross were quick to discover the extent of Liberty Mutual's sex discrimination. They reacted by filing administrative charges of discrimination with the EEOC, and shortly thereafter they sued their boss under Title VII, challenging Liberty Mutual's hiring, classification, assignment, and promotion practices. Needless to say, they won.[20] They also challenged, again under Title VII, Liberty Mutual's denial of equal pay for equal work. Again they won.[21] As we shall see, they obtained broad remedies for their colleagues by suing under Title VII. But they might have obtained more for themselves had they also sued under the Equal Pay Act.

In evaluating the equal pay claims under Title VII, the court incorporated the Equal Pay Act's four criteria—substantially equal skill, effort, and responsibility for jobs performed under similar working conditions—into Title VII. Then the court reviewed the skill, effort, and responsibility of the Claims Adjuster (male) and Claims Representative (female) positions. The purposes and functions of each job, the court found, were "to determine or evaluate the insurance company's potential liability for a given claim and to arrange settlements advantageous to the insurance company without unnecessarily annoying customers. In addition, a prime goal of all these employees was to discourage claimants from contacting lawyers or filing suits."[22] Given the virtually identical functions of the jobs and in view of the identical skills and qualifications needed to perform the jobs, the court held that the jobs involved substantially equal skill, effort, and responsibility. The court had a more difficult time finding that the working conditions were similar, because the Claims Adjusters (male) traveled out of the office more frequently than did the Claims Representatives (female). But because the extra travel was not hazardous, "the slight difference in working conditions here is legally insignificant."[23] Accordingly, the court found that Liberty Mutual had violated Title VII by denying Sandra Wetzel and Mari Ross equal pay for equal work.

At this point, the court considered the scope of the remedies available, and it was then that the differences between Title VII and the Equal Pay Act became apparent. First, there is an initial difference between Title VII and the Equal Pay Act in the practices that can be challenged. Since Title VII is not limited only to correcting equal pay violations—as is the Equal Pay Act—Ms. Wetzel and Ms. Ross successfully used Title VII to remedy Liberty Mutual's many sex discriminatory practices.

Second, there is a difference in the scope of the equal pay remedy available. Under the Equal Pay Act, remedies technically are limited only to the individual "establishment" where the equal pay violation is proven. In this situation, the establishment probably would be the Pittsburgh branch office rather than all 130 of Liberty Mutual's branch offices. Title VII, on the other hand, applies to employers, and remedies may be imposed with regard to all of the employers' offices. Since Ms. Wetzel and Ms. Ross sued under Title VII, prospective relief properly could be obtained with regard to Liberty Mutual's entire operation.

Third, there is a difference in the number of individuals who can benefit from back pay remedies. Under the Equal Pay Act, back pay remedies are limited to the individuals who sue their boss or who affirmatively "opt into" the class by filing written consents with the court. Under Title VII, people can sue on their own behalf and, in a class action, can sue on behalf of all unidentified individuals who have been similarly discriminated against. If the class action lawsuit wins, all of the unidentified persons— members of the class—who come forward to show that they had been similarly discriminated against are entitled to back pay awards. Since Ms. Wetzel and Ms. Ross had their lawsuit certified as a class action under Title VII, thousands of Liberty Mutual's other Claims Representatives (female) became eligible for back pay under Title VII.

Fourth, the amount of back pay available under the Equal Pay Act runs from two or three years prior to the filing of the lawsuit or filing consents with the court. Under Title VII, the back pay period runs from two years prior to the filing of the first administrative charge with the EEOC. Since Ms. Wetzel and Ms. Ross sued only under Title VII, the back pay awards were calculated from two years prior to the date of the first charge.

Fifth, there is yet another difference in the manner in which individuals can benefit from the back pay remedies. Under the Equal Pay Act, named individuals who sue or who affirmatively "opt into" the lawsuit can recover double back pay—referred to as "liquidated damages"—if the employer's equal pay violation was willful. However, there is no such remedy available under Title VII. Because Sandra Wetzel and Mari Ross sued only under Title VII, they were not eligible for double back pay as liquidated damages.

Sandra Wetzel and Mari Ross obtained a lucrative equal pay victory for themselves and their colleagues. If they also had pressed claims of equal pay discrimination under the Equal Pay Act, they might have been able to obtain an even greater remedy for themselves.[24]

A contrasting case is the lawsuit filed by Mary Laffey. Mary Laffey's Equal Pay Act lawsuit against Northwest Airlines resulted in the upgrading of stewardess salaries to purser salaries and an award of three years' back pay and other forms of compensation for Ms. Laffey and for the named stewardesses who opted into the lawsuit.[25] But that lawsuit also was filed under Title VII. As a result, the victorious women also successfully challenged other discriminatory practices unrelated to unequal pay, and they obtained for themselves and for unnamed female employees the maximum back pay available under both laws.

Mary Laffey's basic challenge was to Northwest's payment of higher wages to male pursers than to female stewardesses for the same work. This challenge was successful both under the Equal Pay Act and under Title VII. But Ms. Laffey also challenged as sex discriminatory Northwest's refusal to hire women as pursers, as well as the airline's imposition of maximum-weight requirements on the stewardesses but not on the pursers. These additional challenges, not involving unequal pay, could be brought only under Title VII. By joining a Title VII claim to her Equal Pay Act claim, Mary Laffey was able to attack successfully two sex discriminatory practices that were unlawful under Title VII but not under the Equal Pay Act.

The basic remedies for the equal pay violation were the upward equalization of pay—so that the 1,747 stewardesses would receive the higher pay of the 137 pursers—and the reimbursement of back pay. The total monetary awards, however, were not limited only to Mary Laffey and the named stewardesses. Because they sued not only under the Equal Pay Act but also under Title VII, as a class action, they were able to obtain back pay running from two years prior to the first EEOC charge for all of the stewardesses who had been denied equal pay by Northwest Airlines.

By suing under the Equal Pay Act, they also had an opportunity to seek liquidated damages doubling their back pay awards —a remedy which they obtained. Because they pursued an Equal Pay Act claim in addition to their Title VII claim, Mary Laffey and the stewardesses who affirmatively joined her lawsuit doubled their back pay awards.

Mary Laffey and her colleagues, by winning under the Equal Pay Act and under Title VII, obtained their rights in the broadest and most remunerative way possible. Whenever you assert your rights, you obviously should follow Mary Laffey's example and use all the available laws to your advantage.

Combining the various federal laws not only increases the remedies available to you and your colleagues, *but also may mean the difference between winning and losing.* Illustrative is the equal pay lawsuit filed by Deputy Sheriff Pauline Howard against Ward County, North Dakota. Employed as a deputy sheriff since 1962, Pauline Howard consistently was paid less than the male deputy sheriffs. By the mid-1970s, as a court later pointed out, Lieutenant Howard's place among Ward County's fifteen sheriffs was "third in seniority and no less than fifth in command [but] fifteenth in salary."[26] In fact, several of the men under her direct command earned $150 a month more than she did. Displeased with her low pay, Pauline Howard, in January 1975, filed administrative charges of sex discrimination with the EEOC. Later that year, she sued Ward County both under the Equal Pay Act and under Title VII. Deciding her case in 1976, the court made a potentially crucial error: it improperly held that local governments could not be sued under the Equal Pay Act, and it thus dismissed Pauline Howard's claim under the Equal Pay Act.[27] If Lt. Howard had sued only under the Equal Pay Act, she could have obtained her rights to equal compensation only by appealing the court's erroneous decision to a higher court. But since she also had sued under Title VII, the court next addressed her Title VII claim. As to Title VII, the court first ruled that the Equal Pay Act's four criteria—substantially equal skill, effort, and responsibility for work performed under similar working conditions—were incorporated into Title VII. Applying those factors, the court concluded that Lt. Howard was performing equal work for unequal pay, and rejected as irrelevant Ward County's defense that higher pay for Lt. Howard might result in legitimate demands by other women for higher pay. After finding that Ward County had violated the Equal Pay Act criteria incorporated into Title VII, the court awarded her the Title VII remedies applicable to her situation: back pay from two years prior to the filing of her administrative charge of discrimination, totaling $6,-935.58; termination of any future discrimination against her; and her attorney's fees.[28]

Because Pauline Howard used Title VII in addition to the Equal Pay Act, she won her lawsuit. Yet there are other laws which she also could have used to her advantage. If she had sued Ward County under the Civil Rights Act of 1871, she might have been able to win compensatory pain-and-suffering damages and maybe even punitive damages. If she had filed administrative charges of discrimination with the ORS under the Revenue Sharing Act, she might have been able to prevail against her boss without the need to file a lawsuit. But Pauline Howard did not use these other federal laws. She didn't, probably, because she, like so many other people, was not aware of the availability and scope of all of the seven major laws.

As is by now obvious, all of the applicable laws should be combined whenever possible to ensure that your rights are protected and to win the broadest remedies possible. In fact, there even are isolated laws not covered in this book that sometimes can enhance your remedies even further. Occasionally, for example, individuals can recover additional monetary remedies under state tort laws.[29] People who have been discriminated against by state or local law enforcement agencies that receive federal funding under the Justice System Improvement Act can sometimes obtain a quick remedy by filing a charge of discrimination with the Justice Department's Office of Justice Assistance, Research and Statistics, a step that can threaten the suspension and termination of that federal funding in a manner similar to the method of suspending and terminating revenue sharing funding.[30] And in limited circumstances, victims of discrimination can sue government officials personally under the Fifth or Fourteenth Amendments for monetary damages.[31] But, aside from the use of these and other isolated laws, the fact of the matter is that even the seven major federal laws themselves are rarely used effectively, much less combined to obtain the broadest and quickest remedies.

Of the seven major federal laws, the two that are the least used are the Revenue Sharing Act and Executive Order 11246. There is no particular reason for this neglect other than that they simply are not well-known laws. The lack of knowledge about these two powerful laws is understandable. They are more recent than Title VII. Further, they do not compel employers to post notices explaining your rights under them as is required by several of the other laws. But most important, they became law without any civil rights fanfare in a political environment quite different from the early 1960s, when Title VII was enacted. In fact, the mandatory civil rights enforcement procedure requiring the administrative suspension and termination of revenue sharing funding was added to the Revenue Sharing Act in 1976 virtually without the knowledge of the local government lobbyists, who simply wanted more federal funding regardless of the strings that might be attached.

Despite the lack of general awareness about the Revenue Sharing Act and Executive Order 11246, they nonetheless provide the most potent means available to attack unlawful employment discrimination. The weapon, of course, is the threatened and sometimes actual suspension and termination of valued federal funding and federal contracts. When faced with the threat of such a fate, employer after employer suddenly decides that it is better to continue receiving federal monies than to maintain discriminatory practices. In order to invoke this threat—indeed, in order to obtain your rights under five of the seven federal laws —you first have to file proper, thorough, and timely administrative charges of discrimination.

# Filing **9**
## an Administrative Charge
## of Discrimination

Once you decide to demand your rights to non-discrimination, your first formal step is to file *proper, thorough,* and *timely* administrative charges of discrimination with the appropriate federal agencies. This is not only the first step. It is the most important one. If you misstep, you ordinarily can forget about winning your rights.

As we have seen, five of the major federal laws—the basic and most important of the seven laws—are enforced initially by federal agencies. One agency, the EEOC, enforces the Equal Pay Act, Title VII of the Civil Rights Act of 1964, and the Age Discrimination in Employment Act. Administrative enforcement using the power of the federal purse is accomplished by the ORS under the Revenue Sharing Act and by the OFCCP under Executive Order 11246. In order to initiate administrative enforcement under each law—indeed, in order to sue if you ultimately need to—you first have to file an administrative charge. This should be an easy step. But hundreds if not thousands of people every year have their charges dismissed by the administrative agencies or their lawsuits dismissed by the courts because their charges contained inaccurate or insufficient information, or were filed too late. It bears repeating: *your administrative charges must be proper, thorough, and timely.*

Filing an administrative charge is not a complicated step, but it must be a considered one. Obviously, you first must decide whether to file charges. And you need to know how to file charges. Each of these subjects has already been reviewed in Chapters 1 through 5. Administrative charges are sufficiently important, however, to merit a chapter of their own.

## WHETHER TO FILE CHARGES

The formal step of filing administrative charges of discrimination with the appropriate federal agencies should be taken only if you are certain that you want to enforce your rights under the federal laws prohibiting discrimination. Even if you're sure on this point, you nevertheless might harbor some doubts about initiating formal enforcement. In all events, you must give careful consideration to whether you should file a charge.

Among the reasons for treating this formal step seriously is, first and foremost, the possibility that your boss will retaliate against you. While considering this possibility, you have to keep in mind that your charges must be timely, that the administrative agencies will not necessarily respond very quickly to your charges, and that you just might be able to have the discrimination resolved informally without filing a charge. Though all of these matters should be of concern, the first is the most worrisome.

### Retaliation

Retaliation, as you are aware, occurs when an employer, in response to your efforts to fight discrimination, reacts negatively by harassing you, giving you poor evaluations, demoting you, retaliating in other ways, or even firing you. The risk of retaliation, even today with federal rights to non-discrimination firmly established, is fairly high. As summarized by a federal court in 1978:

> Advocacy of equal rights has seldom been a completely secure vocation. Whether out of fear or for less attractive motives, certain [employers] view the advance of equality as a threat to be opposed.

Those who take up the cause of equal rights run the risk that their persons and property will suffer the consequences of their opponents' hostility.[1]

*Retaliation of course is unlawful.* But the law hasn't stopped employers from retaliating against individuals who file administrative charges of discrimination by firing them[2] or giving them negative recommendations when they look for other jobs.[3] In fact, even when formal charges haven't been filed, employers have fired people who privately accused them of discrimination[4] or who supported the accusations of others.[5]

The overall picture is not entirely this bleak. Not all employers, after all, engage in retaliation. Indeed, the filing of a charge of discrimination sometimes will prompt an employer to remedy at least part of its discrimination.[6] And, on occasion, a charge of discrimination, like a lawsuit, will spur an employer to respond by reforming its employment practices across the board.[7] In any event, it is highly unlikely that any discrimination you encounter will ever be remedied unless you assert your rights. But when you do so, you should appreciate the risk of retaliation. And if you are retaliated against, you then should file amended charges of discrimination alleging unlawful retaliation.

## Filing a Timely Charge

If you can't file timely charges, you simply shouldn't file them. In fact, if you know that your charges will be untimely, you should not even consider filing formal administrative charges, for to do so would gain no benefit for you but would invite overt or subtle retaliation by your boss.

Three of the five major federal laws, as we have seen, have relatively short time periods for filing charges after you have been discriminated against. Charges that are filed with the EEOC under Title VII of the Civil Rights Act of 1964,[8] or under the Age Discrimination in Employment Act[9] ordinarily *must* be filed within 180 days of the discrimination, although these periods may be extended to 300 days if you're in a state that has a state agency with enforcement authority similar to that of the federal EEOC and if you've already filed a charge with that agency for 60 days.[10] Charges that are filed with the OFCCP under Executive Order 11246 also *must* be filed within 180 days, a time period that can be extended by the OFCCP if good cause is shown.[11]

Under two laws there are no time periods. Charges that are filed with the EEOC under the Equal Pay Act,[12] and charges that are filed with the ORS under the Revenue Sharing Act may be filed at any time.[13] This doesn't mean that you should sit on your rights or that you should file charges that are no longer relevant to an employer's current practices. But it does give you a little more time, while also providing you with a safe harbor to charge discrimination in the event you miss the time periods under other applicable laws.

Aside from these two exceptions, remember that most charges must be timely filed. They're your rights, after all, that are at stake.

## Resolution of Your Charges

While you ordinarily must file your charges quickly, the federal agencies do not necessarily respond quickly. In fact, one of the major problems that individuals have encountered in obtaining their rights is the dilatory pace with which the federal agencies have responded to, investigated, and conciliated charges of discrimination. Because of their procrastination and lack of results, the federal agencies in their early years—particularly the EEOC—developed terrible reputations for civil rights enforcement. Although their reputations linger, the agencies actually have significantly improved their enforcement capacities.

An initial cause of agency unresponsiveness was—purely and simply—bureaucratic inefficiency. For reasons that will never be adequately explained, the EEOC during its first decade was simply unable to resolve, much less even properly investigate, charges of discrimination. After individuals had put themselves on the line by filing charges, the EEOC all too often allowed those charges to languish for years without even investigating them. But by the late 1970s, this posture began to change. In the past few years, in fact, the EEOC has had in operation a new rapid charge processing system. EEOC employees are now trained to refine (and, be careful, sometimes reject) charges; the charges are assigned quickly to investigators; and predetermination settlement conferences often bring the charging parties and employers together within weeks after charges are filed and before formal investigations are even initiated. The EEOC's rapid charge processing system is far from perfect and in some respects it is seriously flawed. But it has improved the EEOC's ability to respond quickly to charges.

A more nearly fatal reason for agency delay was the unwillingness of several of the agencies to enforce the law. To be specific, the ORS and the OFCCP, prior to the mid-1970s, virtually refused to use their considerable power of the federal purse to resolve even blatant discrimination. Congress reacted in 1976 to the ORS's obstinacy by amending the Revenue Sharing Act to impose upon the ORS the most detailed, mandatory enforcement procedures that exist even today, procedures that *require* the ORS to investigate and make findings within 90 days after charges are filed.[14] Although a similar mandate was not imposed upon the OFCCP, that agency in 1977 nonetheless finally began to take its enforcement responsibilities seriously. This doesn't mean that either the ORS or the OFCCP now investigates charges as fast as they should—the ORS in fact rarely even initiates an investigation within the required 90 days—but they are acting fairly expeditiously, and when they do render findings, their power of the purse allows them to eliminate illegal discrimination almost overnight.

A final cause of agency sluggishness was the absence of any real enforcement threats sufficient to encourage employers to end their discrimination. This perception of course flowed in part from the agencies' past inability or unwillingness to enforce the law. But it also resulted from uncertainty in the law itself. The law, however, is no longer uncertain. Back pay and other monetary remedies now have become commonplace. And the EEOC, the ORS, and the OFCCP have embarked on ambitious courses of relatively expeditious administrative enforcement. In other words, the imminence of resolute enforcement is now a reality.

All of this is to say that agency enforcement has improved by leaps and bounds in recent years. Charges of discrimination today are being investigated and resolved more quickly than ever before. Nonetheless, especially in view of the huge volume of charges—hundreds of thousands—that are now being filed annually, most charges will not be resolved immediately. So be prepared to wait weeks, months, and in some instances even years before your charges are resolved.

## Informal Settlement

The possibility of retaliation for filing a charge coupled with the probability that your charge will not be resolved quickly by the federal agencies raises one final matter that you should consider before filing a formal charge. Quite simply, you might want to try to resolve the discrimination informally by talking with your supervisor, with whoever else might be in a position to make a difference, or with your employer's equal employment opportunity officer or affirmative action officer (if there is one). Since an informal approach usually is less intimidating to an employer than is a formal administrative charge, you might be able to win a quick end to the discrimination. On the other hand, you might be met with pious claims of non-discrimination, no changes, and possible retaliation. Or you might reach an accommodation that goes only part way, fully satisfying neither you nor your employer, but nonetheless ending the dispute.

Whether or not you attempt an informal settlement, you should keep in mind that most formal charges of discrimination are settled without turning into lawsuits, and that most lawsuits are settled without going to trial. And although you may believe that you are 90 percent to 100 percent right and your employer 90 percent to 100 percent wrong, the truth of the matter ordinarily is not so one-sided. In other words, since formal settlement is a long-run likelihood, an informal settlement at the outset can provide the most convenient and certainly the fastest way of resolving the discrimination.

Despite these realities, early informal settlement is a rarity for rejected applicants and discharged employees, for the simple reason that they have so little leverage against employers. But if you are a current employee, the informal approach may be useful, particularly if you have a good work record and are on friendly terms with your supervisors. Your chances of success are even better if you are a valued employee, if you have never before complained even informally about discrimination, and especially if your employer either is committed to affirmative action, or recently has been investigated or otherwise under pressure from a federal enforcement agency. When most of these factors are in your favor, you probably will find it to be worth your effort to make your dissatisfaction known and to try to achieve an informal settlement.

Regardless of whether you attempt an informal settlement, you always should keep your eyes on a calendar. The time is limited before you have to file your administrative charges.

## HOW TO FILE A CHARGE

Filing a formal charge—assuming that it will be timely—is accomplished in two steps: stating in writing on a government form or in a letter that your employer has discriminated against you; and mailing the form or letter, or taking it personally, to the appropriate federal agencies.

While filing a charge ordinarily is a relatively easy process, remember that your charges should be both *proper* and *thorough*. To be *proper*, your charges ordinarily must contain your name, address, and phone number, and under Title VII of the Civil Rights Act of 1964, your charge must be sworn to.[15] Additionally, although the next steps are not strictly required, the EEOC prefers that all charges under Title VII be written not in a letter but on its official government form, and that the charges be filed not by mailing but by delivering them personally to the nearest EEOC office.

To be *thorough*, your charges should contain at least as much information as is relevant to your claim. Often this means that you will have to do some investigating yourself. To be in the best position, you should quietly try to find out as much as possible about the specific employment practices that you are going to claim are unlawful. Remember, under the federal laws, the burden is on you to show that unlawful discrimination actually occurred. Your proof usually will include written documents, statements from co-workers and colleagues, and statistics—all indicating that unlawful discrimination in fact occurred. In other words, before you file formal charges, you first should find out how much evidence is available.

In the federal investigative and fact-finding processes that begin after you file your charges with the appropriate federal agencies, your burden of proof technically is minimal because the agencies themselves are ultimately obligated to conduct a thorough investigation of all the facts by obtaining the relevant documents, by talking to you and other individuals, and by reviewing the employment statistics. Nonetheless, you should undertake these tasks yourself to ensure that your charges contain as much relevant information as possible, and to guarantee that the federal agencies will receive all the facts and data relevant to your claim. In fact, the information you turn up will be particularly useful if you are filing a charge under Title VII, not only because some EEOC investigations are imprecise if not lackadaisical, but also because the EEOC often convenes predetermination settlement conferences—face-to-face meetings between you and representatives of your employer—before it even investigates your charges.

In any event, once you have gathered your evidence, you are ready to write out your charges. In your charge—it need not be typed; a handwritten charge is fine—you should:

• State your name, address, and phone number.
• Provide the names and business addresses and phone numbers of *all* the parties (employers, unions, supervisors, etc.—all of whom become "respondents" in your charge) that were responsible for the discrimination against you and others.
• Describe fully the nature and scope of the discrimination practiced against you and others.
• Give the dates of the various discriminatory actions.
• Indicate the extent to which the discrimination has been practiced against other people besides you.
• List some examples of the evidence that you have showing that discrimination in fact occurred, and provide work-force imbalance statistics if you have them.

- Sign your name, and if your charge is under Title VII, swear to your charge under oath.

If you provide all this information in each written charge, you will have satisfied all the legal requirements for a *thorough* and *proper* charge under each of the federal laws. The single exception is that in your charge to the OFCCP under Executive Order 11246 you should also indicate that you have been affected by "systemic" discrimination.[16]

Before you file your charge, two additional matters need to be considered. Most important is the fact that *three of the laws—* Title VII, the Revenue Sharing Act, and Executive Order 11246 *—permit your charge to be filed by your representative* (a friend or your lawyer acting on your behalf).[17] This means that if you're worried about immediate retaliation, you can write a charge under three of the laws without identifying yourself, so long as your representative complies with all other filing requirements, such as identifying himself or herself, and, under Title VII, swearing to the charge under oath.[18] Less important is the fact that your charge, while it should be thorough in describing the scope of the discrimination practiced against you, need not detail all of the specific information you've uncovered. Summarizing the facts and all discriminatory actions fairly succinctly in your charges is the recommended course. You can always provide extensive details and supporting documents to the agencies shortly after you file the charge.

When you file a charge of discrimination under Title VII with the EEOC, this process can become a little more difficult. This is because, as noted earlier, the EEOC prefers you to file a charge not in the written format just described but on its own government form (with four carbon copies attached), a form which EEOC officials usually won't send to you.* The EEOC has adopted this practice because it prefers you to come into the nearest EEOC district or area office to obtain and fill out the form in person. Unless your circumstances make it next to impossible for you to appear personally, you should appease the EEOC by complying. Whether or not you actually can appear personally,

---

*A copy of the official government form for filing a charge of discrimination under Title VII is at the end of Chapter 2.

*you don't have to comply with either of these preferences.* [19] You always can mail a letter to the EEOC, so long as it is thorough and sworn to. But since the EEOC enforces your rights, you should try to comply with their administrative preferences.

The EEOC's preferences about the way it wants to receive Title VII charges obviously are more burdensome for you than the requirements under other laws, or even than the strict requirements under Title VII. But remember, Title VII is the best known of all the federal laws, a fact that has led to the filing of nearly 100,000 charges each year and to the creation of the EEOC's unmanageable and uninvestigated backlog of charges. This in turn led the EEOC to adopt its strict preferences for the filing of charges. EEOC officials accordingly not only will encourage you to use the official EEOC charge form and to complete the form in an EEOC office; they sometimes will go further by urging you to limit the scope of your charges. A narrow charge, naturally, makes the EEOC investigation easier and also will lead to an easier resolution. But if the discrimination against you and others has been broad and you are steadfast in wanting to remedy that discrimination, *you should resist any attempts to narrow your charge. You are in control. It is your charge, and you can and should charge your boss with the full extent of the discrimination that has occurred.* So, whenever you do appear personally at an EEOC office to obtain and complete the official government form for filing a charge under Title VII, don't forget that it is your charge and you are in control. If you run into any problems, *you always can attach your own handwritten, informal charge to the official government form.*

## WHERE TO FILE CHARGES

In order to file a proper charge under each of the federal laws applicable to your situation, you should file a separate charge of discrimination under each of the laws with each federal agency that enforces a federal law protecting you from the discrimination you have suffered. In other words, if you possibly have been discriminated against on grounds of sex because you are a woman, on grounds of age because you are forty or older, and on grounds of race because you are black, prepare and file charges on all counts under the applicable laws with the appropriate agencies.

In order to initiate enforcement of the Equal Pay Act, Title VII of the Civil Rights Act of 1964, or the Age Discrimination in Employment Act, you must file your charge with the Equal Employment Opportunity Commission. The addresses of the EEOC's district and area offices are listed at the end of this chapter. The address of the EEOC's main office is stated in each of the first three chapters.

Charges under the Revenue Sharing Act must be filed with the Office of Revenue Sharing, and charges under Executive Order 11246 must be filed with the Office of Federal Contract Compliance Programs. The addresses of these federal agencies are in Chapters 4 and 5. Of the latter two agencies, only the OFCCP maintains regional offices. Their addresses are listed at the end of this chapter.

In filing your charges, remember that they are your charges and that they should concisely describe all the discrimination you have experienced. And make sure you file them on time.

## EEOC District and Area Offices

Unlike most federal agencies, the EEOC is not structurally organized among the ten federal regions. The EEOC, in fact, does not even maintain regional offices; instead it has district and area offices. Nonetheless, in order to make this list readily usable, the EEOC district and area offices are grouped separately by federal region. If you don't know which office you should be in contact with, call the nearest district or area office.

*Region I* • *New England States:* Connecticut, Maine, Massachusetts, New Hampshire, Rhode Island, Vermont

Boston Area Office:        150 Causeway St., Suite 1000
(entire region)           Boston, Massachusetts 02114
                          617 223–4535

*Region II* • *Eastern States:* New York, New Jersey, Puerto Rico, Virgin Islands

| | |
|---|---|
| New York District Office (southern New York, Puerto Rico, and Virgin Islands) | 90 Church St., Room 1301 New York, New York 10007 212 264–7161 |
| Buffalo Area Office: (upstate New York) | One W. Genesee St., Room 320 Buffalo, New York 14202 716 846–4141 |
| Newark Area Office: (New Jersey) | 744 Broad St., Room 502 Newark, New Jersey 07102 201 645–5967 |

*Region III* • *Mid-Atlantic States:* Delaware, District of Columbia, Maryland, Pennsylvania, Virginia, West Virginia

| | |
|---|---|
| Baltimore District Office: (Maryland) | Rotunda Building, Room 210 711 W. 40 St. Baltimore, Maryland 21211 301 962–3932 |
| Norfolk Area Office: (eastern shore of Virginia) | 215 East Plume St. Norfolk, Virginia 23510 804 441–3476 |
| Richmond Area Office: (western Virginia) | 400 N. 8th St., Room 6213 Richmond, Virginia 23219 804 782–2911 |
| Washington Area Office: (metropolitan District of Columbia) | 1717 H St., N.W., Room 402 Washington, D.C. 20006 202 653–6197 |
| Philadelphia District Office: (eastern Pennsylvania and Delaware) | 127 North Fourth St., Room 200 Philadelphia, Pennsylvania 19106 215 597–7784 |
| Pittsburgh Area Office: (western Pennsylvania and West Virginia) | Federal Office Building, Room 2038A 1000 Liberty Avenue Pittsburgh, Pennsylvania 15222 412 644–3444 |

*Region IV* • *Southern States:* Alabama, Florida, Georgia, Kentucky, Mississippi, North Carolina, South Carolina, Tennessee

| | |
|---|---|
| Atlanta District Office: (Georgia) | Citizens Trust Bldg., 10th Floor 75 Piedmont Ave., N.E. Atlanta, Georgia 30303 404 221–4566 |
| Greenville Area Office: (South Carolina) | Bankers' Trust Building, 5th Floor 7 North Laurens St. Greenville, South Carolina 29602 803 233–1791 |
| Birmingham District Office: (Alabama) | 2121 Eighth Ave., North Birmingham, Alabama 35203 205 254–1166 |
| Jackson Area Office: (Mississippi) | Petroleum Building, 5th Floor 200 E. Pascagoula St. Jackson, Mississippi 39201 601 969–4537 |
| Charlotte District Office: (Western North Carolina) | 403 North Tryon St., 2nd Floor Charlotte, North Carolina 28202 704 371–6137 |
| Raleigh Area Office: (eastern North Carolina) | 414 Fayetteville St. Raleigh, North Carolina 27608 919 755–4064 |
| Memphis District Office: (western Tennessee) | 1407 Union Ave., Room 502 Memphis, Tennessee 38104 901 521–2617 |
| Louisville Area Office: (Kentucky) | U.S. Post Office & Courthouse, Room 105 601 West Broadway Louisville, Kentucky 40202 502 582–6082 |
| Nashville Area Office: (eastern Tennessee) | Parkway Towers, Room 1822 404 James Robertson Parkway Nashville, Tennessee 37219 615 215–5820 |

| | |
|---|---|
| Miami District Office: (southern Florida) | DuPont Plaza Center, Room 414 300 Biscayne Blvd. Way Miami, Florida 33131 305 350–4491 |
| Tampa Area Office: (northern Florida) | 700 Twiggs St. Tampa, Florida 33602 813 826–2284 |

*Region V • Midwestern States:* Illinois, Indiana, Michigan, Minnesota, Ohio, Wisconsin

| | |
|---|---|
| Chicago District Office: (Illinois) | Federal Building, Room 234 536 South Clark St. Chicago, Illinois 60605 312 353–2687 |
| Cleveland District Office: (northern Ohio) | Engineers' Building, Room 402 1365 Ontario St. Cleveland, Ohio 44114 216 522–4793 |
| Cincinnati Area Office: (southern Ohio) | Federal Building, Room 7019 550 Main St. Cincinnati, Ohio 45202 513 684–2379 |
| Dayton Area Office: (western Ohio) | Federal Building 200 West 2 St. Dayton, Ohio 45402 513 225–2753 |
| Detroit District Office: (Michigan) | Federal Building, Room 461 231 W. LaFayette St. Detroit, Michigan 48226 313 266–7636 |
| Indianapolis District Office: (Indiana) | Federal Building, Room 456 46 East Ohio St. Indianapolis, Indiana 46204 317 269–7212 |

Milwaukee District Office:
(Wisconsin)

342 N. Water St., Room 612
Milwaukee, Wisconsin 53202
414 224–1185

Minneapolis Area Office:
(Minnesota)

Plymouth Building
12 South Sixth St.
Minneapolis, Minnesota 55414
612 725–6101

*Region VI* • *South-Southwestern States:* Arkansas, Louisiana, New
Mexico, Oklahoma, Texas

Albuquerque Area Office:
(New Mexico)

Western Bank Building, Room
1515
505 Marquette Ave., N.W.
Albuquerque, New Mexico
87101
505 766–2061

Dallas District Office:
(northern Texas)

Corrigan Tower, 6th Floor
212 N. St. Paul
Dallas, Texas 75201
214 767–4607

El Paso Area Office:
(western Texas)

Property Trust Building, Room
E235
2211 East Missouri
El Paso, Texas 79903
915 543–7596

Oklahoma City Area Office:
(Oklahoma)

50 Penn Place, Room 1430
Oklahoma City, Oklahoma
73118
405 231–4912

Houston District Office:
(southern Texas)

Federal Building, Room 1101
2320 LaBranch Ave.
Houston, Texas 77004
713 226–5561

San Antonio Area Office:
(southeastern Texas)

727 E. Durango St., Suite B-601
San Antonio, Texas 78206
512 229–6051

New Orleans District Office:
(Louisiana)

Federal Building, Room 1007
500 Camp St.
New Orleans, Louisiana 70130
504 589–3842

Little Rock Area Office:
(Arkansas)

Federal Building
700 West Capitol
Little Rock, Arkansas 72201
501 378–5901

*Region VII* • *Great Plains States:* Iowa, Kansas, Missouri, Nebraska

St. Louis District Office
(eastern Missouri and Iowa)

1601 Olive St.
St. Louis, Missouri 63103
314 425–5571

Kansas City Area Office:
(western Missouri, Kansas and
Nebraska)

1150 Grand, 1st Floor
Kansas City, Missouri 64106
816 374–5773

*Region VIII* • *Rocky Mountain States:* Colorado, Montana, North
Dakota, South Dakota, Utah, Wyoming

Denver District Office:
(entire region except *Utah,*
which falls under the
jurisdiction of the Phoenix Area
Office in Region IX)

1513 Stout St., 6th Floor
Denver, Colorado 80202
303 837–2771

*Region IX* • *Western States:* Arizona, California, Hawaii, Nevada

Los Angeles District Office:
(southern California)

3255 Wilshire Blvd., 9th Floor
Los Angeles, California 90010
213 798–3400

San Diego Area Office:
(southern California)

Federal Building
880 Front St.
San Diego, California 92101
714 293–5194

Phoenix District Office:
(Arizona and Utah)

201 North Central Ave., Suite
1450
Phoenix, Arizona 85073
602 261–3882

San Francisco District Office:
(northern California)

Grosvenor Plaza, Suite 325
1390 Market St.
San Francisco, California 94102
415 556–0260

Oakland Area Office:
(northern California)

Federal Building
1515 Clay St.
Oakland, California 94612
415 273–7579

San Jose Area Office:
(central California)

Crocker Plaza Building
84 West Santa Clara
San Jose, California 95113
408 275–7200

*Region X* • *Pacific Northwest States:* Alaska, Idaho, Oregon,
Washington

Seattle District Office:
(entire region)

Dexter Horton Building
710 Second Ave.
Seattle, Washington 98104
206 422–0976

# OFCCP Regional Offices

The OFCCP maintains a regional office in each of the ten
federal regions. There also are seventy-one OFCCP area offices.
Listed here are only the regional offices. These offices will refer
charges of discrimination to the area offices, if necessary.

**OFFICE OF FEDERAL CONTRACT COMPLIANCE PROGRAMS**
**U.S. DEPARTMENT OF LABOR**

*Region I*

JFK Building, Room 1612-C
Government Center
Boston, Massachusetts 02203
617 223–4232

*Region II*

1515 Broadway, Room 3308
New York, New York 10036
212 944–3403

*Region III*

Gateway Building, Room 1310
3535 Market St.
Philadelphia, Pennsylvania
19104
215 596–6168

*Region IV*

1371 Peachtree St., N.E.
Room 111
Atlanta, Georgia 30309
404 881–4211

*Region V*

New Federal Building, Room
3952
230 S. Dearborn St.
Chicago, Illinois 60604
312 353–0335

*Region VI*

555 Griffin Square Building
Room 505
Dallas, Texas 75202
214 767–4771

*Region VII*

Federal Building, Room 2000
911 Walnut St.
Kansas City, Missouri 64106
816 374–5384

*Region VIII*

1412 Federal Building
1961 Stout St.
Denver, Colorado 80202
303 837–5011

*Region IX*

Federal Building, Room 11435
450 Golden Gate Ave.
San Francisco, California 94102
415 556–6060

*Region X*

Federal Building, Room 3088
909 First Ave.
Seattle, Washington 98174
206 442–4508

# Finding a Lawyer **10**
# If You Actually Have to
# Sue Your Boss

Understanding employment discrimination law does not mean that it will be easy to win your rights. Your employer probably will not want to give them to you, and certainly will not want to give you back pay or other remedies. To be in the best position to obtain your rights against your boss, you should try to find a lawyer. Certainly, if you intend to sue, you should retain a lawyer.

With more than 400,000 lawyers in the United States, you technically should have no problem finding one. Technicalities aside, you may be likely to experience some difficulty not only in finding *a* lawyer to represent you but also in finding *the right lawyer* to represent you. Some lawyers simply refuse to represent employment discrimination clients. Other lawyers know nothing about employment discrimination law and would not be the best lawyers for you. A few lawyers may charge you too much money in legal fees simply to listen to you describe your case. Your task, very simply, is to find the right lawyer: a lawyer who will represent you, who is knowledgeable about employment discrimination law, and who will charge fees that you are able to pay. The best lawyer for you—and this needs to be emphasized —is not a high-priced lawyer but one who has some experience with and knowledge about employment discrimination law. Finding such a lawyer is easier now than ever before, for the simple reason that employment discrimination law is the fastest-growing specialty in the legal profession.

Before you set out to find a lawyer, there are some basic facts that you should understand about retaining a lawyer. You also should know about what to look for in a lawyer, and where to look for a lawyer. Each of these three considerations is important to finding the right lawyer.

## WHAT YOU SHOULD KNOW BEFORE YOU LOOK FOR A LAWYER

As this book has emphasized, you do not need a lawyer to prepare or to file your administrative charges of discrimination. A lawyer's advice would be helpful. But you can accomplish this step yourself, if you make sure that your charges are proper, thorough, and timely. After you've filed your charges, the federal enforcement agencies usually will investigate and try to resolve them, a procedure which often involves face-to-face negotiations between you and your boss. Again, at this stage, legal representation can be helpful, since lawyers are experienced in forcing action by federal agencies and ordinarily are skilled negotiators. Regardless, your charges frequently will be resolved by the federal enforcement agencies during the administrative negotiations, and this can occur quite satisfactorily without your ever having retained a lawyer. But if you believe that the administrative investigations or negotiations may be difficult, or if you intend to sue, you should bring a lawyer into your case as early as possible.

The basic reason for retaining a lawyer, especially if you intend to sue, arises from the nature of law itself. Like most specialized areas of law, the law of employment discrimination is fairly intricate, quite a bit more complicated in fact than it appears in this book. And although the basic precepts are now established, the law is still developing quickly, with hundreds of new court decisions being handed down each year, decisions that can dispose of your case. Employment lawyers not only are trained to understand the law but they keep up with current developments. They also ordinarily are aware of other laws and procedures, beyond the seven major federal laws covered in this book, that might be useful to you in obtaining your rights to non-discrimination in employment. For example, you might be able to win under various state laws and local ordinances, under labor grievance procedures that vary from union to union, or even under a few minor federal statutory provisions that have application only to isolated situations.[1] Most of this will be of marginal relevance to you, but a lawyer nonetheless is equipped to advise you and to undertake thorough research in all of these areas. Finally, it needs to be pointed out that the law is quite complicated not only in its substance but particularly in court procedures. An otherwise perfect lawsuit can be dismissed because of technical, procedural deficiencies. Lawyers are trained in the technicalities of court procedures and also in the nuts and bolts of filing and winning lawsuits. The practice of law, after all, includes drafting formal complaints that initiate lawsuits, preparing and answering written interrogatories, taking oral depositions of potential witnesses, decision-making concerning which witnesses and experts should testify at trial, trying cases in court and on appeal, and negotiating settlements.

While an attorney's expertise obviously can make the difference between losing and winning, it is true that you are not obligated to retain a lawyer to go to court. You always can represent yourself in your lawsuit under a procedure called proceeding *pro se*—proceeding on your own behalf. This, however, *is not* recommended, even for lawyers who might want to represent themselves. One of the primary reasons for retaining outside counsel is to have a representative who can be objective, who will not pursue a frivolous or unmeritorious case, and who will be able to recognize the possibilities for a fair settlement of the case. For this reason alone, a person who represents himself or herself is thought to have a fool for a client.

In any event, whatever doubts you may harbor about retaining a lawyer ordinarily will dissipate rapidly when you confront your employer in an administrative or judicial forum. It's then that you'll find out that your boss is represented not just by one lawyer but by several of them. Yes, you too should have legal representation. But there's more to understand than this before you look for a lawyer, such as the matter of attorney's fees, the problems caused by big cases, and the decision about whether to proceed in a single action or a class action.

## Attorney's Fees

When you retain a lawyer, you almost always will be confronted with the problem of paying attorney's fees. An hour's consultation may result in little in the way of services, but you still may be stuck with a fee. Representation in even a relatively uncomplicated case will necessitate more of an attorney's time, and will result in more fees. Representation in a complicated or lengthy case will necessitate considerably more time, and will result in even higher fees.

Usually, any lawyer you retain will want to be paid for his or her services on an hourly basis. Depending upon the lawyer's experience, overhead, and location, hourly fees can run from $25 an hour to $200 an hour. On the less expensive end of the scale are attorneys with several years of experience working in fairly unprepossessing offices located in small cities. On the higher end of the scale are attorneys with thirty years of experience working in lavish Wall Street offices in New York City. Don't worry about the higher-priced lawyers, since they ordinarily represent employers, not individuals like you. In any event, even the hourly fees charged by medium-priced lawyers still may seem unduly high. But very little of the fee represents profit. Most of it covers overhead costs such as rent, heating, phones, salaries for secretaries and paralegals, photocopying, stationery, and other office supplies. What remains provides the equivalent of a take-home salary for the attorneys.

In addition to paying the hourly fees of a lawyer, you also will be asked by a lawyer to pay for the actual costs of litigating a lawsuit in court. These litigation costs include small fees required by the courts for filing lawsuits, the bills of a court reporter for transcribing oral depositions and in-court proceedings, and the fees of experts (often statisticians) who assist in the preparation of the case. Even in small lawsuits these costs can exceed $1,000. In big cases against large employers, actual costs can make the filing of a lawsuit so expensive as to be prohibitive.

Lawyer's hourly fees and sometimes court costs do not have to be paid in all situations. On occasion, lawsuits can be brought fairly inexpensively because of contingency fee arrangements, court-awarded attorney's fees, and free legal representation. Don't get too excited. These exceptions are fairly narrow.

*Contingency fees.*   The major variation from hourly fees is a contingency fee. Under this method of billing, a lawyer may agree to take your case contingent upon being paid a percentage of the monetary award you will receive upon winning the case in court or settling it favorably. The percentage ordinarily is set at 30 percent of the monetary award, but the precise terms of a contingency fee arrangement depend upon what you and your lawyer agree upon.

The advantage of a contingency fee arrangement is that you usually will have to pay only the actual costs of litigation until such time as you win a monetary award. Then you will have to pay a percentage of that award to your lawyer. But, because of the uncertainty of payment, lawyers ordinarily will work for a contingency fee only on cases that have a high probability of winning *and* that promise substantial monetary awards. Many employment discrimination cases simply do not fit these categories. Those cases that have a high probability of winning often promise only small amounts of back pay, and many cases that involve potentially substantial sums of back pay and other monetary remedies may not have a high enough probability of winning for a lawyer to risk non-payment by taking the case. Where both criteria are satisfied, however, use of a contingency fee arrangement may allow you to hire a lawyer without incurring substantial, up-front attorney's fees.

*Court-awarded fees.*   Another variation from hourly fees involves court-awarded fees. Each of the six federal laws which authorize you to sue your boss also authorize the courts to order the losing defendant (the employers and unions you sue) to pay the attorney's fees of the prevailing plaintiff (that's you, if you win). But watch out, because four of the laws also authorize fee awards to be paid by you to a prevailing defendant, albeit under considerably more stringent standards. Again, however, the laws differ.

Under two of the laws, the Equal Pay Act and the Age Discrimination in Employment Act, attorney's fees can be awarded *only* to a prevailing plaintiff.[2] If you win, a fee award is virtually automatic. Since there is no authorization of fees for a prevailing defendant, you cannot be assessed your boss's fees even if you lose.[3] The other four laws are not quite as one-sided, since they authorize the courts to order the payment of attorney's fees to the "prevailing party."[4] Despite this neutral language, the authorization of attorney's fees to a "prevailing party" nonetheless has a dual standard that operates in your favor. When you win and thereby become the prevailing party, the court *must* order your boss to pay your attorney's fees unless special circumstances would render the award unjust.[5] When your boss, as a defendant sued by you, wins the case, your boss is the prevailing party, but the court here can order you to pay your boss's attorney's fees under Title VII and under the Revenue Sharing Act *only if* the court finds that your case was frivolous, unreasonable, or groundless, or that you continued to litigate your case after it became groundless.[6] In a lawsuit filed under the Civil Rights Acts of 1866 and 1871 that is won by a defendant, the court can order you to pay fees *only if* the court finds that your lawsuit was brought in bad faith in that it was clearly frivolous or primarily for harassment purposes.[7] Even in the unlikely event that you are assessed your boss's fees, the amount of the fees ordinarily would be minuscule because the courts take into account your inability to pay.[8]

What all of this means is that so long as you have a strong case, and through your lawsuit win merely "some of the benefit" you seek,[9] you *always* will be awarded fees; on the other hand, you rarely can be ordered to pay your boss's fees even if you lose. "Always" may seem to be too strong a word in view of the seemingly discretionary standard that requires a court to order your boss to pay your attorney's fees only if there are no special circumstances which would render the award unjust. In practice, however, there are no such special circumstances. For example, you are entitled to an award of fees from employers who claim that they acted in good faith[10] and from government employers who claim that they were simply required to enforce a law or practice against you.[11] You also are entitled to attorney's fees even if you prevail not in court but rather by settling the case[12] or by otherwise causing your employer to comply voluntarily with the law.[13] And it doesn't matter whether you win minor monetary remedies[14] or substantial monetary remedies.[15] Also irrelevant is the fact that you might have a contingency fee arrangement with your lawyer,[16] have a set fee arrangement,[17] or otherwise are well able to pay your own legal fees.[18] Indeed, you are entitled to court-awarded fees even if you didn't actually pay fees, for example, where your lawyer agreed to represent you for possible court-ordered fees, or where you were lucky enough to obtain free legal representation.[19]

This availability of court-ordered attorney's fees often provides a sufficient incentive for a lawyer to take your case even if the case does not involve large amounts of back pay or other monetary awards. In fact, the certainty of at least some court-ordered award of attorney's fees is more appealing to most lawyers than a percentage contingency fee arrangement. Nonetheless, your lawyer, like you, will want to make sure that you will be the prevailing party. The stronger your case, the better are your chances of finding a lawyer.

*Free legal representation.* The best of all worlds would be free legal representation. This is a rarity, but it is possible in three narrow circumstances. First, there is the possibility of finding a lawyer in the private practice of law who normally charges fees from his or her clients but who will represent you for free simply because your case is one of public importance. This form of *pro bono* practice—for the public good—is infrequent, is undertaken only by a few lawyers, and usually is limited to small, non-time-consuming cases. Given these limitations, you shouldn't expect to find a private lawyer who will represent you for free.

The second possibility of obtaining free legal representation arises not from lawyers in private practice but from salaried lawyers who work for government-funded legal aid and legal services organizations which serve low-income people. Traditionally, "legal aid societies" represented low-income people only in criminal defense cases. In the mid-1960s, legal aid societies were expanded, or "legal services organizations" created, to provide free legal representation to poor people in civil cases—

cases such as employment discrimination, where individuals become "plaintiffs" suing others for violating the law. Many legal
aid and legal services lawyers are among the very best employment discrimination lawyers in the country. In fact, many of the
cases mentioned in this book—especially the cases against state
and local governments—were litigated by these free lawyers. As
is discussed later in this chapter, legal aid societies and legal
services organizations are located in nearly every city in the
country. It's worth your while to see if you are eligible for free
legal representation.

The third possibility involves another category of organization: civil rights organizations. Some of them, like the American
Civil Liberties Union, are well known; others are not. Many of
them represent at least a few clients in employment discrimination cases. A list of these organizations appears later in this
chapter.

Despite the possibility of free legal representation, be aware
that the pool of free lawyers is quite small. Few lawyers in private
practice actually represent employment discrimination clients
for free. And the limited resources of legal aid societies, legal
services organizations, and civil rights organizations prevent
them from representing very many employment discrimination
clients. In most instances, the lawyer you retain will be in private
practice and will charge you fees.

## Big Cases

A potential hurdle to finding a lawyer is the narrow but sometimes insurmountable problem posed by the "big case." A big
case is one which involves multiple claims of discrimination
against a major corporation, union, or government agency that
usually is represented by a plethora of defense lawyers. The
actual costs of litigating a big case can run into tens of thousands
of dollars simply to pay for deposition transcripts, for trial transcripts, for statistical studies on applicant flow and work-force
availability, and for expert witness fees to be paid to statisticians,
industrial psychologists, and test validation experts. The extended time necessary to litigate a big case also means substantial
attorney's fees.

The problem with big cases, in addition to their complexity, is the difficulty of finding the lawyers to bring such a case on behalf of a client who cannot pay either costs or fees on a continuing basis. Because of the expense and the substantial time gap between the filing and the winning of such a lawsuit—sometimes five years or longer—most private lawyers are reluctant to take on such a case on a contingency fee basis or upon hoped-for court-awarded attorney's fees. And because of the limited resources of legal aid societies, legal services organizations, and civil rights organizations, they too are reluctant to accept the big cases.

If your case is not a big case, you aren't faced with this problem. But if yours is a big case, you should expect difficulty in finding a lawyer. This doesn't mean that you shouldn't try. Many of the lawsuits discussed in this book are big cases that were litigated by lawyers on behalf of individuals like you. Some lawyers, after all, are interested in the challenges presented by these cases. You simply have to find the lawyer that will take the big case.

## Individual Cases vs. Class Actions

A final consideration concerns the type of case that you want a lawyer to prepare for you. If you are looking for a lawyer, it is because you have been discriminated against as an individual, and because you want to or have to sue to obtain your rights. You nonetheless sometimes have two options: an individual case or a class action. There are advantages and disadvantages to each.

In an individual case, you will be proceeding on your own, without evident support from your co-workers. This may make you feel isolated. And it may make it easier for your boss to retaliate against you. On the other hand, an individual case is relatively easy to settle because it won't cost your boss very much.

If your co-workers have been discriminated against in a manner similar to the discrimination practiced against you, then you and your colleagues can file a class action lawsuit. In lawsuits filed only under the Equal Pay Act or the Age Discrimination in Employment Act, the other discriminated-against persons must

affirmatively opt into the lawsuit by becoming plaintiffs or by filing written consents with the court. But under the other laws
that authorize private lawsuits, you can file a class action on
behalf of similarly situated, *unidentified* individuals. In either
situation, you'll have the comfort of your colleagues, and you'll
all be working toward a common goal. The problem is that such
a lawsuit can become a costly "big case" for you. And because
your winning could be very costly to your employer, it can be
quite unattractive for your boss to settle. Moreover, once the case
is underway, your employer cannot settle your individual claim
quietly on the side.

Before you talk with a lawyer, you should have weighed these
advantages and disadvantages. And you should be prepared to
discuss the type of case—individual or class action—that you
want to bring.

## WHAT TO LOOK FOR IN A LAWYER

Naturally, you want the best lawyer you can find to represent
you. Ideally, your lawyer should be experienced, knowledgeable,
compatible, and relatively inexpensive. But remember that it is
a two-way street: just as you want a good lawyer, a lawyer wants
a good client. And one of the most important elements to finding
a good attorney is for you to be a knowledgeable and organized
prospective client.

### You, the Prospective Client

Your time is worth money. So is a lawyer's. When you meet
with a lawyer about taking your case, keep in mind that the
lawyer probably is quite busy. He or she will want to learn about
the basis of your case quickly so as to decide whether to represent
you. So come prepared to present your case as succinctly as
possible. You'll have to explain who discriminated against you,
the nature of the discrimination, and the proof you have that
discrimination actually occurred. And be ready to present the
lawyer with written documents relevant to your case. Bring with
you copies of your administrative charges of discrimination and

any administrative findings of discrimination. Especially helpful is a short, typewritten narrative describing the circumstances of the discrimination, indicating the steps you have taken to try to end the discrimination, and listing potential witnesses and documents that support your claims of discrimination.

Be prepared, but don't overdo it. The lawyer simply will want to learn about the essentials of your case and will be pleased to realize that you are a serious potential client.

## Your Prospective Lawyer

The primary qualities you should look for in a lawyer are experience with and knowledge about employment discrimination law. You also will want a lawyer with whom you feel comfortable. And naturally you should shop for a relatively inexpensive lawyer.

*Experience and knowledge.* The legal profession, as opposed to the medical profession, *formally* recognizes very few specialties. Lawyers usually are held out as generalists who are equally as adept at drafting a will as litigating an antitrust case, conducting a real-estate closing as winning a personal injury case, and giving tax advice as defending a criminal case. In reality, most lawyers, at least in large urban areas, are specialists—certainly in the sense that they devote most of their professional time to one or sometimes several specialized areas of law—even though they don't advertise themselves as specialists. One such specialty is employment discrimination law.

Ideally, your lawyer should have some experience with employment discrimination law. Based on the knowledge that you have gained from this book, you are in a good position to ask questions. Don't be shy. Has the lawyer ever been involved in employment discrimination lawsuits? How many? Against whom? What were the results? If the lawyer's answers don't give you confidence in *that* lawyer, move on to another one. You're investing in your future. You can and should shop around.

*Compatibility.* When you retain a lawyer, you are establishing a business relationship. Your lawyer doesn't have to be and indeed shouldn't be your best friend. Nonetheless, you want a lawyer with whom you can be personally compatible. Some people want to be involved in, or at least be apprised of, every aspect of their ongoing litigation. They like to be able to meet with and talk to their lawyer frequently. If you are this kind of person, make sure that this fits into your potential lawyer's style of practice. Other people don't care to talk with their lawyer any more than is absolutely necessary. If this description fits you, be sure your potential lawyer ordinarily practices law in this manner. These considerations are not crucial. Nonetheless, you certainly do not want a lawyer with whom you may develop personal antagonisms.

*Costs and attorney's fees.* Very quickly, if not at the outset, any discussion with a lawyer will involve the topic of costs and attorney's fees. You will want to know the lawyer's rates. (In fact, before you even talk with a lawyer, you should find out whether the lawyer has an initial consultation fee just for discussing your case. Some lawyers do.) The lawyer, in turn, will want to know how much you can pay in costs and fees.

Frequently this money issue will make or break your relationship with the lawyer. Don't offer to pay more than you can afford. Urge the lawyer to consider a contingency fee arrangement. Remind the lawyer that court-ordered attorney's fees are available under the federal laws. If you can't meet the lawyer's price, move on to another lawyer. Before you leave, however, ask him or her for suggestions of other lawyers who might be able to represent you.

During your search for the right lawyer, bury the idea that high-priced lawyers are better than medium-priced ones. It's simply not true. The best lawyer for you is not a high-priced lawyer but one who has some experience with and knowledge about employment discrimination law.

## Client-Lawyer Relationship

Once you are satisfied with a prospective lawyer who agrees to represent you, you both will enter into a formal lawyer-client relationship. In most instances, this formal relationship is signified by the signing of a contract referred to as a "retainer." A retainer obligates your lawyer to perform services on your behalf, and it obligates you to pay for those services in a manner mutually agreed upon.

Two items pertaining to your lawyer's services, which sometimes appear in retainers and sometimes do not, deserve special attention from you. They concern limited representation, and settlements. Limited representation refers to any limitations that a lawyer may impose upon the scope of his or her representation. Usually a lawyer will agree to represent you for all purposes on your case, but sometimes a lawyer will limit the scope of his or her representation, for example, by agreeing to represent you only at trial but not on appeal. You should be wary of any such limitations, because you don't want to be looking for a new lawyer in midstream. If you find the right lawyer, he or she should be your representative from beginning to end.

Settlements provide the most common end to lawsuits. Just as administratively negotiated settlements are the heart of the administrative charge process, so too are lawyer-negotiated settlements the heart of the litigation process. Because employment discrimination law has become more clear in recent years, an increasing number of lawsuits are being settled prior to trial. One of the most important roles of your lawyer is to try to negotiate a settlement which is favorable to you. In a settlement you will always receive less than 100 percent of your demands. But 25 to 50 percent is better than nothing, and nothing is what you will receive if you lose your case in court. Naturally, what you will settle for depends upon the relative strength of your case. In any event, be prepared to tell your lawyer what you want as a minimum remedy.

Both of these topics, limited representation and settlements, are likely to arise during early conversations with your prospective lawyer. If the lawyer doesn't raise these issues, you should. Be ready to oppose limited representation, and be ready to state your settlement terms. Overall, make sure that you and your prospective lawyer understand one another.

# WHERE TO LOOK FOR A LAWYER

Most people who need a lawyer usually find one by asking their friends and co-workers about their lawyers, about lawyers they know, or about lawyers they have heard of. Although this can be a useful process, remember that the lawyer who drafted your uncle's will is not necessarily a good employment discrimination lawyer.

You are most likely to find your lawyer in one of four places: a private law firm, a legal aid or legal services organization, a civil rights organization, or a law school. There are excellent employment discrimination lawyers in each of these four areas.

## Private Law Firms

Private law firms vary tremendously in their size and type of law practice. Some have a hundred lawyers who specialize in business and commercial law. Others have only a few lawyers who specialize in civil rights law or even employment discrimination law. Most law firms fall somewhere in between. Your goal is to filter through these law firms to find the right attorney for you.

Lawyer referral services of local bar associations may be useful to direct you to the right lawyer. The purpose of a lawyer referral service is to match potential clients with lawyers. You can find out if there is a lawyer referral service in your area by calling your local bar association.

In some cities, there are lawyers in private law firms who are willing to represent a few clients *pro bono*. Occasionally, these lawyers form organizations that make it easier for individuals like you to seek free legal representation. The group in New York City is called New York Lawyers for the Public Interest. Similar groups exist in other parts of the country. These organizations usually interview clients and screen cases. If the case is not too difficult and if it appears to have a high probability of success, the organization may refer the case to one of its member attorneys for his or her consideration. If the lawyer agrees to take the case, he or she *may* represent you without charge.

By using both these resources, as well as the word-of-mouth

method among friends and co-workers, you may be fortunate enough to find your way into the office of a small law firm that specializes in employment discrimination law and charges minimal fees. There are dozens of such law firms. The following list, which is hardly exhaustive, indicates the employment law expertise of some of the lawyers in these small private law firms. Although these lawyers are listed by city, they, like all lawyers, usually will represent clients in cities or states far beyond where the lawyers ordinarily work.

*Atlanta:*  Stagg, Wildau, Simpson, Hoy & Oakley
1950 Peachtree Summit
401 West Peachtree, N.W.
Atlanta, Georgia 30308

404 681–1950

A good example of the small, civil-rights-oriented law firms across the country is this five-lawyer firm in Atlanta. Composed of civil rights lawyers and former legal aid attorneys, the law firm specializes in civil rights litigation.

The firm's expert on equal employment opportunity law is Mary Ann B. Oakley, an experienced litigator who devotes more than 80 percent of her practice to employment law. Ms. Oakley has assisted innumerable clients with the preparation and filing of administrative charges of discrimination. She has litigated dozens of cases, including: a successful class action race discrimination lawsuit filed under Title VII against the entire southeastern region of the U.S. Department of Labor; a successful Equal Pay Act case against the city of Atlanta; a successful age discrimination lawsuit against Sears, Roebuck & Co.; a successful Title VII sex discrimination lawsuit against the Georgia Department of Offender Rehabilitation; and a pending equal pay case against the Metropolitan Atlanta Rapid Transit Authority. Most of these cases, among others, have been successfully settled before trial.

*Boston:*  Silverglate, Shapiro & Gertner
33 Broad Street
Boston, Massachusetts 02109

617 723–2624

242 · HOW TO OBTAIN YOUR RIGHTS

Three of the lawyers in this five-lawyer firm devote substantial amounts of their practice to employment discrimination law. Nancy Gertner, who also teaches employment discrimination law at Boston University Law School, focuses more than 50 percent of her practice on employment law. Also heavily involved are Marjorie Heins and Ann Greenblatt.

One of Nancy Gertner's recent victories was a $60,000 settlement on behalf of three women who successfully challenged the sex-segregated unions at Houghton Mifflin's Riverside Press. In another successful sex discrimination lawsuit, Ms. Gertner won a preliminary injunction reinstating a woman professor at Tufts University; she is awaiting a final decision in that case. Ms. Gertner has similar sex discrimination lawsuits against the Massachusetts state college system, against the University of New Hampshire, against Brown, and against Dartmouth.

*Charleston:* McClain & Derfner
123 Meeting Street
P.O. Box 608
Charleston, South Carolina 29402

803 577–3170

Among the many experienced civil rights law firms in the South is this five-lawyer firm composed of Ray McClain, Armand Derfner, Ann Stirling, Steven Metalitz, and Karen Peterson. Approximately 20 percent of their law practice involves employment law generally, and 10 percent specifically involves employment discrimination law.

The lawyers in the firm have litigated a large number of employment discrimination lawsuits and favorably settled dozens of others. They've won an equal pay case for female teachers at a private high school; an equal pay, discharge, and retaliation case against a small business enterprise; a refusal-to-hire case against a grocery chain; and a refusal-to-promote case against the Post Office. They currently are litigating race discrimination cases against a construction company and against a naval engineering facility. They recently won a favorable settlement in a major promotion and disciplinary class action case against the South Carolina State Ports Authority.

*Chicago:* Davis, Miner & Barnhill
14 West Erie
Chicago, Illinois 60610

312 751–1170

This six-member law firm specializing in federal trial work devotes 40 percent of its practice specifically to employment discrimination law. Among its employment experts are Judson H. Miner and Charles Barnhill, both of whom have argued major cases before the Supreme Court.

The lawyers in this firm have represented dozens of clients in successful lawsuits and favorable settlements. In the area of federal employment, they've won an age discrimination case against the Federal Home Loan Bank Board, a race and sex discrimination case against the Veterans Administration, and a race discrimination case against the Department of Transportation. In the private sector they've won a race case against Motorola and innumerable race cases in the construction industry.

*Cleveland:* Stege & Delbaum
1614 Standard Building
Cleveland, Ohio 44113

216 861–0360

A number of small, private firms are composed of civil rights lawyers who previously were employed in salaried civil rights positions. Such is the composition of Stege & Delbaum, whose lawyers previously practiced with the Cleveland Legal Aid Society. One of its lawyers, Edward R. Stege, was Law Reform Director of the Legal Aid Society for nearly a decade.

One of Cleveland's best federal court trial lawyers, Mr. Stege also is an expert in employment discrimination law. In the early 1970s, he successfully litigated a major race discrimination lawsuit under Title VII against the sheet-metal workers' union, the sheet-metal contractors, and the sheet-metal apprenticeship program—opening them up for the first time to minority workers. In another major lawsuit, he successfully sued the Cleveland Police Department for race discrimination under the Civil

Rights Acts of 1866 and 1871. After chipping away at the Police Department's unlawful practices over a period of several years, Mr. Stege became one of the first lawyers to sue also under the Revenue Sharing Act; flowing predictably from the threatened loss of federal funding to the department, the lawsuit shortly thereafter was settled on terms very favorable to Mr. Stege's clients. More recently, Mr. Stege has served as counsel to a Cleveland women's group in two major lawsuits challenging race and sex discrimination in the banking industry.

*Little Rock:* John W. Walker, P.A.
First National Bank Bldg., Suite 1191
Little Rock, Arkansas 72201

501 374–3758

One of the most experienced employment discrimination law firms in the country is this five-lawyer firm headed by John W. Walker. A graduate of Yale Law School in 1964, Mr. Walker returned to Arkansas to found a private law firm which would concentrate on civil rights law. After litigating every important civil rights issue during the 1960s and early 1970s, the firm now focuses nearly 75 percent of its work on employment discrimination law.

Over the years, John Walker and his colleagues have successfully represented hundreds of employment discrimination clients. On behalf of its clients, the firm has sued the Southwestern Bell Telephone Co., Arkansas Power & Light Co., International Paper Company, Georgia Pacific Paper, most of Arkansas' state agencies, nearly all the banks and hospitals in Little Rock, numerous other employers in Arkansas, and several out-of-state employers in Tennessee, Oklahoma, and Texas. Among the firm's many victories is a double back pay judgment under the Equal Pay Act, which at the time represented the largest equal pay award ever made to an individual.

With nearly a hundred pending employment discrimination lawsuits, and with approximately two hundred pending charges of employment discrimination filed with federal agencies, Mr. Walker and his colleagues have their hands full. But they're always open for more business.

*Los Angeles:*  Bersch & Kaplowitz
291 South La Cienga Blvd., Suite 410
Beverly Hills, California 90211

213 652–0681

The members of this four-lawyer firm are Blanche C. Bersch, Karen Kaplowitz, Joan Patsy Ostroy, and Ann C. Scales. All practice employment law. Overall, the firm devotes approximately 35 percent of its law practice to employment discrimination matters.

The firm has represented clients charging race and/or sex discrimination against various employers, including insurance companies and major aerospace companies. Also, because of its success with sex discrimination claims against various ambulance services, Los Angeles residents are beginning to see female ambulance drivers for the first time.

*Memphis:*  Ratner & Sugarmon
Commerce Title Building, Suite 525
Memphis, Tennessee 38103

901 525–8601

Legal experts on employment discrimination law are found not only in small firms. This unique, medium-to-large-size Memphis law firm, which specializes in civil rights litigation, employs fifteen lawyers. Overall, the firm devotes more than 50 percent of its practice to civil rights work, with approximately 25 percent of its practice focusing on employment discrimination law.

Led by employment discrimination experts William Caldwell, Philip Arnold, Richard Fields, Barbara Dickey, and Tom Daniel, the firm has sued, with frequent success through favorable court orders or consent decrees, such employment discrimination defendants as Kroger Stores; Kellogg; Memphis Light, Gas & Water; Kimberly Clark; Illinois Central Railroad; Troxel Mfg. Co.; the University of Tennessee; Methodist Hospital; Bricklayers Union Local No. 1; the Memphis Police Department; the Memphis Fire Department; the Memphis Board of Education; and the Tennessee Department of Employment Security.

*Minneapolis–St. Paul:* Oakes & Kanatz
Park Square Court
400 Sibley Street
St. Paul, Minnesota 55101

612 227–0804

Judith L. Oakes, Viola M. Kanatz, and Kathleen Knutson, the members of this three-lawyer firm, include among their specialties sex discrimination law. This is especially true of Ms. Oakes, who has been successfully litigating sex discrimination employment cases for more than a decade.

Among Ms. Oakes's many cases have been several job classification cases on behalf of "policewomen" who performed jobs similar to those performed by "policemen" but who predictably were paid less, a case challenging the physical fitness exams and promotion practices of the St. Paul Fire Department, a discharge case against an insurance company, an equal pay and retaliatory discharge case against a bank, a hiring case against the campus police at the University of Minnesota, and a promotion case against an oil company.

*New York City:* Clark, Wulf, Levine & Peratis
113 University Place
New York, New York 10003

212 475–3232

This four-lawyer law firm, established in 1977, is composed of several of the most eminent civil rights lawyers in the United States. In the mid-1960s Ramsey Clark, as Attorney General of the United States, was the nation's top law enforcement officer; currently, he chairs the National Advisory Council of the American Civil Liberties Union. Mel Wulf, for more than twenty years, was Legal Director of the American Civil Liberties Union. Alan Levine, for nearly a decade, was a lawyer with the New York Civil Liberties Union. And Kathleen Willert Peratis, in the mid-1970s, was Director of the American Civil Liberties Union's Women's Rights Project. These exceptionally experienced civil rights lawyers specialize in all aspects of civil rights law.

Employment discrimination law and especially sex discrimination law are the specialties of Kathleen Willert Peratis. Her expertise is based upon years of experience both as an author of employment discrimination books and pamphlets and as a lawyer representing a wide variety of discriminated-against clients. One of her many litigation targets was the Philadelphia Police Department, which had refused to employ women as police officers—a practice which Ms. Peratis successfully challenged and changed. Other targets were the fashionable haute-cuisine restaurants of New York City, which refused to hire women as waiters—another sex discriminatory practice which Ms. Peratis challenged and changed.

*San Francisco:* Erickson, Beasley & Hewitt
12 Geary Street
San Francisco, California 94108

415 781–3040

The three partners in this four-lawyer firm formerly were salaried civil rights lawyers. John H. Erickson and Alice M. Beasley both were associated with the NAACP Legal Defense Fund. Henry Hewitt worked with the Legal Aid Society of Alameda County. Each is an expert on employment law, particularly as it affects the federal government.

Approximately 50 percent of the firm's work involves employment litigation, although the lawyers expect this percentage to decrease somewhat in the next few years. Among the cases they have won for their clients are a race and national origin discrimination lawsuit against Naval Air Rework Facility-Alameda, a sex discrimination case against Safeway Stores, a race case against Alameda Contra Costa Transit, and a race and national origin case against a union, Local 3, Operating Engineers.

*Washington, D.C.:* Yablonski, Both & Edelman
1140 Connecticut Avenue, N.W.
Washington, D.C. 20036

202 833–9060

Joseph Yablonski, Jr., Charles R. Both, and Daniel B. Edelman, the three members of this firm, specialize in labor law specifically and employee rights generally. Nearly half the firm's practice focuses on employment discrimination law. Primarily through the involvement of Mr. Edelman, one of Washington, D.C.'s most brilliant lawyers, the firm has represented clients in numerous lawsuits against federal agencies and private companies alike. Among its many lawsuits are a Title VII race case against a federal agency, several Title VII and 1866 Act race cases against private employers, an Equal Pay Act and Title VII case against a private employer, and two national origin discrimination cases against yet another private employer.

The foregoing examples, it bears repeating, are only illustrative of the many small law firms across the country that may represent individuals like you in employment discrimination lawsuits. There are dozens more.

## Legal Aid and Legal Services Organizations

Legal aid societies and legal services organizations are funded by federal, state, and sometimes local and private sources for the express purpose of providing free legal assistance to low-income people who can afford very few services, much less a lawyer. If you are poor or unemployed, you may be eligible for free legal representation from your local legal aid society or legal services organization. This representation ordinarily is top notch because the lawyers in these organizations are experts in areas of the law that most affect poor people: welfare law, housing law, and employment law. If you are eligible for their assistance, and if they agree to represent you, you could not be better represented.

There is a legal aid society and/or a legal services organization in nearly every city in the country. To find the nearest office, simply look in the phone book or call your local government information number for advice. If you have difficulty finding the appropriate local legal aid society or legal services organizations, there are two national organizations you might want to contact. One is:

National Legal Aid and Defender Association [NLADA]
2100 M Street, N.W., Suite 601
Washington, D.C. 20037

202 452–0620

Most legal aid and legal services lawyers or their organizations
are members of the NLADA. The NLADA will be able to refer
you to the appropriate legal services office in your area. Another
national organization you may wish to contact is:

Legal Services Corporation
733 Fifteenth Street, N.W.
Washington, D.C. 20005

202 376–5100

The Legal Services Corporation is an independent federal
agency which provides funding to most legal services organizations. The corporation should be able to refer you to an appropriate legal services office in your area.

## Civil Rights Organizations

Many of the best employment discrimination lawyers in the
country are lawyers on the legal staffs of or otherwise affiliated
with civil rights organizations. Probably the most well known of
all such organizations are the American Civil Liberties Union
and the National Association for the Advancement of Colored
People. But there are dozens of other civil rights organizations
which are not as well known.

Nearly all of these civil rights organizations, or their lawyers,
represent employment discrimination clients. But they do not
necessarily represent many for the simple reason that most of the
organizations in recent years have experienced severe cutbacks
in membership contributions, foundation grants, or both. Even
if these organizations cannot represent you, they may be able to
provide you with assistance in finding a private lawyer.

The following pages contain a list of many of the civil rights
organizations that have knowledge and experience about em-

ployment discrimination law. Because many of the organizations specialize in one form of discrimination law, they have been categorized by their specializations where appropriate.

*Discrimination on all grounds: race, color, national origin, religion, sex, and age*

American Civil Liberties Union
132 West 43 Street
New York, New York 10036

212 944–9800

The ACLU's expertise is in free speech law under the First Amendment. It also is very much involved in discrimination law generally and employment discrimination law in particular. The national office, listed above, directly represents very few clients. Nearly all representation occurs through the ACLU's state affiliates and local chapters across the country. In order to inquire about possible ACLU assistance, you should contact the state ACLU affiliate or local ACLU chapter nearest you.

Center for Constitutional Rights
853 Broadway
New York, New York 10003

212 673–3303

The Center for Constitutional Rights focuses on numerous constitutional issues including discrimination law. It has a very small legal staff, and thus is unable to represent many clients. But it is responsive to ground-breaking issues.

Center for Law in the Public Interest
10203 Santa Monica Boulevard
Los Angeles, California 90067

213 879–5588

Approximately half the legal work of the Center for Law in the Public Interest focuses on employment discrimination law. It

employs a legal staff of nine lawyers, represents clients primarily
in major cases, and concentrates its efforts in California.

Center for Law and Social Policy
1751 N Street, N.W.
Washington, D.C. 20036

202 872–0670

The Center for Law and Social Policy is involved in numerous
civil rights issues. Several of its lawyers are employment discrimination experts who represent employment clients primarily in
and around Washington, D.C.

Lawyers Committee for Civil Rights under Law
733 Fifteenth Street, N.W.
Washington, D.C. 20005

202 628–6700

The Lawyers Committee, with approximately ten staff lawyers, specializes exclusively in all aspects of discrimination law—
primarily on behalf of black persons. It maintains a number of
regional and local offices throughout the country, and it widely
uses the volunteer services of lawyers in private law firms. If the
Lawyers Committee cannot represent you directly, it often can
refer you to a private lawyer who might take your case.

National Employment Law Project
475 Riverside Drive
New York, New York 10027

212 870–2121

NELP, with its ten lawyers, specializes in all aspects of employment law, including employment discrimination law. Funded
primarily by the federal Legal Services Corporation, NELP's
basic role is to assist in employment lawsuits filed on behalf of
poor people by local legal services organizations across the country. Occasionally, NELP will represent low-income clients directly, although more often it will refer potential clients to local
legal services organizations.

National Lawyers Guild
853 Broadway
New York, New York 10003

212 260–1360

The Guild, a membership organization of civil rights lawyers, focuses upon unpopular legal causes, including the right to non-discrimination in employment. The Guild, which maintains offices in most major cities, will not represent you directly but it may refer you to its member lawyers.

Public Advocates
433 Turk Street
San Francisco, California 94102

415 441–8850

Public Advocates employs a handful of civil rights lawyers, several of whom are employment discrimination experts. Formerly well funded by foundation grants, Public Advocates now supports itself in part with court-awarded attorney's fees in employment discrimination cases. Its efforts are concentrated in the Bay Area.

Southern Poverty Law Center
1001 South Hull Street
Montgomery, Alabama 36101

205 264–0268

The Southern Poverty Law Center specializes in the civil rights problems of the poor, and primarily represents poor black people. It focuses its efforts throughout the South.

*Discrimination on grounds of race, color, and national origin*

ACLU Southern Regional Office
52 Fairlie Street, N.W.
Atlanta, Georgia 30303

404 523–2721

The ACLU Southern Regional Office specializes in race discrimination law—particularly voter discrimination law and jury discrimination law, but also employment discrimination law. It employs three lawyers and represents clients throughout the South.

Mexican-American Legal Defense & Education Fund
28 Geary Street
San Francisco, California 94108

415 981–5800

MALDEF specializes in all aspects of discrimination law affecting Mexican-Americans. It employs twenty staff lawyers and, in addition to its national office in San Francisco, has offices in Denver, Los Angeles, and San Antonio. It represents numerous employment discrimination clients and refers others to lawyers in private practice.

National Association for the Advancement of Colored People
1790 Broadway
New York, New York 10019

212 245–2100

The NAACP, the oldest and largest of all civil rights organizations, specializes in race discrimination law on behalf of black persons. It has a small legal staff at its national office, listed above, but it maintains 1,700 state and local NAACP chapters throughout the country. To obtain legal assistance from the NAACP, you should contact the local NAACP chapter closest to you.

NAACP Legal Defense & Education Fund
10 Columbus Circle
New York, New York 10019

212 568–8397

The Legal Defense Fund, an organization entirely separate from the NAACP (except for the shared name), has the largest national legal staff of any civil rights organization. It concentrates on all aspects of race discrimination law and has made employment discrimination law one of its highest priorities. Through its staff attorneys and its expansive network of cooperating private attorneys located mostly in the South, the Legal Defense Fund is the nation's major organization litigating employment discrimination.

National Conference of Black Lawyers
126 West 119 Street
New York, New York 10026

212 866–3501

NCBL, an organization of black lawyers, focuses on all aspects of discrimination law through its national network of lawyers. NCBL does not represent clients directly, but it does refer potential clients to member lawyers in private practice.

Native American Rights Fund
1506 Broadway
Boulder, Colorado 80302

303 447–8760

The Native American Rights Fund specializes in native American issues and represents indigent native Americans. It also refers potential clients to lawyers in private practice.

Puerto Rican Legal Defense & Education Fund
95 Madison Avenue
New York, New York 10016

212 532–8470

The PRLDF specializes in discrimination law—particularly bilingual education law and employment discrimination law. It represents some clients directly.

*Religious discrimination*

American Jewish Committee
165 East 56 Street
New York, New York 10022

212 751–4000

The committee is involved in all aspects of discrimination law, but its primary focus is on religious discrimination in the context of the right to free exercise of religion. With a small legal staff, it mostly refers potential clients to private lawyers.

American Jewish Congress
15 East 84 Street
New York, New York 10028

212 879–4500

The Congress concentrates primarily on religious discrimination issues. It represents few clients, mostly referring prospective clients to private lawyers.

Americans United for Separation of Church & State
8120 Fenton Street
Silver Spring, Maryland 20910

301 589–3707

Americans United primarily is concerned with separation of church and state issues. However, it does refer discrimination clients to private lawyers.

National Coalition for Public Education and Religious Liberty
1201 Sixteenth Street, N.W.
Washington, D.C. 20036

202 833–5412

PEARL, a coalition of religious organizations, is primarily concerned with the separation of church and state in public education. However, it does become involved in employment discrimination issues, and usually refers prospective clients to private lawyers.

*Sex discrimination*

ACLU Women's Rights Project
132 West 43 Street
New York, New York 10036

212 944–9800

The ACLU Women's Rights Project, with four lawyers, is involved in all aspects of sex discrimination law. Its primary emphasis is on employment discrimination law, particularly in nontraditional jobs. Although it mostly provides back-up assistance to ACLU volunteer attorneys litigating sex discrimination cases across the country, it also represents a few clients directly.

NOW Legal Defense & Education Fund
132 West 43 Street
New York, New York 10036

212 354–1225

The NOW Legal Defense Fund, an organization separate from the National Organization of Women (except for the shared name), concentrates on all sex discrimination issues. It has three lawyers on its staff.

WEAL Legal Defense & Education Fund
733 Fifteenth Street, N.W.
Washington, D.C. 20005

202 638–1961

The WEAL Legal Defense Fund is separate from and yet the legal arm of the Women's Equity Action League. Although it is concerned with all aspects of sex discrimination law, its primary emphasis is on women (as students and faculty) in higher education. It represents some clients directly.

Women's Legal Defense & Education Fund
1010 Vermont Avenue, N.W.
Washington, D.C. 20005

202 638–1123

The Women's Legal Defense Fund is involved in all sex discrimination issues with a specific emphasis on employment discrimination law. It represents some clients directly.

## Age discrimination

American Association of Retired Persons
1909 K Street, N.W.
Washington, D.C. 20049

202 872–4700

Although AARP is one of the largest membership organizations in the country, it maintains a very small legal department. It ordinarily does not represent clients directly.

National Senior Citizens Law Center
1636 West 8 Street, Suite 201
Los Angeles, California 90017

213 388–1381

National Senior Citizens Law Center
1424 Sixteenth Street, N.W., Suite 300
Washington, D.C. 20036

202 232–6570

The center, in its two locations, employs twenty lawyers. It specializes in all aspects of age discrimination, especially those which affect poor people. The center provides direct representation to many clients.

The foregoing civil rights organizations in large measure are responsible for the development and growth of employment discrimination law. Most, however, are poorly funded and employ only a few lawyers. As much as they'd like to represent you and many other clients, they often are unable to do so.

## Law Schools

A final resource in your search for an attorney is provided by the faculties of the nearly two hundred law schools in the country. Approximately half the law schools have employment discrimination seminars and a smaller number have employment discrimination clinics. Some of these clinics assist clients in employment discrimination lawsuits. Law students perform much of the legal research. But it is one of the professors who would be your lawyer.

If there is a law school in your city—there probably is—you should find out if it has an employment discrimination clinic. It may be able to represent you. Even if the law school does not have a clinic, you may be able to find a law professor who will represent you.

Finding the right lawyer sometimes will be tedious. But more employment discrimination charges and lawsuits are being filed every year. In response, law firms and lawyers in every city are expanding their horizons to gain expertise in employment discrimination law. Even if you encounter some difficulty finding the right lawyer, it is an easier task now than ever before. It certainly is easier for you than it was for the many people who won the lawsuits discussed in this book. These groundbreakers somehow found lawyers in private practice, in legal aid and legal services organizations, in civil rights organizations, and in law schools.

• Junior-high-school teachers Jo Carol LaFleur and Ann Elizabeth Nelson were required to take mandatory maternity leaves by their boss, the Cleveland Board of Education. They sued and won.[20] They had found an expert in sex discrimination law, Jane M. Picker, an attorney with a private law firm in Cleveland.

• Gerald Carter was one of the many blacks who had been denied employment by the Minneapolis Fire Department. As a result of his successful lawsuit, the department was required to eliminate its discriminatory use of written tests, high-school diploma requirements, and no arrest record requirements.[21] As a poor person, Gerald Carter had obtained free legal representation from Luther Granquist and other staff lawyers with the Minneapolis Legal Aid Society.

• Dianne Rawlinson and Brenda Meith were denied employment by the Alabama Board of Corrections and by the Alabama

Department of Public Safety, respectively, because of sex discriminatory minimum-height and -weight requirements. They sued and won.[22] They had found legal representation from staff lawyers with a civil rights organization, the Southern Poverty Law Center.

• Jane Monell was required to take an unpaid maternity leave by her boss, the New York City Department of Social Services. She sued and won.[23] Her chief lawyer was law professor Oscar Chase of Brooklyn Law School.

Because of the success of these lawsuits, and because of the success of the administrative charges and lawsuits filed by so many other discriminated-against people, you now are in a good position to be able to obtain your rights to non-discrimination merely through the filing of an administrative charge of discrimination. You also are in a better position than ever before to find a skilled attorney to represent you if you should have to sue your boss.

Remember, the federal laws set forth in this book were enacted for your benefit. Unless you take advantage of them, your boss may continue to take advantage of you.

# Notes

## 1: WINNING EQUAL PAY FOR EQUAL WORK

1. *Corning Glass Works v. Brennan*, 417 U.S. 166, 195 (1974) (citation omitted) (emphasis in original).
2. *Bullock* v. *Pizza Hut, Inc.*, 429 F.Supp. 424, 430 (M.D. La. 1977).
3. 29 U.S.C. §206(d)(1). The federal regulations interpreting the Equal Pay Act are in a state of flux. The regulations cited herein are those issued by the Wage and Hour Division of the U.S. Department of Labor. Effective July 1, 1979, enforcement of the Equal Pay Act was transferred to the EEOC pursuant to Presidential Reorganization Plan No. 1 of 1978, 43 Fed.Reg. 19807 (May 9, 1978). See note 68, *infra*. Under its new authority, the EEOC has indicated that it intends to promulgate new regulations under the Act. 44 Fed. Reg. 38670 (July 2, 1979). The EEOC regulations will be issued in proposed form some time in 1981, and will be collected in 29 C.F.R. Part 1620. Until the EEOC's final regulations are issued, the old regulations remain in effect.
4. 29 U.S.C. §§201, *et seq.*
5. 29 U.S.C. §206(d)(1). Compare *Brennan* v. *Goose Creek Ind. School Dist.*, 519 F.2d 53 (5th Cir. 1975) (school district, not each separate school, is the "establishment"), with *Wetzel* v. *Liberty Mutual Insurance Company*, 449 F.Supp. 397 (W.D. Pa. 1978) (each separate branch office, not the company overall, is the "establishment").
6. 29 U.S.C. §§203(r) & (s). See also 29 C.F.R. §800.5.
7. 29 U.S.C. §203(s).
8. *Katzenbach* v. *McClung*, 379 U.S. 294 (1964). See also *Heart of Atlanta Motel, Inc.* v. *United States*, 397 U.S. 241 (1964) (service

to clients who travel in interstate commerce brings the enterprise within interstate commerce).

9. 29 U.S.C. §203(e)(2)(A), and §203(x). This protection of federal employees was added in 1974, when Congress enacted the Fair Labor Standards Amendments of 1974, Pub.L. 93–259 (April 8, 1974), 88 Stat. 55.

Equal pay regardless of sex is required in the federal government by another federal law, the Classification Act, 5 U.S.C. §5101, a law which requires equal pay for substantially equal work but does not authorize back pay remedies for violations of the law. See *Haneke* v. *Secretary of H.E.W.*, 535 F.2d 1291 (D.C.Cir. 1976).

10. In 1974 Congress extended minimum wage and hence equal pay protection to state and local government employees. See notes 11 and 12, *infra*. The extended minimum wage protection, however, did not last very long. In 1976, the Supreme Court held that the application of the minimum wage law to state and local government employees was unconstitutional. *National League of Cities* v. *Usery*, 426 U.S. 833 (1976), *overruling Maryland* v. *Wirtz*, 392 U.S. 183 (1968). Since the reasoning of the decision does not apply to the Equal Pay Act, the federal courts have uniformly held the Equal Pay Act continues to protect state and local government employees. E.g., *Marshall* v. *A & M Consolidated Independent School District*, 605 F.2d 186 (5th Cir. 1979); *Pearce* v. *Wichita County*, 590 F.2d 128 (5th Cir. 1979); *Marshall* v. *Kent State University*, 589 F.2d 255 (6th Cir. 1978); *Marshall* v. *Owensboro-Daviess County Hospital*, 581 F.2d 116 (6th Cir. 1978); *Usery* v. *Charleston County School District*, 558 F.2d 1169 (4th Cir. 1977); *Usery* v. *Allegheny County Institution District*, 544 F.2d 148 (3d Cir. 1976), *cert. denied*, 430 U.S. 946 (1977).

11. 29 U.S.C. §203(e)(2)(C).

12. 29 U.S.C. §203(e)(2) and §203(s)(5).

13. 29 U.S.C. §203(x). See also 29 U.S.C. §203(c)(2) and §203(s)(5).

14. 29 U.S.C. §213(a)(1).

15. 29 U.S.C. §203(d).

16. 29 U.S.C. §§206(d)(2) & (4). See *Hodgson* v. *Baltimore Regional Joint Board, Amalgamated Clothing Workers*, 462 F.2d 180 (4th Cir. 1972).

17. 29 C.F.R. §§800.110–800.116.

18. See *Los Angeles* v. *Manhart*, 435 U.S. 702 (1978); *EEOC* v. *Colby College*, 589 F.2d 1139 (1st Cir. 1978).

19. 29 U.S.C. §206(d)(1) (emphasis added).
20. *Shultz* v. *Wheaton Glass Co.,* 421 F.2d 259, 265 (3d Cir), *cert. denied,* 398 U.S. 905 (1970), applying 29 C.F.R. §800.122. See also all the other cases cited in these footnotes.
21. *Katz* v. *School District of Clayton,* 557 F.2d 153, 156 (8th Cir. 1977) (citation omitted).
22. *Id.*
23. *Laffey* v. *Northwest Airlines, Inc.,* 567 F.2d 429 (D.C. Cir. 1976), *cert. denied,* 434 U.S. 1086 (1978).
24. *Peltier* v. *City of Fargo,* 533 F.2d 374 (8th Cir. 1976).
25. *DiSalvo* v. *Chamber of Commerce of Greater Kansas City,* 568 F.2d 593 (8th Cir. 1978), *aff'g* 416 F.Supp. 844 (W.D. Mo. 1976).
26. See note 21, *supra.*
27. See note 23, *supra.*
28. See note 24, *supra.*
29. See note 25, *supra;* see also *Marshall* v. *School Board, Hermitage School District,* 599 F.2d 1220 (3d Cir. 1979) (the Equal Pay Act also applies to temporary job assignments).
30. *Corning Glass Works* v. *Brennan,* 417 U.S. 188, 206 (1974) (citation omitted).
31. 42 U.S.C. §2000e–2(a)(1).
32. 42 U.S.C. §2000e–2(h).
33. *DiSalvo* v. *Chamber of Commerce of Greater Kansas City,* 568 F.2d 593, 596 (8th Cir. 1978). At the same time, Title VII's prohibition of sex discrimination in setting compensation is broader than the Equal Pay Act's prohibition of unequal pay for equal work. See *Gunther* v. *County of Washington,* 602 F.2d 882, 889 –891 (9th Cir. 1979), *reh. denied,* 623 F.2d 1317 (7th Cir. 1980).
34. 29 C.F.R. §800.125.
35. *DiSalvo* v. *Chamber of Commerce of Greater Kansas City,* 568 F.2d 593 (8th Cir. 1978), *aff'g* 416 F.Supp. 844 (W.D. Mo. 1976).
36. *Hodgson* v. *Miller Brewing Co.,* 457 F.2d 221 (7th Cir. 1972).
37. *Brennan* v. *City Stores, Inc.,* 479 F.2d 235 (5th Cir. 1973). Compare *Brennan* v. *Cain Sloane Co.,* 502 F.2d 200 (6th Cir. 1974).
38. *Brennan* v. *Sears, Roebuck & Co.,* 410 F.Supp. 84 (N.D. Iowa 1976).
39. 29 C.F.R. §800.127.
40. 29 C.F.R. §800.128.
41. *Shultz* v. *American Can Co.—Dixie Products,* 424 F.2d 356 (8th Cir. 1970).
42. E.g., *Brennan* v. *South Davis Community Hosp.,* 538 F.2d 859

(10th Cir. 1976); *Brennan* v. *Owensboro-Daviess County Hosp.*, 523 F.2d 1013 (6th Cir. 1975); *Brennan* v. *Prince William Hosp. Corp.*, 503 F.2d 282 (4th Cir. 1974), *cert. denied*, 420 U.S. 972 (1975); *Hodgson* v. *Brookhaven Gen. Hosp.*, 436 F.2d 719 (5th Cir. 1970). Contra, e.g., *Hodgson* v. *Golden Isles Nursing Home*, 468 F.2d 1256 (5th Cir. 1972).

43. *Brennan* v. *Goose Creek Ind. School Dist.*, 519 F.2d 53, 58 (5th Cir. 1975). But see *Marshall* v. *Dallas Independent School District*, 605 F.2d 191 (5th Cir. 1979); *Marshall* v. *Building Maintenance Corp.*, 587 F.2d 567 (2d Cir. 1978).

44. *Brennan* v. *Sears, Roebuck & Co.*, 410 F.Supp. 84, 93 (N.D. Iowa 1976) (emphasis in original).

45. 29 C.F.R. §800.129.

46. *Dunlop* v. *General Electric Co.*, 401 F.Supp. 1353 (W.D. Va. 1975).

47. *Laffey* v. *Northwest Airlines, Inc.*, 567 F.2d 429 (D.C. Cir. 1976), *cert. denied*, 434 U.S. 1086 (1978). See also *Hodgson* v. *American Bank of Commerce*, 447 F.2d 416 (5th Cir. 1971).

48. 29 C.F.R. §800.132.

49. *Hodgson* v. *Miller Brewing Co.*, 457 F.2d 221 (7th Cir. 1972).

50. *Corning Glass Works* v. *Brennan*, 417 U.S. 188 (1974).

51. *Peltier* v. *City of Fargo*, 533 F.2d 374 (8th Cir. 1976).

52. 29 U.S.C. §215(a)(3).

53. *Bullock* v. *Pizza Hut, Inc.*, 429 F.Supp. 424 (M.D.La. 1977).

54. A truly major exception in the minimum wage law exempts executives, administrators, and professionals from minimum wage protection. 29 U.S.C. §213(a)(1). This exception, however, does not exist with regard to the Equal Pay Act. 29 U.S.C. §213(a). Accordingly, executives, administrators, and professionals are protected by the Equal Pay Act.

55. 29 U.S.C. §§213(a)(3), (5), (6), (8), and (10), respectively. See generally 29 U.S.C. §213.

56. 29 U.S.C. §§206(d)(1)(i)–(iv).

57. 29 C.F.R. §800.142; cf., *Corning Glass Works* v. *Brennan*, 417 U.S. 188 (1974).

58. *Corning Glass Works* v. *Brennan*, 417 U.S. 188 (1974).

59. *Brennan* v. *Victoria Bank & Trust Co.*, 493 F.2d 896 (5th Cir. 1974). See also notes 60 and 61, *infra*.

60. E.g., *Hodgson* v. *Behrens Drug Co.*, 475 F.2d 1041 (5th Cir. 1973), *cert. denied*, 414 U.S. 822 (1973); *Hodgson* v. *Security National Bank*, 460 F.2d 57 (8th Cir. 1972); *Hodgson* v. *Fairmont Supply Co.*, 454 F.2d 490 (4th Cir. 1972).

61. *Marshall* v. *Security Bank & Trust Co.*, 572 F.2d 276 (10th Cir. 1978). But see *EEOC* v. *Aetna Insurance Co.*, 616 F.2d 719 (4th Cir. 1980).
62. *Usery* v. *Allegheny County Institution District*, 544 F.2d 148 (3d Cir. 1976).
63. *Brennan* v. *Victoria Bank & Trust Co.*, 493 F.2d 896 (5th Cir. 1974).
64. *DiSalvo* v. *Chamber of Commerce of Greater Kansas City*, 416 F.Supp. 844, 853 (W.D. Mo. 1976), *aff'd*, 568 F.2d 593 (8th Cir. 1978).
65. 29 C.F.R. §800.149. See *Marshall* v. *A & M Consolidated Independent School District*, 605 F.2d 186 (5th Cir. 1979).
66. 29 C.F.R. §800.151.
67. *Id.*
68. Prior to July 1, 1979, the federal agency responsible for administering and enforcing the Equal Pay Act with regard to private employers and state and local governments was the Wage and Hour Division of the U.S. Department of Labor. With regard to federal employment, administration and enforcement of the Act was carried out by the Civil Service Commission. Effective July 1, 1979, however, administration and enforcement of the Equal Pay Act was transferred to the EEOC pursuant to Presidential Reorganization Plan No. 1 of 1978, 43 Fed. Reg. 19807 (May 9, 1978).
69. *Id.*
70. E.g., *Carter* v. *Marshall*, 457 F.Supp. 38 (D.D.C. 1978). See generally 29 U.S.C. §204(f).
71. See *Usery* v. *Ritter*, 547 F.2d 528 (10th Cir. 1977); see also, *Dunlop* v. *J.D.C.N., Inc.*, 67 F.R.D. 505 (E.D.Mich. 1975).
72. 29 U.S.C. §216(c), and §217.
73. 29 U.S.C. §216(c) and §217 incorporate the statute of limitations set forth in §6 of the Portal-to-Portal Act, 29 U.S.C. §255. For a definition of willfulness, see *Marshall* v. *A & M Consolidated Independent School District*, 605 F.2d 186 (5th Cir. 1979). The statute of limitations also operates as a limitation on the amount of back wages available. See, e.g., *Brennan* v. *Sears, Roebuck & Co.*, 410 F.Supp. 84 (N.D. Iowa 1976) (three-year limitation applicable to a willful violation).
74. 29 U.S.C. §§216(b) & (c).
75. *Id.* E.g., *Usery* v. *Board of Education*, 418 F.Supp. 1037 (W.D. Pa. 1976).

76.  See note 73, *supra;* see also, *Tavernaris* v. *Beaver School District,* 454 F.Supp. 355 (W.D.Pa. 1978).
77.  29 U.S.C. §§216(b) & (c). See *Kinney Shoe Corp.* v. *Vorhes,* 564 F.2d 859 (9th Cir. 1977); *Schmidt* v. *Fuller Brush Co.,* 527 F.2d 532 (8th Cir. 1975); *Kuhn* v. *Philadelphia Electric Co.,* 487 F. Supp. 974 (E.D. Pa. 1980); *Roberts* v. *Western Airlines,* 425 F. Supp. 416 (N.D.Cal. 1976).
78.  29 U.S.C. §§216(b) & (c).
79.  *Id.*
80.  *Id.*
81.  29 U.S.C. §216(b).
82.  *Id.* See *Horner* v. *Mary Institute,* 613 F.2d 706 (8th Cir. 1980). On the other hand, a court can order you to pay an employer's fees if your lawsuit was brought in bad faith. See generally *Alyeska Pipeline Service Co.* v. *Wilderness Society,* 421 U.S. 240 (1975).
83.  *Hodgson* v. *Miller Brewing Co.,* 457 F.2d 221 (7th Cir. 1972). See also *Bullock* v. *Pizza Hut, Inc.,* 429 F.Supp. 424 (M.D. La. 1977).
84.  *Laffey* v. *Northwest Airlines, Inc.,* 567 F.2d 429 (D.C. Cir. 1976), *cert. denied,* 434 U.S. 1086 (1978), *on remand,* 481 F.Supp. 199 (D.D.C. 1979).

### 2: IMPLEMENTING THE BILL OF RIGHTS OF EMPLOYMENT LAW

1.  401 U.S. 424, 430, 432 (1971).
2.  42 U.S.C. §2000e(b), §2000e–2(a).
3.  *Id.*
4.  42 U.S.C. §§2000e(d) & (e), §2000e–2(c).
5.  42 U.S.C. §§2000e(b) (d) & (e), §2000e–2(d).
6.  42 U.S.C. §2000e(c), §2000e–2(b).
7.  42 U.S.C. §2000e–16(a).
8.  *Brown* v. *General Services Administration,* 425 U.S. 820 (1976).
9.  42 U.S.C. §2000e–2.
10.  42 U.S.C. §2000e(k), added by Pub.L. 95–555 (Oct. 31, 1978), 92 Stat. 2076.
11.  See cases cited in notes 71 & 72, *infra,* which were overruled by Pub.L. 95–555 (Oct. 31, 1978), 92 Stat. 2076.
12.  42 U.S.C. §2000e–2(a).
13.  42 U.S.C. §2000e–2(c).
14.  42 U.S.C. §2000e–2(d).

15. 42 U.S.C. §2000e–2(b).
16. 42 U.S.C. §2000e–3(b).
17. 42 U.S.C. §2000e–3(a).
18. E.g., *Local 189, Papermakers and Paperworkers* v. *United States,* 416 F.2d 980 (5th Cir. 1969), *cert. denied,* 397 U.S. 919 (1970); *Quarles* v. *Phillip Morris, Inc.,* 279 F.Supp. 505 (E.D. Va. 1968).
19. *Rios* v. *Local 638, Steamfitters,* 326 F.Supp. 198 (S.D.N.Y. 1971), and 360 F.Supp. 979 (S.D.N.Y. 1973), *aff'd,* 501 F.2d 622 (2d Cir. 1974).
20. *Phillips* v. *Martin Marietta Corp.,* 400 U.S. 542 (1971). See also *In re Airline Cases,* 582 F.2d 1142 (7th Cir. 1978) (policy of denying employment to, discharging, or firing women who are mothers but not men who are fathers violates Title VII).
21. *Sprogis* v. *United Air Lines,* 444 F.2d 1194 (7th Cir.), *cert. denied,* 404 U.S. 991 (1971).
22. *United States* v. *Chicago,* 549 F.2d 415 (7th Cir.), *cert. denied,* 434 U.S. 875 (1977).
23. 29 C.F.R. §1607.3.
24. 401 U.S. 424 (1971).
25. *Id.,* at 432, 431 (1971) (emphasis in original).
26. The discriminatory impact principle is modified by two caveats when the EEOC or the Department of Justice enforces Title VII. First, the federal enforcement agencies have a "bottom line" policy which focuses upon the impact of an employer's total selection process for a job. If the total selection process does not have a discriminatory impact, the federal enforcement agencies ordinarily will not inquire into the impact or validity of any specific component of the selection process unless the component is one which has an obvious discriminatory impact and is not job-related—such as minimum height and weight requirements and no arrest record requirements.

Second, the discriminatory impact of an entire selection process or of a significant component thereof is determined by an 80 percent rule (or four-fifths rule). Under the 80 percent rule, the federal enforcement agencies will not regard a selection process as having a discriminatory impact unless the selection rate for a racial minority group or for women is less than 80 percent of the rate for the group (usually whites or males) with the highest selection rate. The 80 percent rule is calculated by first determining the selection rate of each racial or sexual group and then by determining whether any group has a selection rate of less than 80 percent of the highest selection rate. For example:

| Applicants | Hires | Selection Rate | 80% Rule |
|---|---|---|---|
| 80 white | 48 | 48/60 = 80% | |
| 40 black | 12 | 12/40 = 30% | 30/60 = 50% |

In this example, a comparison of the black selection rate of 30 percent with the white selection rate of 60 percent shows that the black selection rate is one-half or 50 percent of the white rate. Since 50 percent is less than the 80 percent of the 80 percent rule, discriminatory impact is present.

Neither of these two policies is a legal definition of adverse discriminatory impact. Rather, both are simply rules which the federal enforcement agencies follow in their administrative and prosecutorial discretion.

These policies, adopted by the EEOC and the Department of Justice along with other federal enforcement agencies, are set forth in the Uniform Guidelines on Employee Selection Procedures, 43 Fed. Reg. 38290 (Aug. 25, 1978); 29 C.F.R. §1607 [EEOC], and 28 C.F.R. Part 50 [Department of Justice].

27.  *Griggs* v. *Duke Power Co.,* 401 U.S. 424, 432, 431 (1971).
28.  *Id.* at 431 (1971).
29.  *Id.*
30.  *Vogler* v. *McCarty, Inc.,* 294 F.Supp. 368 (E.D. La. 1968), *aff'd sub nom., Local 53 Insulators & Asbestos Workers* v. *Vogler,* 407 F.2d 1047 (5th Cir. 1969), cited with approval in *Teamsters* v. *United States,* 431 U.S. 324, 349 n.32 (1977).
31.  E.g., *Meith* v. *Dothard,* 418 F.Supp. 1169 (M.D. Ala. 1976), *aff'd sub nom., Dothard* v. *Rawlinson,* 433 U.S. 321 (1977). See also, *United States* v. *Lee Way Motor Freight, Inc.,* 625 F.2d 918 (10th Cir. 1979); *Horace* v. *Pontiac,* 624 F.2d 765 (6th Cir. 1980); *United States* v. *Virginia,* 620 F.2d 1018 (4th Cir. 1980); *Blake* v. *Los Angeles,* 595 F.2d 1367 (9th Cir. 1979).
32.  E.g., *Gregory* v. *Litton Systems, Inc.,* 472 F.2d 631 (9th Cir. 1972).
33.  E.g., *Green* v. *Missouri Pacific Railroad Co.,* 523 F.2d 1290 (8th Cir. 1975).
34.  E.g., *United States* v. *Chicago,* 549 F.2d 415 (7th Cir.), *cert. denied,* 434 U.S. 875 (1977).
35.  E.g., *Wallace* v. *Debron Corp.,* 494 F.2d 674 (8th Cir. 1974).
36.  E.g., *Donnell* v. *General Motors Corp.,* 576 F.2d 1292 (8th Cir. 1978); *Johnson* v. *Goodyear Tire & Rubber Co.,* 491 F.2d 1364, 1371–1372 (5th Cir. 1974); *United States* v. *Georgia Power Co.,* 474 F.2d 906, 918 (5th Cir. 1973).

37. E.g., *Ensley Branch NAACP* v. *Seibels,* 616 F.2d 812 (5th Cir. 1980); *United States* v. *Chicago,* 549 F.2d 415 (7th Cir.), *cert. denied,* 434 U.S. 875 (1977); *United States* v. *Jacksonville Terminal Co.,* 451 F.2d 418 (5th Cir. 1971), *cert. denied,* 406 U.S. 906 (1972). See generally the cases cited in notes 22, 26–29, and 31 to Chapter 4.

38. A number of public employers in recent years have argued that Congress has the power only to prohibit intentional discrimination and that Title VII accordingly cannot bar practices which only have a discriminatory impact. Although this issue has not yet been specifically ruled on by the Supreme Court, the argument has been uniformly rejected by every court of appeals which has considered it. E.g., *United States* v. *Virginia,* 620 F.2d 1018 (4th Cir. 1980); *Scott* v. *Anniston,* 597 F.2d 897 (5th Cir. 1979); *Blake* v. *Los Angeles,* 595 F.2d 1367 (9th Cir. 1979); *United States* v. *Chicago,* 573 F.2d 416 (7th Cir. 1978); *Firefighters Institute for Racial Equality* v. *St. Louis,* 549 F.2d 506 (8th Cir.), *cert. denied,* 434 U.S. 819 (1977).

39. *Rowe* v. *General Motors Corp.,* 457 F.2d 348, 356 (5th Cir. 1972).

40. 29 C.F.R. §1607.4 and §607.15.

41. *Hester* v. *Southern Railway Co.,* 497 F.2d 1374, 1381 (5th Cir. 1974); see also, *New York City Transit Authority* v. *Beazer,* 440 U.S. 568 (1979); *EEOC* v. *Navajo Refining Co.,* 593 F.2d 988 (10th Cir. 1979).

42. The federal guidelines, the Uniform Guidelines on Employee Selection Procedures, have been adopted by five federal agencies (the Equal Employment Opportunity Commission, Office of Personnel Management, Department of Justice, Department of Labor, and Department of the Treasury) and are set forth in 29 C.F.R. §1607. The Uniform Guidelines incorporate by reference the American Psychological Association's *Standards for Educational & Psychological Tests* (Washington, D.C. 1974).

    The standards in the Uniform Guidelines are given great deference by the courts. See, e.g., *Firefighters Institute for Racial Equality* v. *St. Louis,* 616 F.2d 350 (8th Cir. 1980); *Allen* v. *Mobile,* 464 F.Supp. 433 (S.D. Ala. 1978).

43. *Spurlock* v. *United Air Lines, Inc.,* 475 F.2d 216 (10th Cir. 1972).

44. *Rice* v. *St. Louis,* 607 F.2d 791 (8th Cir. 1979); *Townsend* v. *Nassau County Medical Center,* 558 F.2d 117 (2d Cir. 1977), *cert. denied,* 434 U.S. 1015 (1978); see also, *Scott* v. *University of Delaware,* 455 F.Supp. 1102 (D.Del. 1978), *vacated on other grounds,* 601 F.2d 76 (3d Cir. 1979).

45. 411 U.S. 792 (1973).
46. *Id.*, at 802.
47. *Id.* at 804.
48. *Id.* at 802.
49. *Gates* v. *Georgia-Pacific Corp.*, 492 F.2d 292 (9th Cir. 1974). See also *Sweeney* v. *Board of Trustees of Keene State College*, 604 F.2d 106 (1st Cir. 1979), *Kamberos* v. *GTE Automatic Electric, Inc.*, 603 F.2d 598 (7th Cir. 1979).
50. *Gilmore* v. *Kansas City Terminal Railway*, 509 F.2d 48 (8th Cir. 1975).
51. *King* v. *Yellow Freight System, Inc.*, 523 F.2d 879 (8th Cir. 1975); see also, *Naraine* v. *Western Electric Co.*, 507 F.2d 590 (8th Cir. 1974).
52. 42 U.S.C. §2000e–2(a)(1); see also, the EEOC Guidelines on Discrimination Because of Sex, 29 C.F.R. §1604.11, as amended by 45 Fed.Reg. 74676 (Nov. 10, 1980).
53. *Barnes* v. *Costle*, 561 F.2d 983 (D.C. Cir. 1977).
54. *Garber* v. *Saxon Business Products*, 552 F.2d 1032 (4th Cir. 1977); see also, *Miller* v. *Bank of America*, 600 F.2d 211 (9th Cir. 1979).
55. *Tompkins* v. *Public Service Electric & Gas Co.*, 568 F.2d 1044 (3d Cir. 1977).
56. 42 U.S.C. §2000e–3(a).
57. E.g., *Berg* v. *LaCrosse Cooler Co.*, 612 F.2d 1041 (7th Cir. 1980); *Sias* v. *City Demonstration Agency*, 588 F.2d 692 (9th Cir. 1978); *Pettway* v. *American Cast Iron Pipe Co.*, 411 F.2d 998 (5th Cir. 1969).
58. *EEOC* v. *Liberty Mutual Ins. Co.*, 346 F.Supp. 675 (N.D. Ga. 1972), *aff'd*, 475 F.2d 579 (5th Cir. 1973); cf., *Drew* v. *Liberty Mutual Ins. Co.*, 480 F.2d 69 (5th Cir. 1973), *cert. denied*, 417 U.S. 935 (1974). See also *Mitchell* v. *Mid-Continent Spring Co. of Kentucky*, 583 F.2d 275 (6th Cir. 1978), *cert. denied*, 441 U.S. 992 (1979).
59. *Novotny* v. *Great American Federal Savings & Loan Assn.*, 584 F.2d 1235 (3d Cir. 1978) *(en banc)*, *rev'd on other grounds*, 442 U.S. 366 (1979). See also, *Eichman* v. *Indiana State University*, 597 F.2d 1104 (7th Cir. 1979).
60. *Rutherford* v. *American Bank of Commerce*, 565 F.2d 1162 (10th Cir. 1977); see also, *Shehadeh* v. *Chesapeake & Potomac Tel. Co.*, 595 F.2d 711 (D.C. Cir. 1978); *Pantchenko* v. *C. B. Dolge Co., Inc.*, 581 F.2d 1052 (2d Cir. 1978).

61. *Hochstadt* v. *Worcester Foundation for Experimental Biology*, 545 F.2d 222, 230 (1st Cir. 1976). Cf., *Ammons* v. *Zia Co.*, 448 F.2d 117 (10th Cir. 1971).

62. 42 U.S.C. §2000e–2(j).

63. *Teamsters* v. *United States*, 431 U.S. 324, 339 n.20 (1977).

64. *Hazelwood School District* v. *United States*, 433 U.S. 299 (1977).

65. *Teamsters* v. *United States*, 431 U.S. 324, 339 (1977).

66. E.g., *Reed* v. *Arlington Hotel Co., Inc.*, 476 F.2d 721, 723 (8th Cir. 1973), *cert. denied*, 414 U.S. 854 (1974); *Parham* v. *Southwestern Bell Tel. Co.*, 433 F.2d 421, 426 (8th Cir. 1970); cf., *Davis* v. *Califano*, 613 F.2d 957 (D.C.Cir. 1979) (statistics alone created a prima facie case of disparate treatment discrimination). But see *Williams* v. *Tallahassee Motors, Inc.*, 607 F.2d 689 (5th Cir. 1979).

67. E.g., *EEOC* v. *Navajo Refining Co.*, 593 F.2d 988 (10th Cir. 1979). See generally *Furnco Construction Corp.* v. *Waters*, 438 U.S. 567 (1978). See also *New York City Transit Authority* v. *Beazer*, 440 U.S. 568 (1979).

68. *Espinoza* v. *Farah Manufacturing Co.*, 414 U.S. 86 (1973). See generally the EEOC Guidelines on Discrimination because of National Origin, 29 C.F.R. Part 1606, and see the recently proposed revision thereof, 45 Fed. Reg. 62728 (Sept. 19, 1980).

69. *Diaz* v. *Pan American World Airways, Inc.*, 442 F.2d 385 (5th Cir.), *cert. denied*, 404 U.S. 950 (1971).

70. *Blum* v. *Gulf Oil Corp.*, 597 F.2d 936 (5th Cir. 1979); *Smith* v. *Liberty Mutual Ins. Co.*, 569 F.2d 325 (5th Cir. 1978); see also *DeSantis* v. *Pacific Tel. & Tel. Co., Inc.*, 608 F.2d 327 (9th Cir. 1979).

71. *General Electric Co.* v. *Gilbert*, 429 U.S. 125 (1976).

72. *Nashville Gas Co.* v. *Satty*, 434 U.S. 136 (1977).

73. 42 U.S.C. §2000e(k), added by Pub. L. 95–555 (Oct. 31, 1978), 92 Stat. 2076.

74. 42 U.S.C. §2000e(b).

75. 42 U.S.C. §2000e–1, §2000e–2(e)(2).

76. 42 U.S.C. §2000e–2(i).

77. 42 U.S.C. §2000e(f).

78. 42 U.S.C. §2000e–2(g).

79. 42 U.S.C. §2000e–2(h).

80. 42 U.S.C. §2000e–2(e).

81. 42 U.S.C. §2000e(j).

82. 42 U.S.C. §2000e–2(h).

83. 42 U.S.C. §2000e–11.
84. 42 U.S.C. §2000e–2(h). The Equal Pay Act is set forth at 29 U.S.C. §206(d).
85. It has been argued by employers that since the Equal Pay Act applies only to jobs that in fact are substantially equal in performance, the Equal Pay Act accordingly "authorizes" differential pay for jobs which are different in performance although equal in value. In one instance, this argument succeeded in immunizing different-paid job categories (e.g., women as clerical workers vs. men as plant workers) from equal-pay violations under Title VII. *Christensen* v. *Iowa,* 563 F.2d 353 (8th Cir. 1977). Compare *Gunther* v. *County of Washington,* 602 F.2d 882, 889–891 (9th Cir. 1979), *reh. denied,* 623 F.2d 1317 (9th Cir. 1980).
86. *Los Angeles* v. *Manhart,* 435 U.S. 702 (1978); *Gunther* v. *County of Washington,* 602 F.2d 882 (9th Cir. 1979), *reh. denied,* 623 F.2d 1317 (9th Cir. 1980).
87. *Orr* v. *Frank R. MacNeill & Son, Inc.,* 511 F.2d 166, 170 (5th Cir.), *cert. denied,* 423 U.S. 865 (1975).
88. *Laffey* v. *Northwest Airlines,* 567 F.2d 429 (D.C. Cir. 1976), *cert. denied,* 434 U.S. 1086 (1978).
89. 42 U.S.C. §2000e–2(e).
90. *Dothard* v. *Rawlinson,* 433 U.S. 321, 333–334 (1977); see also 29 C.F.R. §1604.2(a).
91. *Diaz* v. *Pan American World Airways,* 442 F.2d 385, 388 (5th Cir.) (emphasis in original), *cert. denied,* 404 U.S. 950 (1971).
92. *Id.,* see also 29 C.F.R. §§1604.2(a)(i)–(iii).
93. *Bowe* v. *Colgate-Palmolive Co.,* 416 F.2d 711 (7th Cir. 1969); *Weeks* v. *Southern Bell Telephone & Telegraph Co.,* 408 F.2d 228 (5th Cir. 1969).
94. 29 C.F.R. §1604.2(a)(2).
95. *Dothard* v. *Rawlinson,* 433 U.S. 321, 335 (1977).
96. *Manley* v. *Mobile County, Alabama,* 441 F.Supp. 1351, 1357–1358 (S.D. Ala. 1977) (emphasis by the court), quoting from *Dothard* v. *Rawlinson,* 433 U.S. 321, 335 (1977).
97. *Id.* See also *Gunther* v. *Iowa State Men's Reformatory,* 612 F.2d 1079 (8th Cir. 1980).
98. 42 U.S.C. §2000e(j).
99. *Trans World Airlines, Inc.* v. *Hardison,* 432 U.S. 63, 79 (1977).
100. *Id.* at 84 (footnote omitted).
101. Federal employees are not at all affected by the Supreme Court's decision in *Hardison.* Quite apart from Title VII, federal employees are allowed time off for all religious holidays under the

Federal Employees Flexible and Compressed Work Schedule Act of 1978, 5 U.S.C. §5550a.

102. *Yott* v. *North American Rockwell Corp.*, 602 F.2d 904 (9th Cir. 1979); *Anderson* v. *General Dynamics Convair Aerospace Division*, 589 F.2d 397 (9th Cir. 1978); *McDaniel* v. *Essex Int'l, Inc.*, 571 F.2d 338 (6th Cir. 1978); see also, *Redmond* v. *GAF Corp.*, 574 F.2d 897 (7th Cir. 1978).

103. *Brown* v. *General Motors Corp.*, 601 F.2d 956 (8th Cir. 1979); *Wren* v. *T.I.M.E.–D.C., Inc.*, 595 F.2d 441 (8th Cir. 1979); *Jordan* v. *North Carolina National Bank*, 565 F.2d 72 (4th Cir. 1977).

104. 42 U.S.C. §2000e–3(h).

105. *Teamsters* v. *United States*, 431 U.S. 324, 346 n.28 (1977).

106. *Id.*

107. E.g., *Acha* v. *Beame*, 531 F.2d 648 (2d Cir. 1976).

108. *Teamsters* v. *United States*, 431 U.S. 324 (1977). See also *California Brewers Ass'n* v. *Bryant*, 444 U.S. 598 (1980). But see the EEOC Statement on Layoffs and Equal Employment Opportunity, 45 Fed. Reg. 60832 (Sept. 12, 1980).

109. *Acha* v. *Beame*, 570 F.2d 57 (2d Cir. 1978).

110. The Supreme Court's decision in *Franks* v. *Bowman Transportation Co.*, 424 U.S. 747 (1976), awarding retroactive seniority to discriminated-against individuals, was reaffirmed and expanded in *Teamsters* v. *United States*, 431 U.S. 324, 356–377 (1977).

111. 42 U.S.C. §2000e–11. Cf., *Personnel Administrator of Massachusetts* v. *Feeney*, 442 U.S. 256 (1979) (veterans' preference also is lawful under the Civil Rights Act of 1871).

112. See Affirmative Action Appropriate Under Title VII, 29 C.F.R. §1608. See also Policy Statement on Affirmative Action, adopted in 29 C.F.R. §1607.13, and §1607.17.

113. *United Steelworkers of America* v. *Weber*, 443 U.S. 193 (1979). The permissibility of numerical affirmative action plans in public employment, which must be judged not only under Title VII but also under the Civil Rights Act of 1871 and the Fourteenth Amendment's guarantee of equal protection of the laws, has not yet been finally resolved by the Supreme Court. Recent lower-court decisions, however, have upheld such plans. See *Local Union No. 135, IBEW* v. *Hartford*, 625 F.2d 416 (2d Cir. 1980); *United States* v. *Miami*, 614 F.2d 1322 (5th Cir. 1980); *Detroit Police Officers Ass'n* v. *Young*, 608 F.2d 671 (6th Cir. 1979); *Baker* v. *Detroit*, 483 F.Supp. 930 (E.D.Mich. 1979); *Doores* v. *McNamara*, 476 F.Supp. 987 (W.D.Mo. 1979). This issue is currently before the Supreme Court in *Minnick* v. *California De-*

*partment of Corrections,* No. 79–1213, with a decision expected by June 1981.

114. E.g., 42 U.S.C. §2000e–4, §2000e–5, §2000e–8, §2000e–9, and §2000e–12.

115. 42 U.S.C. §2000e–5(b).

116. *Id.* See generally 29 C.F.R. §§1601.6–1601.12; and the EEOC Compliance Manual, Charges, §1.5.

117. For example, where an individual's charge is not sworn to, the EEOC has no jurisdiction over the charge and thus cannot later bring a lawsuit on behalf of the individual. *EEOC* v. *Appalachian Power Co.,* 568 F.2d 354 (4th Cir. 1978). See also cases cited in notes 119–121, 135, and 136, *infra.*

118. 42 U.S.C. §2000e–5(e). See generally *Mohasco Corp.* v. *Silver,* 48 USLW 4851 (U.S. June 23, 1980). See also note 122, *infra.*

119. *International Union of Electrical, Radio and Machine Workers* v. *Robbins & Myers, Inc.,* 429 U.S. 229 (1976).

120. If the discrimination actually is "continuing," this may extend indefinitely the time period for filing the EEOC charge. See, e.g., *Verzosa* v. *Merrill, Lynch, Pierce, Fenner & Smith,* 589 F.2d 974 (9th Cir. 1978) (continuing refusal to promote); *Bethel* v. *Jendoco Const. Co.,* 570 F.2d 1168, 1173–1175 (3d Cir. 1978) (continuing refusal to rehire); *Clark* v. *Olinkraft, Inc.,* 556 F.2d 1219 (5th Cir. 1977), *cert. denied,* 434 U.S. 1069 (1978) (continuing denial of promotion and of equal pay); *Williams* v. *Norfolk & Western Ry.,* 530 F.2d 539 (4th Cir. 1975) (continuing denial of seniority). But see *United Air Lines, Inc.* v. *Evans,* 431 U.S. 553 (1977), where the Supreme Court held that denial of retroactive seniority is not a continuing violation. Most acts of discrimination, in fact, have been held not to be "continuing." See, e.g., *Smith* v. *American President Lines, Ltd.,* 571 F.2d 102 (2d Cir. 1978) (discharge); *Smith* v. *Arkansas State OEO,* 538 F.2d 226 (8th Cir. 1976) (refusal to hire).

121. E.g., *Rudolph* v. *Wagner Electric Corp.,* 586 F.2d 90 (8th Cir. 1978), *cert. denied,* 441 U.S. 924 (1979); *Prophet* v. *Armco Steel, Inc.,* 575 F.2d 579 (5th Cir. 1978).

122. 42 U.S.C. §2000e–5(c). This automatic deferral policy was approved by the Supreme Court in *Love* v. *Pullman Co.,* 404 U.S. 522 (1972).

123. 42 U.S.C. §2000e–5(b). Note that the evidence gathered by the EEOC during its investigation and conciliation cannot be provided to charging parties prior to the filing of their lawsuits. *EEOC* v. *Joseph Horne Co.,* 607 F.2d 1075 (4th Cir. 1979); *Burl-*

*ington Northern, Inc.* v. *EEOC,* 582 F.2d 1097 (7th Cir. 1978), *cert. denied,* 440 U.S. 930 (1979); *Sears, Roebuck & Co.* v. *EEOC,* 581 F.2d 941 (D.C. Cir. 1978). Contra *H. Kessler & Co.* v. *EEOC,* 472 F.2d 1147 (5th Cir. 1973) *(en banc).*

124. 42 U.S.C. §2000e–5(f)(1), §2000e–6.
125. 42 U.S.C. §2000e–8(c).
126. 42 U.S.C. §2000e–5(f)(2).
127. E.g., *EEOC* v. *Liberty Mutual Ins. Co.,* 346 F.Supp. 675 (N.D. Ga. 1972), *aff'd,* 475 F.2d 579 (5th Cir. 1973).
128. 42 U.S.C. §2000e–5(f)(1).
129. 42 U.S.C. §2000e–6. See *United States* v. *Fresno School District,* 592 F.2d 1088 (9th Cir. 1979) (Department of Justice is authorized to sue public employers).
130. 42 U.S.C. §2000e–5(f)(1). See *Nevilles* v. *EEOC,* 511 F.2d 303 (8th Cir. 1975).
131. 42 U.S.C. §2000e–5(f)(1).
132. See *Jones* v. *WFY Radio/RKO General,* 626 F.2d 576 (7th Cir. 1980); *Luna* v. *Int'l Ass'n of Machinists and Aerospace Workers Local #36,* 614 F.2d 529 (5th Cir. 1980); *Spanos* v. *Penn Central Transportation Co.,* 470 F.2d 806 (3d Cir. 1972); cf., *Harris* v. *Walgreen's Distribution Center,* 456 F.2d 588, 590 (6th Cir. 1972).
133. *Tompkins* v. *Public Service Electric & Gas Co.,* 568 F.2d 1044 (3d Cir. 1977). See note 55 and accompanying text, *supra.*
134. 42 U.S.C. §2000e–5(e). See notes 118–121 and accompanying text, *supra.*
135. 42 U.S.C. §2000e–5(f). Failure to sue within 90 days after receipt of the right-to-sue letter will result in the dismissal of your lawsuit. *Bradshaw* v. *Zoological Society of San Diego,* 569 F.2d 1066 (9th Cir. 1978); *Page* v. *U.S. Industries, Inc.,* 556 F.2d 346 (5th Cir. 1977), *cert. denied,* 434 U.S. 1045 (1978). But see *Sambuto* v. *A.T.&T.,* 544 F.2d 1333 (5th Cir. 1977), and *DeMatteis* v. *Eastman Kodak Co.,* 520 F.2d 409 (2d Cir. 1975), where the courts dismissed lawsuits on the grounds that the 90-day period to file suit begins to run not upon receipt of the right-to-sue letter but upon earlier receipt of a notice that the EEOC charge has been dismissed.
136. *McDonnell Douglas Corp.* v. *Green,* 411 U.S. 792, 798 (1973); see also *International Union of Electrical, Radio and Machine Workers* v. *Robbins & Myers, Inc.,* 429 U.S. 229 (1976); *Alexander* v. *Gardner-Denver Co.,* 415 U.S. 36 (1974). Note that one court has recently held that Title VII's requirements are not jurisdictional

but are subject to equitable tolling, *Hart* v. *J. T. Baker Chemical Corp.*, 598 F.2d 829 (3d Cir. 1979). See also *Leake* v. *University of Cincinnati*, 605 F.2d 255 (6th Cir. 1979); *Chappell* v. *Emco Machine Works Co.*, 601 F.2d 1295 (5th Cir. 1979), and cases cited therein.

137. See notes 118–121, *supra*.
138. See note 135, *supra*.
139. *Drew* v. *Liberty Mutual Ins. Co.*, 480 F.2d 69 (5th Cir. 1973), *cert. denied*, 417 U.S. 935 (1974); cf., *Hochstadt* v. *Worcester Foundation for Experimental Biology*, 545 F.2d 222 (1st Cir. 1976) (the court applied the exception without strictly upholding its validity).
140. E.g., *Williams* v. *General Foods Corp.*, 492 F.2d 399, 404–405 (7th Cir. 1974).
141. E.g., *Jenkins* v. *Blue Cross Mutual Hosp. Ins., Inc.*, 538 F.2d 164 (7th Cir. 1976); *Smith* v. *Delta Air Lines, Inc.*, 486 F.2d 512 (5th Cir. 1973).
142. See generally *Sanchez* v. *Standard Brands, Inc.*, 431 F.2d 455 (5th Cir. 1970).
143. E.g., *Garvin* v. *American Life Ins. Co.*, 416 F.Supp. 1087, 1091 –1092 (D. Del. 1976).
144. E.g., *Carr* v. *Conoco Plastics, Inc.*, 295 F.Supp. 1281, 1284–1285 (N.D. Miss. 1969), *aff'd*, 423 F.2d 57 (5th Cir.), *cert. denied*, 400 U.S. 951 (1970).
145. *McDonnell Douglas Corp.* v. *Green*, 411 U.S. 792, 798 (1973).
146. *Id.*
147. E.g., *Dent* v. *St. Louis–San Francisco Ry. Co.*, 406 F.2d 399 (5th Cir. 1969).
148. E.g., *Cox* v. *United States Gypsum Co.*, 409 F.2d 289 (7th Cir. 1969).
149. Some of the procedural difficulties in filing an employment discrimination class action are outlined in *East Texas Motor Freight System, Inc.* v. *Rodriguez*, 431 U.S. 395 (1977); see also, *General Telephone Co. of the Northwest, Inc.* v. *EEOC*, 48 U.S.L.W. 4513 (U.S. May 12, 1980).
150. *Albemarle Paper Co.* v. *Moody*, 422 U.S. 405, 414 n.8 (1975). Unlike the requirements under the Equal Pay Act and under the Age Discrimination in Employment Act, discriminated-against individuals need not affirmatively opt into the class to be included in a Title VII class action. See, e.g., *Rule* v. *International Ass'n of Bridge Workers*, 568 F.2d 558 (8th Cir. 1977).

151. 42 U.S.C. §2000e–16, and 5 C.F.R. §§713, *et seq.*, now incorporated into 29 C.F.R. §1613. Although appeals from the final agency decision formerly were taken to the U.S. Civil Service Commission, such appeals now are taken to the EEOC. See Civil Rights Reorganization Plan No. 1 (1978), 43 Fed. Reg. 19807 (May 9, 1978).

152. *Id.*

153. *Richardson* v. *Wiley,* 569 F.2d 140 (D.C.Cir. 1977) (lawsuit dismissed because of failure to meet the time periods); see also *Scott* v. *Perry,* 569 F.2d 1064 (9th Cir. 1978) (lawsuit dismissed because administrative complaint did not sufficiently allege discrimination); but see *Allen* v. *United States,* 542 F.2d 176 (3d Cir. 1976).

154. *Chandler* v. *Roudebush,* 425 U.S. 840 (1976).

155. *McDonnell Douglas Corp.* v. *Green,* 411 U.S. 792 (1973).

156. *Brown* v. *General Services Administration,* 425 U.S. 820 (1976).

157. *Albemarle Paper Co.* v. *Moody,* 422 U.S. 405, 418 (1975).

158. *Franks* v. *Bowman Transportation Co.,* 424 U.S. 747 (1976).

159. See notes 183–185, *infra.*

160. *DeGrace* v. *Rumsfeld,* 614 F.2d 796 (1st Cir. 1980); *Richerson* v. *Jones,* 551 F.2d 918, 926–928 (3d Cir. 1977); *Pearson* v. *Western Electric Co.,* 542 F.2d 1150 (10th Cir. 1976); *EEOC* v. *Detroit Edison Co.,* 515 F.2d 301, 308–310 (6th Cir. 1975), *vac'd & rem'd on other grounds,* 431 U.S. 951 (1977).

161. *Id.* See also *Grayson* v. *Wickes Corp.,* 607 F.2d 1194, 1196 (7th Cir. 1979), and cases cited therein.

162. E.g., *United States* v. *Jacksonville Terminal Co.,* 451 F.2d 418, 457 (5th Cir. 1971), *cert. denied,* 406 U.S. 906 (1972).

163. *Pettway* v. *American Cast Iron Pipe Co.,* 494 F.2d 211, 248 nn.99 –100 (5th Cir. 1974).

164. *Id.* See also, e.g., *Hairston* v. *McLean Trucking Co.,* 520 F.2d 226, 235 (4th Cir. 1976).

165. *Teamsters* v. *United States,* 431 U.S. 324 (1977).

166. *Id.* at 356–377.

167. *Franks* v. *Bowman Transportation Co.,* 424 U.S. 747 (1976).

168. *Teamsters* v. *United States,* 431 U.S. 324, 356–377 (1977).

169. *Albemarle Paper Co.* v. *Moody,* 422 U.S. 405, 422 (1975).

170. *Id.* See also, e.g., *Pettway* v. *American Cast Iron Pipe Co.,* 494 F.2d 211, 260–263 (5th Cir. 1974). There is no doubt about the legal authority of the EEOC and the Department of Justice to obtain classwide back pay for all discriminated-against persons.

See *General Telephone Co. of the Northwest, Inc.* v. *EEOC,* 48 U.S.L.W. 4513 (U.S. May 12, 1980).

171. E.g., *Pettway* v. *American Cast Iron Pipe Co.*, 494 F.2d 211, 263 nn.155–156 (5th Cir. 1974), and cases cited therein.
172. E.g., *Fitzgerald* v. *Sirloin Stockade, Inc.*, 624 F.2d 945 (10th Cir. 1980); *Patterson* v. *American Tobacco Co.*, 535 F.2d 257, 269 (4th Cir.), *cert. denied,* 429 U.S. 920 (1976). In some instances, front pay has been awarded as an alternative to reinstatement. See *EEOC* v. *Pacific Press Publishing Association,* 482 F.Supp. 1291 (N.D.Cal. 1979).
173. 42 U.S.C. §2000e–5(g).
174. *Id.*
175. *Manley* v. *Mobile County, Alabama,* 441 F.Supp. 1351 (S.D. Ala. 1977). See note 84 and accompanying text, *supra.*
176. Unemployment-compensation benefits usually are deducted from back pay. E.g., *Head* v. *Timken Roller Bearing Co.*, 486 F.2d 870 (6th Cir. 1973); *Bowe* v. *Colgate-Palmolive Co.*, 416 F.2d 711, 721 (7th Cir. 1969). Public-assistance benefits, however, are not deductible from back pay awards. E.g., *EEOC* v. *Enterprise Association Steamfitters,* Local 638, 542 F.2d 579, 591 –592 (2d Cir. 1976).
177. E.g., *EEOC* v. *Contour Chair Lounge Co.*, 596 F.2d 809 (8th Cir. 1979).
178. See notes 179–181, *infra.*
179. E.g., *Bridgeport Guardians* v. *Bridgeport Civil Service Commission,* 482 F.2d 1333 (2d Cir. 1973) (50 percent of future hires to be minorities until a representational goal is reached); *Carter* v. *Gallagher,* 452 F.2d 327 (8th Cir.), *cert. denied,* 406 U.S. 950 (1972) (33 percent of future hires to be minority until a representational goal is reached). Both of these cases were cited with approval in *Regents of the University of California* v. *Bakke,* 438 U.S. 265, 301 (1978) (Powell, J.). Subsequent to *Bakke,* courts have approved similar hiring orders. E.g., *Morrow* v. *Dillard,* 580 F.2d 1284 (5th Cir. 1978).
180. E.g., *Rios* v. *Local 638, Steamfitters,* 501 F.2d 622 (2d Cir. 1974), *on remand,* 400 F.Supp. 983 (S.D.N.Y. 1975).
181. E.g., *United States* v. *Chicago,* 549 F.2d 415 (7th Cir.), *cert. denied,* 434 U.S. 875 (1977).
182. See note 180, *supra.*
183. See cases cited in notes 5 and 9–19 to Chapter 10.
184. 42 U.S.C. §2000e–5(k).
185. *Christiansburg Garment Co.* v. *EEOC,* 434 U.S. 412 (1978).

186. *Sweeney* v. *Board of Trustees of Keene State College,* 569 F.2d 169, 179 (1st Cir.), *vacated and remanded,* 439 U.S. 24 (1978), *initial decision reinstated and aff'd,* 604 F.2d 106 (1st Cir. 1979).
187. *Id.* For another tenure case, see *Kunda* v. *Muhlenberg College,* 621 F.2d 532 (3d Cir. 1980).

## 3: PROTECTING THE COMING OF AGE

1. *EEOC* v. *Janesville,* 480 F.Supp. 1375 (W.D.Wis. 1979), rev'd 630 F.2d 1254 (7th Cir. 1980).
2. *United Air Lines* v. *McMann,* 434 U.S. 192 (1977).
3. 29 U.S.C. §630. The ADEA has been amended several times. The most recent and substantial amendments were in the Age Discrimination in Employment Act Amendments of 1978, Pub.L. 95–256 (April 6, 1978), 92 Stat. 189.
   The federal regulations interpreting the ADEA are in a state of flux. The original ADEA regulations were issued by the Wage and Hour Division of the U.S. Department of Labor. See 29 C.F.R. Part 860. Effective July 1, 1979, however, enforcement of the ADEA was transferred to the EEOC pursuant to Presidential Reorganization Plan No. 1 of 1978, 43 Fed.Reg. 19807 (May 9, 1978). See notes 41 and 64, *infra.* Under its new authority, the EEOC recently issued proposed regulations which, for the most part, follow the old ones. 44 Fed.Reg. 68858 (Nov. 30, 1979). The final ADEA regulations will be issued by the EEOC probably in 1981, and will be collected in 29 C.F.R. Part 1625. The regulations cited herein are the EEOC's proposed regulations, prematurely cited to 29 C.F.R. Part 1625.
4. 29 U.S.C. §623 prohibits age discrimination generally; and 29 U.S.C. §631(a) limits the protection of the ADEA "to individuals who are at least forty years of age but less than seventy years of age."
5. 29 U.S.C. §633a.
6. 29 U.S.C. §633a. This protection without an upper age limit became effective September 30, 1978. *Cf. Christie* v. *Marston,* 551 F.2d 1080 (7th Cir. 1977).
7. *Rodriguez* v. *Taylor,* 569 F.2d 1231 (3d Cir. 1977), *cert. denied,* 436 U.S. 913 (1978).
8. 29 C.F.R. §1625.2(a).
9. 29 U.S.C. §621(b).
10. *Laugesen* v. *Anaconda Co.,* 510 F.2d 307, 317 (6th Cir. (1975).

See also *Loeb* v. *Textron, Inc.,* 600 F.2d 1003 (1st Cir. 1979); *Cleverly* v. *Western Electric Co.,* 594 F.2d 638 (8th Cir. 1979); *Cova* v. *Coca-Cola Bottling Co. of St. Louis,* 574 F.2d 958 (8th Cir. 1978); *Geller v. Markham,* 481 F.Supp. 835 (D.Conn. 1978).

11. 29 U.S.C. §623(a)(1).

12. *Id.*

13. 29 U.S.C. §623(a)(2).

14. *Coates* v. *National Cash Register Co.,* 433 F.Supp. 655 (W.D. Va. 1977).

15. 29 U.S.C. §623(b).

16. 29 U.S.C. §623(e).

17. 29 C.F.R. §1625.4.

18. *Hodgson* v. *Approved Personnel Services, Inc.,* 529 F.2d 760 (4th Cir. 1975). But see *Brennan* v. *Paragon Employment Agency, Inc.,* 489 F.2d 752 (2d Cir. 1974) (approving a similar ad).

19. 29 U.S.C. §623(d).

20. See note 3, *supra.*

21. See notes 4 & 6, *supra.*

22. 29 U.S.C. §623(f)(1).

23. 29 C.F.R. §1625.6.

24. See *Hodgson* v. *Greyhound Lines, Inc.,* 499 F.2d 859 (7th Cir. 1974), *cert. denied,* 419 U.S. 1122 (1975) (upholding a maximum age limit of thirty-five for bus drivers); and *Usery* v. *Tamiami Trails Tours, Inc.,* 531 F.2d 224 (5th Cir. 1976) (similarly upholding an age limitation for bus drivers; see also *Murnane* v. *American Airlines, Inc.,* 482 F.Supp. 135 (D.D.C. 1979) (upholding an age limitation of forty for hiring pilots).

25. *Houghton* v. *McDonnell Douglas Corp.,* 553 F.2d 561 (8th Cir.), *cert. denied,* 434 U.S. 966 (1977); see also *EEOC* v. *Janesville,* 480 F.Supp. 1375 (W.D.Wis. 1979); compare *Houghton* v. *McDonnell Douglas Corp.,* 627 F.2d 858 (8th Cir. 1980).

26. 29 U.S.C. §§623(f)(1)&(3); 29 C.F.R. §1625.7.

27. *Brennan* v. *Reynolds & Co.,* 367 F.Supp. 440 (N.D.Ill. 1973); see also, *Houser* v. *Sears, Roebuck & Co.,* 627 F.2d 756 (5th Cir. 1980).

28. *Walker* v. *Pettit Construction Co., Inc.,* and *Frith* v. *Eastern Air Lines, Inc.,* 605 F.2d 128 (4th Cir. 1979).

29. *Schulz* v. *Hickok Manufacturing Co., Inc.,* 358 F.Supp. 1208 (N.D.Ga. 1973). But cf., *Hannan* v. *Chrysler Motors Corp.,* 443 F.Supp. 802 (E.D.Mich. 1978) (layoff of older employees during a financial austerity program does not violate the ADEA).

30. *Marshall* v. *Arlene Knitwear, Inc.,* 454 F.Supp. 714, 724 (E.D.N.Y. 1978).

31. *United Air Lines, Inc.* v. *McMann,* 434 U.S. 192 (1977).
32. See note 3, *supra,* and notes 34–40, *infra.*
33. See *Morelock* v. *NCR Corp.,* 586 F.2d 1096 (6th Cir. 1978), *cert. denied,* 441 U.S. 906 (1979) (reduction-in-force layoffs pursuant to a bona fide seniority system do not violate the ADEA). Compare *McCorstin* v. *United States Steel Corp.,* 621 F.2d 749 (5th Cir. 1980).
34. 29 U.S.C. §623(f)(2).
35. The increased ADEA protection from ages sixty-five through sixty-nine in state, local, and private employment became effective on January 1, 1979. See *Kuhar* v. *Greensburg-Salem School District,* 616 F.2d 676 (3d Cir. 1980), holding that this increased protection is not retroactive.
36. 29 U.S.C. §633a. This increased protection became effective on September 30, 1978. See note 6, *supra.*
37. Actually, Congress also allowed a fourth exception, which no longer is in effect. Under this temporary exception, some unionized employees could be mandatorily retired at sixty-five or older, at least until January 1, 1980. Specifically, any employee who was covered by a collective bargaining agreement as of September 1, 1977, could be mandatorily retired from ages sixty-five through sixty-nine until expiration of the agreement but in no event later than January 1, 1980. In other words, employees sixty-five through sixty-nine in this category could be mandatorily retired for a limited period of time. However, after the expiration of the collective bargaining agreement, and in no event later than January 1, 1980, these employees cannot be mandatorily retired prior to age seventy.
38. 29 U.S.C. §631(d). See also 29 U.S.C. §631(b); 29 C.F.R. §1625.11.
39. 29 U.S.C. §631(c)(1); 29 C.F.R. §1625.12.
40. 29 U.S.C. §633a(b).
41. Prior to July 1, 1979, the federal agency responsible for administering and enforcing the ADEA was the Wage and Hour Division of the U.S. Department of Labor. Administration and enforcement of the ADEA was transferred to the EEOC pursuant to Presidential Reorganization Plan No. 1 of 1978, 43 Fed. Reg. 19807 (May 9, 1978).
42. 29 U.S.C. §626(d). See notes 53–61, *infra,* and accompanying text.
43. State deferral is required by 29 U.S.C. §633(b); *Oscar Mayer Co.* v. *Evans,* 441 U.S. 750 (1979). Automatic deferral is EEOC policy, 29 C.F.R. §1601.13, a policy upheld in *Love* v. *Pullman Co.,* 404 U.S. 522 (1972).

44. 29 U.S.C. §§626(a),(b)&(d). Cf. *Marshall* v. *Sun Oil Co. of Pa.*, 592 F.2d 563 (10th Cir. 1979).
45. 29 U.S.C. §626(a).
46. 29 U.S.C. §626(b).
47. *Id.* The legislative history of the ADEA Amendments of 1978 makes clear "that conciliation is not a jurisdictional prerequisite to maintaining a cause of action under the [ADEA]." Conference Report, H.R. Rep. No. 95–950, 95th Cong., 2d Sess., 12 (1978). Cf., *Brennan* v. *Ace Hardware Corp.*, 495 F.2d 368 (8th Cir. 1974).

    Similarly, the EEOC may sue without the need for it or the aggrieved individual to file a charge of discrimination with the appropriate state agency. *Marshall* v. *Chamberlain Mfg. Corp.*, 601 F.2d 100 (3d Cir. 1979).
48. 29 U.S.C. §626(e)(1) incorporates the statute of limitations set forth in §6 of the Portal-to-Portal Act, 29 U.S.C. §255. The statute of limitations also operates as a limitation on the amount of back wages available.
49. 29 U.S.C. §626(e)(2). This tolling period was added by the ADEA Amendments of 1978.
50. 29 U.S.C. §626(c). An individual's lawsuit can be later terminated if the EEOC subsequently sues on the individual's behalf. Compare *EEOC* v. *Janesville*, 480 F.Supp. 1375 (W.D.Wis. 1979), with *Jones* v. *Janesville*, 488 F.Supp. 795 (W.D.Wis. 1980).
51. See note 48, *supra.*
52. See note 49, *supra.*
53. 29 U.S.C. §626(d).
54. 29 U.S.C. §626(d)(1). See, e.g., *Templeton* v. *Western Union Telegraph Co.*, 607 F.2d 89 (5th Cir. 1979), and cases cited therein.
55. 29 U.S.C. §626(d)(2). Two courts have broadly construed this 300-day period by applying it to any individual in a state where a state enforcement agency exists, regardless of whether a timely charge was filed with that agency or whether the agency acted on a particular charge. *Davis* v. *Calgon Corp.*, 627 F.2d 674 (3d Cir. 1980); *Bean* v. *Crocker National Bank*, 600 F.2d 754 (9th Cir. 1979). Contra *Ciccone* v. *Textron, Inc.*, 616 F.2d 1216 (1st Cir. 1980).
56. 29 U.S.C. §633(b); see *Oscar Mayer Co.* v. *Evans*, 441 U.S. 750 (1979); *Simpson* v. *Whirlpool Corp.*, 604 F.2d 997 (6th Cir. 1979); *Gabrielle* v. *Chrysler Corp.*, 604 F.2d 996 (6th Cir. 1979).
57. *Id.*
58. See note 43, *supra.*

59. As a result of the ADEA Amendments of 1978, the 180-day filing period in 29 U.S.C. §626(d)(1) need not necessarily be complied with. The legislative history indicates that "the 'charge' requirement is not a jurisdictional prerequisite to maintaining an action under the ADEA and . . . therefore equitable modification for failing to file within the time period will be available to plaintiffs under this Act." Conference Report, H.R. Rep. No. 95–950, 95th Cong., 2d Sess., 12 (1978), accompanying the Age Discrimination in Employment Act Amendments of 1978. See *Wright* v. *Tennessee*, 628 F.2d 949 (6th Cir. 1980) (*en banc*), and cases cited therein.

60. *Shell Oil Co.* v. *Dartt*, 434 U.S. 99 (1977), *aff'g by an equally divided court* 539 F.2d 1256 (10th Cir. 1976); see also, *Kephart* v. *Institute of Gas Technology*, 581 F.2d 1287 (7th Cir. 1978) (employer's failure to post a notice advising employees of their rights under the ADEA tolls the 180-day limitation period); *Thomas* v. *E. I. DuPont de Nemours & Co., Inc.*, 574 F.2d 1324 (5th Cir. 1978).

61. *Quina* v. *Owens-Corning Fiberglass Corp.*, 575 F.2d 1115, 1118 (5th Cir. 1978); see also, *Larson* v. *American Wheel and Brake, Inc.*, 610 F.2d 506 (8th Cir. 1979).

62. See 29 U.S.C. §626(b) incorporating by reference 29 U.S.C. §216(b). Pursuant to this section, most courts have limited ADEA class action representation to include only those persons who have filed written consents with the court. E.g., *LaChapelle* v. *Owens Illinois, Inc.*, 513 F.2d 286 (5th Cir. 1975), *aff'g* 64 F.R.D. 96 (N.D. Ga. 1974); *Hill* v. *Continental Oil Co.*, 58 F.R.D. 636 (E.D. Tex. 1973). But see *Blankenship* v. *Ralston Purina Co.*, 62 F.R.D. 35 (N.D. Ga. 1973). Cf., *Morelock* v. *NCR Corp.*, 586 F.2d 1096 (6th Cir. 1978), *cert. denied*, 441 U.S. 906 (1979) (individuals who are named plaintiffs in a lawsuit need not file written consents).

    Individuals who file written consents, thereby opting into the class, need not have filed any administrative charges of discrimination. See *Bean* v. *Crocker National Bank*, 600 F.2d 754 (9th Cir. 1979).

63. 29 U.S.C. §633a(d).

64. Do *not* send your notice to the United States Civil Service Commission. It formerly had but no longer has the responsibility for enforcing the ADEA in federal employment. See 29 U.S.C. §633a. Under Presidential Reorganization Plan No. 1 of 1978, 43 Fed. Reg. 19807 (May 9, 1978), the federal enforcement responsi-

bility pertaining to non-discrimination in federal employment was shifted to the EEOC.

65. 29 U.S.C. §633a(d).

66. 29 U.S.C. §633a(c)&(d). See also 29 U.S.C. §626(c)(1).

67. See generally 29 U.S.C. §§626(b)&(c) specifying various remedies and incorporating those in 29 U.S.C. §§216 and 217. For an example of equitable, rightful place remedies, see *DeFries* v. *Haarhues*, 488 F.Supp. 1037 (C.D. Ill. 1980).

68. *Marshall* v. *Arlene Knitwear, Inc.*, 454 F.Supp. 715 (E.D.N.Y. 1978).

69. *Cleverly* v. *Western Electric Co.*, 594 F.2d 638 (8th Cir. 1979).

70. 29 U.S.C. §626(b) and 29 U.S.C. §216(b).

71. *Id.*

72. *Id.* See generally *EEOC* v. *Gilbarco, Inc.*, 615 F.2d 985 (4th Cir. 1980).

73. *Mistretta* v. *Sandia Corp.*, 18 EPD ¶8852 (D.N.M. 1978). See also *Wehr* v. *Burroughs Corp.*, 619 F.2d 276 (3d Cir. 1980).

74. 29 U.S.C. §626(c)(2). Cf., *Lorillard* v. *Pons*, 434 U.S. 575 (1978).

75. *Slatin* v. *Stanford Research Institute*, 590 F.2d 1292 (4th Cir. 1979); *Vazquez* v. *Eastern Airlines, Inc.*, 579 F.2d 107 (1st Cir. 1978); *Dean* v. *American Security Insurance Co.*, 559 F.2d 1036 (5th Cir. 1977), *cert. denied*, 434 U.S. 1066 (1978); *Rogers* v. *Exxon Research & Engineering Co.*, 550 F.2d 834 (3d Cir. 1977), *cert. denied*, 434 U.S. 1022 (1978). Contra *Wise* v. *Olan Mills, Inc.*, 485 F.Supp. 542 (D. Colo. 1980).

76. *Walker* v. *Pettit Const. Co., Inc.*, 605 F.2d 128 (4th Cir. 1979); *Murphy* v. *American Motor Sales Corp.*, 570 F.2d 1226 (5th Cir. 1978); *Dean* v. *American Security Insurance Co.*, 559 F.2d 1036 (5th Cir. 1977), *cert. denied*, 434 U.S. 1066 (1978); contra, *Kennedy* v. *Mountain States Tel. & Tel. Co.*, 449 F.Supp. 1008 (D.Colo. 1978).

77. 29 U.S.C. §626(b) incorporates the "remedies" provided in §16(b) of the Fair Labor Standards Act, 29 U.S.C. §216(b); one such remedy is the payment of attorney's fees only to plaintiffs. See, e.g., *Rodriguez* v. *Taylor*, 569 F.2d 1231 (3d Cir. 1977), *cert. denied*, 436 U.S. 913 (1978).

78. See *Cova* v. *Coca-Cola Bottling Co. of St. Louis*, 574 F.2d 958, 962 (8th Cir. 1978). On the other hand, a court can award fees against you if your lawsuit was brought in bad faith. See generally *Alyeska Pipeline Service Co.* v. *Wilderness Society*, 421 U.S. 240 (1975).

79. See *Coates* v. *National Cash Register Co.*, 433 F.Supp. 655 (W.D.

Va. 1977). Most courts, however, have held that pain-and-suffering damages and punitive damages are not available under the ADEA. See notes 75 & 76, *supra*.
80.  *Schulz* v. *Hickok Mfg. Co.*, 358 F.Supp. 1208, 1216 (N.D. Ga. 1973).
81.  *Id.* at 1215–1216.

#### 4: USING A LAW DESIGNED TO BRING DISCRIMINATORY LOCAL GOVERNMENTS TO THEIR KNEES

1.  *United States* v. *Chicago*, 549 F.2d 415, 447 (7th Cir.) (Pell, J., dissenting), *cert. denied*, 434 U.S. 875 (1977).
2.  *United States* v. *Chicago*, 385 F.Supp. 543 (N.D.Ill. 1974).
3.  *United States* v. *Chicago*, 395 F.Supp. 329 (N.D.Ill. 1975).
4.  *United States* v. *Chicago*, 549 F.2d 415, 439 n.36 (7th Cir.), *cert. denied*, 434 U.S. 875 (1977).
5.  The major provisions of the Revenue Sharing Act prohibiting discrimination and governing enforcement are in §122 of the Act, 31 U.S.C. §1242. Other civil rights provisions are contained in §124 and §125 of the Act, 31 U.S.C. §1244 and §1245, respectively.

As noted in the text, the original 1972 Act was reenacted as amended in 1976 by the State and Local Fiscal Assistance Amendments of 1976, Pub.L. No. 94–488 (Oct. 13, 1976), 90 Stat. 2341, 31 U.S.C. §§1221, *et seq.* The Act was reenacted without change in the fall of 1980.

The Revenue Sharing Act, however, did suffer one major change in 1980 as a result of congressional budget-cutting action. Specifically, although the Act authorizes the provision of revenue-sharing payments to the fifty states, Congress in 1980 eliminated state funding from the revenue sharing program. Thus, although the civil rights provisions in §122 of the Act, 31 U.S.C. §1242, address state governments as well as local governments, this chapter refers to the Act as applicable only to local governments.

Another victim of congressional budget cutting in 1980 was the federal funding provided to state and local law enforcement agencies by the Law Enforcement Assistance Administration [LEAA]. As part of the Justice System Improvement Act of 1979, Pub.L. No. 96–157 (Dec. 27, 1979), 93 Stat. 1167, 42 U.S.C. §§3701, *et seq.*, the civil rights provisions in §815(c) of that Act,

42 U.S.C. §3789d(c) [formerly §518(c) of the Crime Control Act, 42 U.S.C. §3766(c)] prohibit discrimination and compel enforcement in a manner virtually identical to the civil rights provisions of the Revenue Sharing Act. In view of the LEAA's lapsed funding, however, this powerful method of civil rights enforcement against state and local law enforcement agencies is no longer viable.

6. 31 U.S.C. §1242(a)(1).

7. 31 C.F.R. §51.2(1) and §51.51(1). This is the same definition as in the old "interim" regulation previously in 31 C.F.R. §51.51(i).

At the time this book was completed, the ORS's regulations were subject to minor uncertainties. In late 1979, the ORS reorganized its old "interim" regulations and published a new set of proposed regulations in 44 Fed.Reg. 77356 (Dec. 31, 1979). Aside from renumbering, the proposed regulations are virtually identical to the old "interim" regulations in 42 Fed.Reg. 18632 (April 6, 1977), and in 43 Fed.Reg. 31927 (July 24, 1978). The regulations relied on herein are the ORS's proposed regulations, cited prematurely to 31 C.F.R. Part 51.

8. 31 U.S.C. §1242(a)(2).

9. 31 U.S.C. §1242 (a)(1). The Revenue Sharing Act also prohibits employment discrimination on grounds of handicapped status, *id.*, a form of discrimination not discussed in this book. Although the Act does prohibit age discrimination generally, *id.*, it does not forbid age discrimination in employment. See note 40, *infra.*

10. 31 C.F.R. §51.52(a).

11. 31 C.F.R. §51.52(b)(3). See also 31 C.F.R. §51.52(b)(6).

12. 31 C.F.R. §51.53(a).

13. The ORS has adopted the EEOC's guidelines on discrimination based upon sex, national origin, and religion. See 31 C.F.R. §51.-54, §51.57, and §51.58, respectively. The ORS also has adopted the Uniform Guidelines on Employee Selection Procedures. See 31 C.F.R. §51.53(b).

14. *United States* v. *Chicago,* 549 F.2d 415, 440 (7th Cir.), *cert. denied,* 434 U.S. 875 (1977). Cf. *United States* v. *Virginia,* 620 F.2d 1018 (4th Cir. 1980) (non-discrimination provisions of the Crime Control Act).

15. *Id.*

16. *Manley* v. *Mobile County, Alabama,* 441 F.Supp. 1351 (S.D.Ala. 1977).

17. *Peltier* v. *Fargo,* 533 F.2d 374 (8th Cir. 1976).

18. *Firefighters Institute for Racial Equality* v. *St. Louis,* 549 F.2d

506 (8th Cir.), *cert. denied,* 434 U.S. 819 (1977); see also *Firefighters Institute for Racial Equality* v. *St. Louis,* 588 F.2d 235 (8th Cir. 1978).

19. See notes 11, 13, and 14, *supra.* The illegality of disparate impact discrimination is modified by two caveats when the ORS or the Department of Justice enforces the Revenue Sharing Act. First, the federal enforcement agencies have a "bottom line" policy under which they ordinarily will not inquire into the impact or validity of an individual component (e.g., a test or oral interview) of a selection process so long as the total selection process does not result in a disparate impact. Second, the discriminatory impact of an entire selection process and of any significant component thereof is determined by an 80 percent rule (or "four-fifths rule") which means that a selection process is considered to be discriminatory only if the selection rate for a racial minority group or for women is less than 80 percent of the rate for the group (usually whites or males) with the highest selection rate.

These somewhat intricate policies are discussed in the text and notes of Chapter 2 with regard to federal enforcement of Title VII. The same policies have been adopted by the ORS for federal enforcement of the Revenue Sharing Act. See Uniform Guidelines on Employee Selection Procedures, 43 Fed.Reg. 38290 (Aug. 25, 1978), adopted by the ORS in 31 C.F.R. §51.53(b), and attached thereto as Appendix A.

20. See notes 1–4, *supra.* See also *Pennsylvania* v. *O'Neill,* 348 F.Supp. 1084 (E.D.Pa. 1972), *aff'd in relevant part,* 473 F.2d 1029 (3d Cir. 1973) (Philadelphia).

21. *United States* v. *Chicago,* 573 F.2d 416 (7th Cir. 1978).

22. *United States* v. *Buffalo,* 457 F.Supp. 612 (W.D.N.Y. 1978).

23. *Officers for Justice* v. *Civil Service Commission,* 395 F.Supp. 378 (N.D.Cal. 1975). For other cases striking down minimum-height requirements, see, e.g., *Dothard* v. *Rawlinson,* 433 U.S. 321 (1977); *Horace* v. *Pontiac,* 624 F.2d 765 (6th Cir. 1980); *United States* v. *Virginia,* 620 F.2d 1018 (4th Cir. 1980); *Blake* v. *Los Angeles,* 595 F.2d 1367 (9th Cir. 1979); *United States* v. *Buffalo,* 457 F.Supp. 612 (W.D.N.Y. 1978). As to physical agility tests, see, e.g., *Harless* v. *Duck,* 619 F.2d 611 (6th Cir. 1980).

24. *Crockett* v. *Green,* 339 F.Supp. 912 (E.D.Wis. 1975), *aff'd,* 534 F.2d 715 (7th Cir. 1976). See also *United States* v. *Milwaukee,* 481 F.Supp. 1162 (E.D.Wis. 1979), holding completion of the Milwaukee Fire Department's training course for firefighters to be a discriminatory and unlawful requirement for paramedics.

25. *Dozier* v. *Chupka*, 395 F.Supp. 836 (S.D.Ohio 1975).
26. *Carter* v. *Gallagher*, 452 F.2d 315 (8th Cir. 1971), *modified on other grounds*, 452 F.2d 327 (8th Cir.) (*en banc*), *cert. denied*, 406 U.S. 950 (1972).
27. *Boston Chapter, NAACP, Inc.* v. *Beecher*, 504 F.2d 1017 (1st Cir. 1974), *cert. denied*, 421 U.S. 910 (1975) (Boston); *Harper* v. *Mayor & City Council*, 486 F.2d 1134 (4th Cir. 1973) (Baltimore); *Firefighters Institute for Racial Equality* v. *St. Louis*, 549 F.2d 506 (8th Cir. 1977) (St. Louis); *Fowler* v. *Schwarzwalder*, 348 F.Supp. 844 (D. Minn. 1972), 351 F.Supp. 721 (D. Minn. 1972) (St. Paul); *Vulcan Society* v. *Civil Service Commission*, 490 F.2d 387 (2d Cir. 1973) (New York); *Western Addition Community Organization* v. *Alioto*, 340 F.Supp. 1351 (N.D. Cal. 1972), 360 F.Supp. 733 (N.D. Cal. 1973), 369 F.Supp. 77 (N.D. Cal. 1973) (San Francisco), respectively. But see *Friend* v. *Leidinger*, 588 F.2d 61 (4th Cir. 1978) (Richmond).
28. *Bridgeport Guardians* v. *Civil Service Commission*, 482 F.2d 1333 (2d Cir. 1973) (Bridgeport); *Pennsylvania* v. *O'Neill*, 348 F.Supp. 1084 (E.D.Pa. 1972), *aff'd in relevant part*, 473 F.2d 1029 (3d Cir. 1973) (Philadelphia); *Shield Club* v. *Cleveland*, 370 F.Supp. 251 (N.D. Ohio 1972) (Cleveland); *Afro-American Patrolmen's League* v. *Duck*, 503 F.2d 294 (6th Cir. 1974) (Toledo), respectively. See also *Kirkland* v. *New York State Department of Correctional Services*, 520 F.2d 420 (2d Cir. 1975), *cert. denied*, 429 U.S. 823 (1976), *on remand as to remedy*, 482 F.Supp. 1179 (S.D.N.Y. 1980); *United States* v. *New York*, 475 F.Supp. 1103 (S.D.N.Y. 1979).
29. *Cooper* v. *Allen*, 467 F.2d 836 (5th Cir. 1972).
30. See generally the Uniform Guidelines on Employee Selection Procedures, 43 Fed.Reg. 38290 (Aug. 25, 1978), adopted by the ORS in 31 C.F.R. §51.53(b) and attached thereto as Appendix A.
31. *Allen* v. *Mobile*, 464 F.Supp. 433 (S.D.Ala. 1978).
32. See generally *McDonnell Douglas Corp.* v. *Green*, 411 U.S. 792 (1973).
33. *Corley* v. *Jackson Police Department*, 566 F.2d 994 (5th Cir. 1978).
34. The EEOC Guidelines on Sex Discrimination, 29 C.F.R. §1604, which specifically prohibit sexual harassment, have been adopted by the ORS. See 31 C.F.R. §51.54.
35. 31 C.F.R. §51.52(b)(5). Retaliation against you by a local government also violates your First Amendment rights to freedom of speech. *Simpson* v. *Weeks*, 570 F.2d 240 (8th Cir. 1978) (individ-

ual awarded $3 nominal damages and $5,000 punitive damages).
See also *Givhan* v. *Western Line Consolidated School District*,
439 U.S. 410 (1979).

36.　See notes 1–4, *supra*. For a general discussion on the use of
statistics, see the text accompanying notes 63–66 in Chapter 2.
See also the cases cited in *United States* v. *Miami*, 614 F.2d 1322
(5th Cir. 1980).

37.　See note 26, *supra*.

38.　*Morrow* v. *Crisler*, 479 F.2d 960 (5th Cir. 1973), *reaff'd en banc*,
491 F.2d 1053 (5th Cir.), *cert. denied*, 419 U.S. 895 (1974).

39.　*NAACP* v. *Allen*, 340 F.Supp. 703 (N.D.Ala. 1972), *aff'd*, 493
F.2d 614 (5th Cir. 1974).

40.　The exclusion of *employment* discrimination based upon age
from the Revenue Sharing Act presents somewhat of an anomaly
because §122 of the Act does mention age discrimination, 31
U.S.C. §1242(a)(1). But, rather than prohibiting it directly, §122
incorporates the protections of the Age Discrimination Act of
1975, 42 U.S.C. §§6101, *et seq.*, a law which prohibits age discrimination generally but which specifically exempts employment discrimination, 42 U.S.C. §6103(c)(1). In other words, because of this incorporation, the Revenue Sharing Act does forbid
some forms of age discrimination but *not* age discrimination in
employment.

　　The age discrimination law referred to above is different from
the Age Discrimination in Employment Act of 1967, a law which
does prohibit age discrimination in employment, and which is
discussed in Chapter 3.

41.　Three of Title VII's exceptions—those allowing sex discrimination authorized by the Equal Pay Act, permitting the continu-
ance of bona fide seniority systems, and allowing veterans' preferences—are referred to neither in the Revenue Sharing Act nor
in the federal regulations interpreting the Act. The Act's general
ban on discrimination thus should prevail over any attempt by an
employer to invoke one of these three Title VII exceptions under
the separate and independent Revenue Sharing Act. See, e.g.,
*Johnson* v. *Railway Express Agency, Inc.*, 421 U.S. 454 (1975),
holding that the employment discrimination laws are separate
and independent from each other.

42.　See note 13, *supra*. See also 31 C.F.R. §51.53(d).

43.　E.g., *United States* v. *Chicago*, 549 F.2d 415, 440 (7th Cir.), *cert.
denied*, 434 U.S. 875 (1977).

44.　42 U.S.C. §2000e(j).

45. 31 U.S.C. §1242(a)(1).
46. The EEOC Guidelines on Affirmative Action Appropriate under Title VII, 29 C.F.R. §1608, have been adopted by the ORS. See 31 C.F.R. §51.61(b), and Appendix F thereto. Although the constitutionality of such voluntary affirmative action in public employment has not yet been decided by the Supreme Court, lower federal courts have upheld it. See note 113 to Chapter 2, and note 46 to Chapter 7.
47. *Id.* See, e.g., *Morrow* v. *Dillard*, 580 F.2d 1284 (5th Cir. 1978); *United States* v. *New York*, 475 F.Supp. 1103 (N.D.N.Y. 1979); see also *United States* v. *Los Angeles*, 595 F.2d 1386, 1390 (9th Cir. 1979).
48. If the local government which discriminated against you is a law enforcement agency which has received funding from the federal Law Enforcement Assistance Administration under the Justice System Improvement Act of 1979 or under the predecessor Crime Control Acts, see note 5, *supra;* you can quickly learn a vast amount about your employer's practices by reviewing its written Equal Employment Opportunity Program, a document required to be maintained by nearly all recipients of LEAA funding. See 28 C.F.R. Part 42.300.
49. 31 C.F.R. §51.62(a).
50. *Id.*
51. 31 U.S.C. §1245(1). See generally 31 C.F.R. §51.62–§51.68.
52. 31 U.S.C. §1242(c)(4).
53. The various enforcement steps are set forth in 31 U.S.C. §§1242(b), (d) & (e), and in 31 C.F.R. §51.64–§51.68. First, within 10 days of its finding of non-compliance, the ORS must send a notice of that non-compliance to the local government involved. Within 30 days thereafter, the local government informally may present evidence to the ORS. The ORS then must make a formal determination of non-compliance or compliance. If the determination is non-compliance, the ORS must suspend all revenue sharing funding unless the local government within 10 days of the determination enters into a compliance agreement or requests a formal hearing before an administrative law judge. If a hearing is requested, it must be initiated within 30 days of the request. Within 30 days of the beginning of the hearing, the administrative law judge must issue a preliminary finding as to whether the local government is "not likely to prevail." If there is a finding that the local government is not likely to prevail, the ORS must immediately suspend all funding. If the administrative

law judge, after completion of the hearing, determines non-compliance, the ORS 31 days thereafter must suspend funding or continue the previous suspension. The administrative law judge, in his or her discretion, may order termination of funding.

54. 31 C.F.R. §51.63.
55. 31 U.S.C. §1242(d)(2); 31 C.F.R. §51.66(e).
56. 31 U.S.C. §1242(c)(1).
57. 31 U.S.C. §§1242(b), (d) & (e).
58. *Id.* See note 53, *supra.*
59. 31 U.S.C. §1242(b)(2).
60. 31 U.S.C. §1242(c)(2).
61. 31 C.F.R. §51.59(a).
62. 31 U.S.C. §1242(g). See, e.g., *United States* v. *Miami,* 614 F.2d 1332 (5th Cir. 1980); *United States* v. *Buffalo,* 457 F.Supp. 612 (W.D.N.Y. 1978).
63. *Id.*
64. The Revenue Sharing Act on its face makes clear that lawsuits are to supplement, not replace, administrative enforcement. Thus, regardless of the filing of a lawsuit, the ORS is still required to proceed with its mandatory enforcement procedures. See generally *United States* v. *Milwaukee,* 449 F.Supp. 949 (E.D.Wis. 1978).
65. 31 U.S.C. §1244(a). Even if your government does not now receive funding, it may be sued so long as it received funding at the time it discriminated against you. *United States* v. *New Jersey,* 473 F.Supp. 1199 (D.N.J. 1979).
66. 31 U.S.C. §1244(d).
67. 31 U.S.C. §1244(b).
68. 31 U.S.C. §1244(e). See *Cohen* v. *West Haven Board of Police Commissioners,* 485 F.Supp. 958 (D. Conn. 1980).
69. This is the standard under Title VII. See *Christiansburg Garment Co.* v. *EEOC,* 434 U.S. 412 (1978). No court has yet decided whether this standard or the more rigorous bad faith standard applicable to losing plaintiffs under 42 U.S.C. §1988, see Chapters 6 and 7, is more appropriate under the Revenue Sharing Act.
70. 31 U.S.C. §1242(g), and §1244(b). See generally *United States* v. *Milwaukee,* 457 F.Supp. 1009 (E.D.Wis. 1978).
71. *Id.* See, e.g., *United States* v. *New York,* 475 F.Supp. 1103 (N.D.N.Y. 1979).
72. *Id.*
73. *Id.* See *United States* v. *New Jersey,* 473 F.Supp. 1179 (D.N.J. 1979).

## 5: TERMINATING LUCRATIVE FEDERAL CONTRACTS TO DISCRIMINATORY PRIVATE EMPLOYERS

1. *EEOC* v. *American Telephone and Telegraph Co.*, 365 F.Supp. 1105 (E.D. Pa. 1973), *modified*, 506 F.2d 735 (3d Cir. 1974), *proceedings on supplemental order*, 419 F.Supp. 1022 (E.D. Pa. 1976), *aff'd*, 556 F.2d 167 (3d Cir. 1977), *cert. denied*, 438 U.S. 915 (1978).

2. E.O. 11246, 30 Fed.Reg. 12319 (Sept. 24, 1965), actually is the successor of many similar orders issued since World War II. E.O. 11246 itself has been amended on several occasions, with the most important amendments occurring through E.O. 11375, 32 Fed. Reg. 14303 (Oct. 13, 1967), which added the prohibition against sex discrimination, and through E.O. 12086, 43 Fed.Reg. 46501 (Oct. 10, 1978), which consolidated all enforcement into the Office of Federal Contract Compliance Programs. The complete text of the amended Executive Order is set out in the notes following 42 U.S.C.A. §2000e.

   Some of the federal regulations interpreting the Executive Order were subject to minor uncertainties at the time this book was written. All of the OFCCP's regulations are codified in 41 C.F.R. Parts 60–1, *et seq.* Late in 1979, the OFCCP issued a partial set of proposed regulations, 44 Fed.Reg. 77006 (Dec. 28, 1979), which proposed changes in some of the old regulations and renumbered others. Other amended regulations appear in 45 Fed.Reg. 9271 (Feb. 12, 1980). The regulations cited herein are the proposed regulations, adopted as final in 45 Fed.Reg. 86216 (Dec. 30, 1980), and cited prematurely to 41 C.F.R. Parts 60–1, *et seq.*

3. E.O. 11246, §202, §301.

4. E.O. 11246, §§201–215.

5. E.O. 11246 §§301–304.

6. 41 C.F.R. §60–1.3.

7. 41 C.F.R. §60–1.5(a). This limitation is authorized by E.O. 11246, §204.

8. 41 C.F.R. §60–1.40 and §60–2.1(a). This limitation similarly is authorized by E.O. 11246, §204.

9. *Pan American World Airways* v. *Marshall*, 439 F.Supp. 487 (S.D.N.Y. 1977).

10. 41 C.F.R. §60–1.3.

11. *Crown Central Petroleum Corp.* v. *Kleppe*, 424 F.Supp. 744, 748 (D. Md. 1976).

12.    41 C.F.R. §60–1.3.
13.    E.O. 11246, §302(a).
14.    41 C.F.R. §60–1.3. See generally E.O. 11246, §301, which incor-
       porates the contractual requirements of E.O. 11246, §202; see
       also, note 7, *supra.*
15.    *Id.* Compare note 8, *supra.*
16.    41 C.F.R. §60–1.5(a).
17.    *Contractors Ass'n of Eastern Pa.* v. *Secretary of Labor,* 311
       F.Supp. 1002 (E.D.Pa. 1970), *aff'd,* 442 F.2d 159 (3d Cir.), *cert.
       denied,* 404 U.S. 854 (1971).
18.    E.O. 11246, §202 and §301; 41 C.F.R. §60–1.4 and §60–4.3.
19.    *Id.*
20.    *Id.* Contractors also are obligated not to discriminate on grounds
       of handicapped status under §503 of the Rehabilitation Act of
       1973, 29 U.S.C. §793, a law that also is enforced through contract
       compliance by the OFCCP.
21.    Office of Federal Contract Compliance Programs Task Force,
       *Preliminary Report on the Revitalization of the Federal Contract
       Program,* 110–111 (Sept. 1977).
22.    Similar to the manner in which disparate impact discrimination
       is modified by two caveats when the EEOC enforces Title VII,
       the illegality of disparate impact discrimination is modified by
       the same two caveats when the OFCCP or the Department of
       Justice enforces Executive Order 11246. First, the federal en-
       forcement agencies have a "bottom line" policy under which
       they ordinarily will not inquire into the impact or validity of an
       individual component (e.g., a test or oral interview) of a selection
       process so long as the total selection process does not result in a
       disparate impact. Second, the discriminatory impact of an entire
       selection process and of any significant component thereof is
       determined by an 80 percent rule (or "four-fifths rule") which
       means that a selection process is considered to be discriminatory
       only if the selection rate for a racial minority group or for women
       is less than 80 percent of the rate for the group (usually whites
       or males) with the highest selection rate.
       These somewhat intricate policies are discussed in the text and
       notes of Chapter 2 with regard to federal enforcement of Title
       VII. The same policies have been adopted by the OFCCP for
       federal enforcement of Executive Order 11246. See Uniform
       Guidelines on Employee Selection Procedures, 43 Fed.Reg.
       38290 (Aug. 25, 1978); 41 C.F.R. Part 60–3.

23. Sexual harassment, in fact, is specifically forbidden by the Executive Order. See 41 C.F.R. §60–20.8.

24. In some respects, the discriminatory practices prohibited by the Executive Order are more extensive than those forbidden by Title VII. See, e.g., the OFCCP's Sex Discrimination Guidelines, 41 C.F.R. Part 60–20.

25. 41 C.F.R. §60–2.10. See generally 41 C.F.R. §60–2.

26. *Id.*

27. 41 C.F.R. §60–2.11.

28. *Id.*

29. *Id.* Additionally, affirmative action on behalf of women requires the inclusion of females in management-training programs. See 41 C.F.R. §60–20.6.

30. 41 C.F.R. §60–2.11(b).

31. *Id.* See also 41 C.F.R. §60–2.12(i).

32. See generally 41 C.F.R. Part 60–2.

33. 41 C.F.R. §60–2.23(a).

34. 41 C.F.R. §60–2.12(i) and §60–2.21; see also 41 C.F.R. §60–1.40(b).

35. 41 C.F.R. §60–4. See also notes 14, 15, and 18, *supra.*

36. See note 17, *supra.*

37. 41 C.F.R. Part 60–4, §60–4.3, and §60–4.6. The required inclusion of women was added in 1978, see 43 Fed.Reg. 14899 (April 7, 1978).

38. 41 C.F.R. §60–1.28.

39. E.g., *United States* v. *New Orleans Public Service, Inc.,* 553 F.2d 459, 465 (5th Cir. 1977), *vacated and remanded on other grounds,* 436 U.S. 942 (1978), *order reinstated on remand,* 480 F.Supp. 705 (E.D.La. 1979). See also the cases cited in the Fifth Circuit's opinion, 553 F.2d at 465–468, and in *Liberty Mutual Insurance Co.* v. *Friedman,* 485 F.Supp. 695 (D.Md. 1979).

40. E.g., *Southern Illinois Builders Ass'n* v. *Ogilvie,* 471 F.2d 680 (7th Cir. 1972); *Contractors Ass'n of Eastern Pa.* v. *Secretary of Labor,* 442 F.2d 159 (3d Cir.), *cert. denied,* 404 U.S. 854 (1971). See also *Weber* v. *Kaiser Aluminum & Chemical Corp.,* 563 F.2d 216 (5th Cir. 1977), *reh. denied,* 571 F.2d 337 (5th Cir. 1978), *rev'd,* 443 U.S. 193 (1979).

41. 41 C.F.R. §60–1.5(a) and §60–4.1.

42. *Id.* 41 C.F.R. §60–2.1(a).

43. 41 C.F.R. §60–1.5(a)(5).

44. 41 C.F.R. §60–1.5(a)(6).

45. 41 C.F.R. §60–1.5(c).

46. 41 C.F.R. §60–20.3(b).
47. 41 C.F.R. §60–50.3.
48. E.g., *Crown Zellerbach Corp.* v. *Marshall,* 441 F.Supp. 1110 (E.D. La. 1977).
49. E.O. 11246, §201 and §401.
50. See notes 58–77 *infra.* See also E.O. 12086, 43 Fed. Reg. 46501 (Oct. 10, 1978), consolidating all enforcement responsibilities in the OFCCP.
51. Office of Federal Contract Compliance Programs Task Force, *Preliminary Report on the Revitalization of the Federal Contract Compliance Program,* 23 (Sept. 1977).
52. Affirmative action programs must be available for inspection. See note 34, *supra.*
53. See generally 41 C.F.R. §60–1.20 and §60–1.21.
54. 41 C.F.R. §60–1.24(a).
55. Office of Federal Contract Compliance Programs Task Force, *Preliminary Report on the Revitalization of the Federal Contract Compliance Program,* xxii, 9, 141 (Sept. 1977).
56. 41 C.F.R. §60–1.24(a).
57. *Freeman* v. *Schultz,* 468 F.2d 120 (D.C.Cir. 1972); *Hadnott* v. *Laird,* 463 F.2d 304 (D.C.Cir. 1972); *Braden* v. *University of Pennsylvania,* 343 F.Supp. 836 (W.D.Pa. 1972), *rev'd on other grounds,* 477 F.2d 1 (3d Cir. 1973); see also, *Farkas* v. *Texas Instruments,* 375 F.2d 629 (5th Cir.), *cert. denied,* 389 U.S. 977 (1967); *Farmer* v. *Philadelphia Electric Co.,* 329 F.2d 3 (3d Cir. 1964); cf., *Rogers* v. *Frito Lay, Inc.,* 611 F.2d 1074 (5th Cir. 1980) (there is no implied cause of action under §503 of the Rehabilitation Act of 1973, 29 U.S.C. §793, a law also enforced through contract compliance by the OFCCP). On the other hand, several courts have held that individuals can sue the federal officials responsible for enforcing the Executive Order, e.g., *Legal Aid Society of Alameda County* v. *Brennan,* 608 F.2d 1319 (9th Cir. 1979); *Percy* v. *Brennan,* 394 F.Supp. 800 (S.D.N.Y. 1974).
58. E.O. 11246, §206(a); 41 C.F.R. §60–1.20, §60–1.21.
59. E.O. 11246, §206(b); 41 C.F.R. §60–1.24. See also the Proposed Memorandum of Understanding between the EEOC and the OFCCP, 45 Fed.Reg. 27071 (April 22, 1980); and see the OFCCP Federal Contract Compliance Manual, §6–20.1.
60. 41 C.F.R. §60–1.24(b).
61. 41 C.F.R. §60–1.23(a).
62. *Id.*
63. 41 C.F.R. §60–1.22.

64. 41 C.F.R. §§60–1.24(b) and (c); see generally E.O. 11246, §206(b).
65. 41 C.F.R. §60–1.24(c)(1).
66. 41 C.F.R. §60–1.24(c)(3).
67. See the OFCCP Federal Contract Compliance Manual, §6–40.5, and Figure 6–1.
68. 41 C.F.R. §60–1.23(b).
69. E.O. 11246, §209(a)(5) [contractors with federal contracts]; see also, E.O. 11246, §303(b)(1) [construction contractors with federally assisted construction contracts].
70. E.O. 11246, §209(a)(6) [contractors with federal contracts]; see also E.O. 11246, §303(b)(2) [construction contractors with federally assisted construction contracts]. In fact, a contractor can be debarred merely for refusing to comply with discovery requests made by the OFCCP as part of a compliance review. See *Uniroyal, Inc.* v. *Marshall,* 482 F.Supp. 364 (D.D.C. 1979).
    The OFCCP in the past used a third method of enforcement. Under this third method, the OFCCP could "pass over" non-complying contractors on up to two future contracts. Employers challenged this method because no hearing procedure was provided. Compare *Crown Zellerbach Corp.* v. *Marshall,* 441 F.Supp. 1110 (E.D.La. 1977) (no formal hearing is required), with *Pan American World Airways* v. *Marshall,* 439 F.Supp. 487 (S.D.N.Y. 1977) (a formal hearing is required). The OFCCP now has abandoned this "pass over" procedure.
71. E.O. 11246, §202, §301.
72. When the OFCCP finds retaliation or is confronted with a contractor's refusal to provide compliance information, the OFCCP may initiate economic sanctions through a shortened, preliminary administrative proceeding. 41 C.F.R. §60–1.29(e). Cf. *Uniroyal, Inc.* v. *Marshall,* 482 F.Supp. 364 (D.D.C. 1979) (a contractor can be debarred for refusing to provide compliance information to the OFCCP).
73. E.O. 11246, §209(b) and §303(c); 41 C.F.R. §60–1.29.
74. 41 C.F.R. §60–1.25.
75. *Id.* See also 41 C.F.R. §60–1.29 and 41 C.F.R. Part 60–30.
76. See E.O. 11246, §208(b), which allows contractors an opportunity for a hearing before debarment can be imposed, and E.O. 11246, §303(c), which allows federally assisted construction contractors an opportunity for a hearing before debarment can be imposed and even before a contract can be canceled, terminated, or suspended; see also, 41 C.F.R. §60–1.30; and see 41 C.F.R. Part 60–30.

77.     41 C.F.R. §60–1.31.
78.     E.O. 11246, §209(a)(2); see also, E.O. 11246, §303(b)(3). Lawsuits
        by the Department of Justice are also authorized in other situa-
        tions, see E.O. 11246, §207, §209(a)(3), §304; see generally, 41
        C.F.R. §60–1.29(f).
79.     *Id.*
80.     *United States* v. *New Orleans Public Service, Inc.,* 553 F.2d 459
        (5th Cir. 1977), *vacated and remanded on other grounds,* 436
        U.S. 942 (1978), *order reinstated on remand,* 480 F.Supp. 705
        (E.D.La. 1979); see also, *United States* v. *Mississippi Power &*
        *Light Co.,* 553 F.2d 480 (5th Cir. 1977), *vacated and remanded*
        *on other grounds,* 436 U.S. 942 (1978); *United States* v. *Duquesne*
        *Light Co.,* 423 F.2d 507 (W.D.Pa. 1976).
81.     *United States* v. *Allegheny-Ludlum Industries, Inc.,* 517 F.2d
        826 (5th Cir. 1975), *cert. denied,* 425 U.S. 944 (1976).
82.     41 C.F.R. §60–1.29(f)(1). See *United States* v. *New Orleans Public*
        *Service, Inc.,* 553 F.2d 459, 473 (5th Cir. 1977), *vacated and*
        *remanded on other grounds,* 436 U.S. 942 (1978), *order reinstated*
        *on remand,* 480 F.Supp. 705 (E.D.La. 1979).
83.     Compare 41 C.F.R. §60–1.26(a) and §60–2.1(b) with 41 C.F.R. §60
        –1.29(f)(2).
84.     *Id.* See also notes 78–81, *supra.*
85.     *Id.*
86.     See note 1, *supra.*
87.     See note 81, *supra.*
88.     E.g., *United States* v. *Duquesne Light Co.,* 423 F.Supp. 507, 509
        (W.D.Pa. 1976).
89.     *American Cyanamid Co.* v. *Roudebush,* 411 F.Supp. 1220
        (S.D.N.Y. 1976).

**6: INCREASING THE MONETARY REMEDIES AVAILABLE IF YOU
HAVE TO SUE YOUR BOSS**

1.      *Garner* v. *Giarrusso,* 571 F.2d 1330, 1332 (5th Cir. 1978).
2.      This reference to "Section 1981" actually is to its current codifi-
        cation in 42 U.S.C. §1981. Historically, both §1981 and its com-
        panion, 42 U.S.C. §1982, derive from §1 of the Civil Rights Act
        of 1866. Both have thus been interpreted in a similar manner.
        E.g., *Tillman* v. *Wheaton-Haven Recreation Ass'n,* 410 U.S. 431
        (1973); *Jones* v. *Alfred H. Mayer Co.,* 392 U.S. 409 (1968). Al-
        though this chapter focuses on §1981, some reference will be

made to §1982, and to 42 U.S.C. §1988, a remedial companion to §1981; and also to 42 U.S.C. §1985(3), a companion law which also prohibits discrimination in the private sector, *Griffin* v. *Breckenridge*, 403 U.S. 88 (1971).

All of the foregoing laws are grouped herein, quite inaccurately, under the phrases "the Civil Rights Act of 1866" or "the 1866 Act" to avoid undue confusion in the text of this chapter.

3.  *Jones* v. *Alfred H. Mayer Co.*, 392 U.S. 409 (1968) [§1982].
4.  *Johnson* v. *Railway Express Agency, Inc.*, 421 U.S. 454 (1975).
5.  See, e.g., the cases cited in *Johnson* v. *Railway Express Agency, Inc.*, 421 U.S. 454, 459 n.6 (1975).
6.  *Garner* v. *Giarrusso*, 571 F.2d 1330 (5th Cir. 1978); *Harkless* v. *Sweeny Independent School District*, 554 F.2d 1353 (5th Cir.), *cert. denied*, 434 U.S. 966 (1978).
7.  *Sullivan* v. *Little Hunting Park, Inc.*, 396 U.S. 229 (1969); *Tillman* v. *Wheaton-Haven Recreational Ass'n*, 517 F.2d 1141 (4th Cir. 1975).
8.  *Allen* v. *Amalgamated Transit Union*, 554 F.2d 876 (8th Cir. 1977), *cert. denied*, 434 U.S. 891 (1978).
9.  *Brown* v. *General Services Administration*, 425 U.S. 820 (1976).
10. Although Title VII does not cover military personnel in the armed services, one court has held that even there the 1866 Act is inapplicable. *Johnson* v. *Alexander*, 572 F.2d 1219 (8th Cir. 1978).
11. 42 U.S.C. §1981.
12. See generally cases cited in *Johnson* v. *Railway Express Agency, Inc.*, 421 U.S. 454, 459 n.6 (1975).

There has been some disagreement about the extent to which the 1866 Act prohibits discrimination on grounds of national origin. Some courts have held that national origin discrimination is forbidden only if joined with a claim of discrimination on grounds of color. See cases collected in *Patel* v. *Holley House Motels*, 483 F.Supp. 374 (S.D.Ala. 1979); cf., *Sethy* v. *Alameda County Water District*, 545 F.2d 1157 (9th Cir. 1976) (the 1866 Act prohibits discrimination against a dark-skinned person of Indian descent). Other courts have held that the 1866 Act protects members of any distinct minority group such as Mexican-Americans. E.g., *Manzanares* v. *Safeway Stores, Inc.*, 593 F.2d 968 (10th Cir. 1979). The Supreme Court has not definitively decided this issue. Cf., *McDonald* v. *Santa Fe Trail Transportation Co.*, 427 U.S. 327 (1976) (whites are protected); *Graham* v. *Richardson*, 403 U.S. 365 (1971) (aliens are protected).

13. *Id.*
14. *Brown* v. *Gaston County Dyeing Machine Co.*, 457 F.2d 1377 (4th Cir.), *cert. denied*, 409 U.S. 982 (1972).
15. These principles were established under Title VII by the Supreme Court in *McDonnell Douglas Corp.* v. *Green*, 411 U.S. 792 (1973). On two occasions the Supreme Court has referred to disparate treatment discrimination as a form of intentional discrimination. *Furnco Construction Corp.* v. *Waters*, 438 U.S. 567 (1978); *Teamsters* v. *United States*, 431 U.S. 324, 335 n.15 (1977). The disparate treatment principles have been uniformly applied by the courts in lawsuits under the 1866 Act. *Kinsey* v. *First Regional Securities, Inc.*, 557 F.2d 830 (D.C.Cir. 1977); *Sabol* v. *Snyder*, 524 F.2d 1009 (10th Cir. 1975); *Long* v. *Ford Motor Co.*, 496 F.2d 500 (6th Cir. 1974).
16. *Kinsey* v. *First Regional Securities, Inc.*, 557 F.2d 830, 839 (D.C.Cir. 1977).
17. *Id.*
18. *Dothard* v. *Rawlinson*, 433 U.S. 321 (1977); *Albemarle Paper Co.* v. *Moody*, 422 U.S. 405 (1975); *Griggs* v. *Duke Power Co.*, 401 U.S. 424 (1971).
19. *Washington* v. *Davis*, 426 U.S. 229 (1976).
20. *Davis* v. *Los Angeles*, 566 F.2d 1334 (9th Cir. 1977), *vacated as moot*, 440 U.S. 625 (1979); cf., *Johnson* v. *Ryder Truck Lines, Inc.*, 575 F.2d 471, 474 (4th Cir. 1978), *cert. denied*, 440 U.S. 979 (1979) (the 1866 Act is to be interpreted consistently with Title VII).
21. *Davis* v. *Los Angeles*, 566 F.2d 1334 (9th Cir. 1977), *vacated as moot*, 440 U.S. 625 (1979). Contra *Craig* v. *Los Angeles*, 626 F.2d 659 (9th Cir. 1980).
22. *Mescall* v. *Burrus*, 603 F.2d 1266 (7th Cir. 1979); *Grigsby* v. *North Mississippi Medical Center*, 586 F.2d 457, 460–461 (5th Cir. 1978); *Williams* v. *DeKalb County*, 582 F.2d 2 (5th Cir. 1978).
23. *United Black Firefighters of Norfolk* v. *Hirst*, 604 F.2d 844 (4th Cir. 1979); *Dawson* v. *Pastrick*, 600 F.2d 70 (7th Cir. 1979); *Richardson* v. *Pennsylvania Department of Health*, 561 F.2d 489, 493 (3d Cir. 1977); cf., *Johnson* v. *Alexander*, 572 F.2d 1219 (8th Cir.), *cert. denied*, 439 U.S. 986 (1978).
24. *Los Angeles* v. *Davis*, 440 U.S. 625 (1979), *vacated as moot* 566 F.2d 1334 (9th Cir. 1977).
25. Even if the 1866 Act ultimately is held to bar only intentional discrimination, this will *not* affect the illegality of overt dis-

crimination, which of course is intentional discrimination, or of disparate treatment discrimination, which has been presumed by the courts to be intentional discrimination. See note 15, *supra.*

26. *Teamsters* v. *United States*, 431 U.S. 324, 339–340 n.20 (1977); see also *Castaneda* v. *Partida*, 430 U.S. 482 (1977).

27. See, e.g., *Sethy* v. *Alameda County Water District*, 545 F.2d 1157 (9th Cir. 1976).

28. As is set forth in Chapter 2, one of Title VII's exceptions allows the use of seniority systems regardless of their discriminatory impact upon minorities and women so long as the seniority systems are bona fide (meaning that they are real, not fictitious) and were not created with an intent to discriminate. 42 U.S.C. §2000e –2(h). *Teamsters* v. *United States*, 431 U.S. 324 (1977). Since the 1866 Act contains no such exception, persons who have been discriminated against by employers' seniority systems have argued that the systems are unlawful under the 1866 Act. In one instance, this argument was successful—with the result that the seniority system was struck down. *Bolden* v. *Pennsylvania State Police*, 578 F.2d 912 (3d Cir. 1978). In several other cases, however, this argument has lost because the courts applied the bona fide seniority system exception in Title VII to the 1866 Act. *Pettway* v. *American Cast Iron Pipe Co.*, 576 F.2d 1157, 1191–1192 n.37 (5th Cir. 1978), *cert. denied*, 439 U.S. 896 (1979); *Johnson* v. *Ryder Truck Lines, Inc.*, 575 F.2d 471 (4th Cir. 1978), *cert. denied*, 440 U.S. 979 (1979); see also *Sledge* v. *J. P. Stevens & Co., Inc.*, 585 F.2d 625 (4th Cir. 1978), *cert. denied*, 440 U.S. 981 (1979).

Whether Title VII's exceptions will be grafted onto the 1866 Act by the courts is an issue similar to whether the 1866 Act prohibits practices with a discriminatory effect or only those practices which are intentionally discriminatory. Until the Supreme Court decides the issue, it depends upon which court you are in.

29. The permissibility of such affirmative action under the 1866 Act is presumed because the legislative purposes of the 1866 Act were identical to the purposes of Title VII, a law which allows voluntary affirmative action. *United Steelworkers of America* v. *Weber*, 443 U.S. 193 (1979). See *Detroit Police Officers Ass'n* v. *Young*, 608 F.2d 671 (6th Cir. 1979). Whether voluntary affirmative action is also permissible under the 1871 Act is another matter. See note 46 to Chapter 7.

30. See *Carter* v. *Gallagher,* 452 F.2d 327 (8th Cir.), *cert. denied,* 406 U.S. 950 (1972), cited with approval in *Regents of the University of California* v. *Bakke,* 438 U.S. 265, 301 (1978) (Powell, J.). See also *Davis* v. *Los Angeles,* 566 F.2d 1334 (9th Cir. 1977), *vacated as moot,* 440 U.S. 625 (1979).

31. *Johnson* v. *Railway Express Agency, Inc.,* 421 U.S. 454 (1975).

32. E.g., *Carter* v. *Gallagher,* 452 F.2d 315 (8th Cir. 1971), *modified on other grounds, en banc,* 452 F.2d 327 (8th Cir.), *cert. denied,* 406 U.S. 950 (1972).

33. *Johnson* v. *Railway Express Agency, Inc.,* 421 U.S. 454 (1975); *Garner* v. *Giarrusso,* 571 F.2d 1330 (5th Cir. 1978).

34. *Johnson* v. *Railway Express Agency, Inc.,* 421 U.S. 454 (1975).

35. *Id.*

36. *Prophet* v. *Armco Steel Inc.,* 575 F.2d 579 (5th Cir. 1978); *Dupree* v. *Hutchins Brothers,* 521 F.2d 236 (5th Cir. 1976).

37. *Keyse* v. *California Texas Oil Corp.,* 590 F.2d 45 (2d Cir. 1978).

38. *Waters* v. *Wisconsin Steel Works of Int'l Harvester Co.,* 427 F.2d 476 (7th Cir.), *cert. denied,* 400 U.S. 911 (1970).

39. *Boudreaux* v. *Baton Rouge Marine Contracting Co.,* 437 F.2d 1011, 1017 n.16 (5th Cir. 1971).

40. *Page* v. *U.S. Industries, Inc.,* 556 F.2d 346, 351–354 (5th Cir. 1977), *cert. denied,* 434 U.S. 1045 (1978).

41. *Johnson* v. *Railway Express Agency, Inc.,* 421 U.S. 454 (1975).

42. *Johnson* v. *Railway Express Agency, Inc.,* 421 U.S. 454, 460 (1975); see also *Sullivan* v. *Little Hunting Park, Inc.,* 396 U.S. 229 (1969); *Jones* v. *Alfred H. Mayer Co.,* 392 U.S. 409 (1968).

43. *Brown* v. *Gaston County Dyeing Machine Co.,* 457 F.2d 1377 (4th Cir.), *cert. denied,* 409 U.S. 982 (1972).

44. E.g., *Sethy* v. *Alameda County Water District,* 545 F.2d 1157 (9th Cir. 1976).

45. Cf., *Carey* v. *Piphus,* 435 U.S. 247 (1978) (Civil Rights Act of 1871).

46. *Harkless* v. *Sweeny Independent School District,* 427 F.2d 319, 323–324 (5th Cir. 1970), *cert. denied,* 400 U.S. 991 (1971); see also 446 F.Supp. 457 (S.D.Tex.), *aff'd,* 608 F.2d 594 (5th Cir. 1979).

47. *Id.*

48. *Garner* v. *Giarrusso,* 571 F.2d 1330, 1332 (5th Cir. 1978).

49. E.g., *Claiborne* v. *Illinois Central R.R.,* 583 F.2d 143, 153–154 (5th Cir. 1978) ($50,000); *Allen* v. *Amalgamated Transit Union,* 554 F.2d 876 (8th Cir. 1977), *cert. denied,* 434 U.S. 891 (1978) ($15,000); *Sabol* v. *Snyder,* 524 F.2d 1009 (10th Cir. 1975) ($1,000).

50. 42 U.S.C. §1988. See *Sethy* v. *Alameda County Water District,* 602 F.2d 894 (1979).

51. *Id.* See also *Harkless* v. *Sweeny Independent School District,* 608 F.2d 594 (5th Cir. 1979).

52. This "bad faith" standard is set forth in the legislative history of the Civil Rights Attorneys Fees Awards Act of 1976, 42 U.S.C. §1988. See generally H.R.Rep. No. 95–1558, 94th Cong., 2d Sess., 7 (1976); S.Rep. No. 94–1011, 94th Cong., 2d Sess., 5 (1976). This standard is considerably more favorable to a losing plaintiff than is the standard under Title VII, which allows fees to be assessed against a losing plaintiff whose lawsuit was frivolous, unreasonable, or groundless, or who continued to litigate after it clearly became so. *Christiansburg Garment Co.* v. *EEOC,* 434 U.S. 412 (1978).

53. *Claiborne* v. *Illinois Central R.R.,* 583 F.2d 143 (5th Cir. 1978). See also *Sethy* v. *Alameda County Water District,* 545 F.2d 1157 (9th Cir. 1976) (reinstatement and $35,000 in damages).

54. 347 U.S. 483, 495 (1954).

55. *Sabol* v. *Snyder,* 524 F.2d 1009, 1012–1013 (10th Cir. 1975). See note 15, *supra.*

### 7: OBTAINING FURTHER REMEDIES FROM STATE AND LOCAL GOVERNMENTS

1. *Hill* v. *Nettleton,* 455 F.Supp. 514 (D.Colo. 1978).

2. This reference to "Section 1983" is to its current codification in 42 U.S.C. §1983. Although the focus of this chapter is Section 1983, there necessarily will be discussion of 42 U.S.C. §1988, and of the First and Fourteenth Amendments to the U.S. Constitution. All of the foregoing are grouped, quite inaccurately, under the phrases "the Civil Rights Act of 1871" or "the 1871 Act" in order to avoid undue confusion in the text of this chapter. (Excluded from this chapter is any discussion of 42 U.S.C. §1985 and of the criminal statutes derived from the 1871 Act.)

Section 1983, as its language indicates, technically does not prohibit discrimination but rather only makes "liable" any person who does discriminate "under color of" state law; the actual discrimination is prohibited by the Fourteenth Amendment and occasionally by the First and Fourteenth Amendments. Any person suing under the 1871 Act thus should allege a violation of the Fourteenth Amendment and liability under 42 U.S.C. §1983.

3. *District of Columbia* v. *Carter,* 409 U.S. 418 (1973) (this exclusion also includes the District of Columbia). Compare *Davis* v. *Passman,* 442 U.S. 228 (1979), allowing a cause of action against federal officials directly under the equal protection component of the Fifth Amendment.

4. On occasion, however, where a state or local government's practices become closely interconnected with those of a non-governmental private entity, the private entity may be covered by 42 U.S.C. §1983 because it is acting under color of state law. *Adickes* v. *S. H. Kress & Co.,* 398 U.S. 144 (1970) (discrimination by private lunch counter enforced by local police is unlawful discrimination under color of state law); *Burton* v. *Wilmington Parking Authority,* 365 U.S. 715 (1961) (discrimination in private restaurant on property leased from the state is unlawful discrimination under color of state law). A court of appeals has even held that private charitable foundations which owe their existence to state-granted tax-exempt status might be covered by 42 U.S.C. §1983 and hence prohibited from engaging in employment discrimination. *Jackson* v. *Statler Foundation,* 496 F.2d 623 (2d Cir. 1974), *cert. denied,* 420 U.S. 927 (1975). Most private employers, however, do not act under color of state law and thus are not covered by 42 U.S.C. §1983.

5. See *Chapman* v. *Houston Welfare Rights Organization,* 441 U.S. 600 (1979).

6. 42 U.S.C. §1983.

7. In some circumstances, an individual even can sue directly under the Constitution to remedy employment discrimination. See *Davis* v. *Passman,* 442 U.S. 228 (1979).

8. Equal protection, as noted, is not the only Fourteenth Amendment right relating to discrimination which is enforced through the 1871 Act. Another important right enforced through the 1871 Act is the right to due process of law. Since the right to substantive due process in some instances means the right not to be subjected to arbitrary treatment, it sometimes has been a useful tool to combat employment discrimination. For example, state and local government mandatory maternity leave policies have been challenged through 42 U.S.C. §1983 as sex discriminatory in violation of equal protection and as arbitrary in violation of due process. Although both claims were before the Supreme Court in *Cleveland Board of Education* v. *LaFleur,* 414 U.S. 632 (1974), the Court decided only the due process issue in holding that the mandatory maternity leave policies were unlawful.

9. *Brown* v. *Board of Education of Topeka,* 347 U.S. 483 (1954), *overruling Plessy* v. *Ferguson,* 163 U.S. 537 (1896).
10. Most lower courts prior to 1976, in fact, had held that forbidden discrimination included not just intentional discrimination but also practices which merely had a discriminatory effect. See generally the cases cited in *Washington* v. *Davis,* 426 U.S. 229, 244 n.12 (1976); see also 426 U.S. at 269 n.12, 270 n.13 (Brennan, J., dissenting).
11. *Washington* v. *Davis,* 426 U.S. 229 (1976).
12. See *Furnco Construction Corp.* v. *Waters,* 438 U.S. 567 (1978); *Teamsters* v. *United States,* 431 U.S. 324, 335 n.15 (1977); see also *Ramirez* v. *Sloss,* 615 F.2d 163 (5th Cir. 1980); and see note 15 to Chapter 6.
13. *Washington* v. *Davis,* 426 U.S. 229 (1976). Although this case was brought against the District of Columbia and hence technically did not involve the equal protection clause or 42 U.S.C. §1983, see note 3, *supra,* the Supreme Court based its decision on equal protection principles.

    Even if a practice is not intentionally discriminatory and thus not a violation of equal protection under 42 U.S.C. §1983, the practice nonetheless may be unlawful under Title VII's prohibition against disparate impact discrimination. See, e.g., *Ensley Branch NAACP* v. *Seibels,* 616 F.2d 812 (5th Cir. 1980). See generally Chapter 2.
14. *Personnel Administrator of Massachusetts* v. *Feeney,* 442 U.S. 256 (1979).
15. *Arlington Heights* v. *Metro. Housing Development Corp.,* 429 U.S. 252, 265–266 (1977) (emphasis added).
16. *Arlington Heights* v. *Metro. Housing Development Corp.,* 429 U.S. 252, 266–267 (1977). A seventh element is the use of "a selection procedure that is susceptible to abuse." *Castaneda* v. *Partida,* 430 U.S. 482, 494 (1977). In other words, a subjective practice such as use of an oral interview procedure may be intentionally discriminatory. But again, the entire background of the challenged practice must be reviewed.
17. *Teamsters* v. *United States,* 431 U.S. 324, 339–340 n.20 (1977). See also *Castaneda* v. *Partida,* 430 U.S. 482 (1977).
18. *Harkless* v. *Sweeny Independent School District,* 554 F.2d 1353, 1357–1358 (5th Cir.), *cert. denied,* 434 U.S. 966 (1977); see also *Blake* v. *Los Angeles,* 595 F.2d 1367, 1383–1385 (9th Cir. 1979); *Williams* v. *Anderson,* 562 F.2d 1081 (8th Cir. 1977); *Richardson*

v. *Pennsylvania Dept. of Health,* 561 F.2d 489 (3d Cir. 1977); compare, *Marshall* v. *Kirkland,* 602 F.2d 1282 (8th Cir. 1979).

19.	Discrimination on grounds of race, color, or national origin includes not only discrimination against black persons but also discrimination against all members of "discrete and insular minorities," *United States* v. *Carolene Products Co.,* 304 U.S. 144, 152 n.4 (1938). See, e.g., *Castaneda* v. *Partida,* 430 U.S. 482 (1977) (Chicanos); *Keyes* v. *School District No. 1,* 413 U.S. 189 (1973) (blacks & Chicanos); *Hernandez* v. *Texas,* 347 U.S. 475 (1954) (Chicanos); *Oyama* v. *California,* 332 U.S. 633 (1948) (Japanese); *Yick Wo* v. *Hopkins,* 118 U.S. 356 (1886) (Chinese).

20.	*Dunn* v. *Blumstein,* 405 U.S. 330, 342–343 (1972).

21.	*San Antonio School District* v. *Rodriguez,* 411 U.S. 1, 28 (1973), paraphrasing *United States* v. *Carolene Products Co.,* 304 U.S. 144, 152 n.4 (1938).

22.	*Sherbert* v. *Verner,* 374 U.S. 398 (1963).

23.	Chief Justice Warren Burger has emphasized the strictness of this standard by writing that no state "has ever satisfied this seemingly insurmountable standard, and I doubt that one ever will, for it demands nothing less than perfection." *Dunn* v. *Blumstein,* 405 U.S. 330, 363 (1972) (Burger, C.J., dissenting).

	Until recently, there were only two cases in history where a compelling state interest was found to exist as a sufficient justification for discrimination. Both cases involved official discrimination against Japanese-Americans during World War II, a context which the Supreme Court characterized as conditions of "gravest, imminent danger to the public safety," *Korematsu* v. *United States,* 323 U.S. 214, 218 (1944), and as "conditions of great emergency," *Hirabayashi* v. *United States,* 320 U.S. 81, 111 (1943) (Murphy, J., concurring).

24.	*Sherbert* v. *Verner,* 374 U.S. 398 (1963).

25.	*Foley* v. *Connelie,* 435 U.S. 291, 296 (1978), quoting from *Sugarman* v. *Dougall,* 413 U.S. 634, 647 (1973).

26.	*Foley* v. *Connelie,* 435 U.S. 291 (1978).

27.	*Ambach* v. *Norwick,* 441 U.S. 68 (1979).

28.	*Sugarman* v. *Dougall,* 413 U.S. 634 (1973). Similarly, a rule of the United States Civil Service Commission requiring citizenship for nearly all federal civil service jobs was struck down in *Hampton* v. *Mow Sun Wong,* 426 U.S. 88 (1976). Subsequently, however, President Ford required citizenship for nearly all federal jobs by issuing Executive Order 11935, see 5 C.F.R. §7.4, a requirement which has been upheld by the courts. *Mow Sun Wong* v. *Campbell*, 626 F.2d 739 (9th Cir. 1980); *Vergara* v. *Hampton*, 581 F.2d 1281 (7th Cir. 1978), *cert. denied*, 441 U.S. 905 (1979).

29. *In re* Griffiths, 413 U.S. 717 (1973).

30. *Examining Board* v. *Flores de Otero*, 426 U.S. 572 (1976).

31. *Frontiero* v. *Richardson*, 411 U.S. 677, 678–691 (1973) (plurality opinion of Brennan, J., with Douglas, White, and Marshall, JJ.).

32. *Craig* v. *Boren*, 429 U.S. 190, 197 (1976). This formulation has sometimes varied. See cases cited in note 33, *infra*.

33. See, e.g., *Califano* v. *Webster*, 430 U.S. 313 (1977); *Stanton* v. *Stanton*, 421 U.S. 7 (1975); *Weinberger* v. *Wiesenfeld*, 420 U.S. 636 (1975); see also *Reed* v. *Reed*, 404 U.S. 71 (1971).

34. *Frontiero* v. *Richardson*, 411 U.S. 677 (1973).

35. See *Geduldig* v. *Aiello*, 417 U.S. 484 (1974).

36. Several years after its decision in *Geduldig*, the Supreme Court also held that Title VII's prohibition against sex discrimination did not necessarily prohibit sex discrimination involving pregnancy. *General Electric Co.* v. *Gilbert*, 429 U.S. 125 (1976). This latter decision was overruled by Congress in 1978 when it amended Title VII to clarify that sex discrimination involving pregnancy is unlawful under Title VII. See 42 U.S.C. §2000e(k), discussed in the text accompanying notes 10 and 11 to Chapter 2.

37. *F. S. Royster Guano Co.* v. *Virginia*, 253 U.S. 412, 415 (1920).

38. *McGowan* v. *Maryland*, 366 U.S. 420, 425–426 (1961).

39. *Massachusetts Board of Retirement* v. *Murgia*, 427 U.S. 307, 311, 314–315 (1976).

40. *Martin* v. *Tamaki*, 607 F.2d 307 (9th Cir. 1979); *Johnson* v. *Lefkowitz*, 566 F.2d 866 (2d Cir. 1977), *cert. denied*, 440 U.S. 945 (1979). See also *Vance* v. *Bradley*, 440 U.S. 93 (1979) (upholding mandatory retirement for foreign-service officials).

41. *Lamb* v. *Scripps College*, 627 F.2d 1015 (9th Cir. 1980); *Palmer* v. *Ticcione*, 576 F.2d 459 (2d Cir. 1978), *cert. denied*, 440 U.S. 945 (1979); see also, *Kuhar* v. *Greensburg-Salem School District*, 616 F.2d 676 (3d Cir. 1980); but cf., *Gault* v. *Garrison*, 569 F.2d 993 (7th Cir. 1977), *cert. denied*, 440 U.S. 945 (1979) (motion to dismiss denied).

42. *Trafelet* v. *Thompson*, 594 F.2d 623 (7th Cir.), *cert. denied*, 444 U.S. 906 (1979).

43. See Chapter 3.

44. *Givhan* v. *Western Line Consolidated School District*, 439 U.S.

410 (1979). See also, *Simpson* v. *Weeks,* 570 F.2d 240 (8th Cir. 1978).

45. *Hill* v. *Nettleton,* 455 F.Supp. 514 (D.Colo. 1978).

46. The permissibility of numerical goals and timetables under the Fourteenth Amendment's guarantee of equal protection of the laws was not finally decided in *Regents of the University of California* v. *Bakke,* 438 U.S. 265 (1978), where only five Justices expressed their views—voting in favor of its permissibility by four to one. In the wake of *Bakke,* the lower federal courts have uniformly held such affirmative action permissible. *United States* v. *Miami,* 614 F.2d 1322 (5th Cir. 1980); *Detroit Police Officers Assn.* v. *Young,* 608 F.2d 671 (6th Cir. 1979); *Baker* v. *Detroit,* 483 F.Supp. 930 (E.D.Mich. 1979); *Doores* v. *McNamara,* 476 F.Supp. 987 (W.D.Mo. 1979). A Supreme Court decision on this issue is expected in June 1981 in the case of *Minnick* v. *California Department of Corrections,* No. 79–1213.

47. *Regents of the University of California* v. *Bakke,* 438 U.S. 265, 301–309 (1978) (Powell, J.); *Morrow* v. *Dillard,* 580 F.2d 1284 (5th Cir. 1978).

48. *Johnson* v. *Railway Express Agency, Inc.,* 421 U.S. 454 (1975).

49. *Monroe* v. *Pape,* 365 U.S. 167 (1961). Note that this part of *Monroe* was not overruled in *Monell* v. *Department of Social Services of the City of New York,* 436 U.S. 658 (1978). See also *Carter* v. *Gallagher,* 452 F.2d 315 (8th Cir. 1971), *modified on other grounds, en banc,* 452 F.2d 327 (8th Cir.), *cert. denied,* 406 U.S. 950 (1972).

50. *Johnson* v. *Railway Express Agency, Inc.,* 421 U.S. 454 (1975); *O'Sullivan* v. *Felix,* 233 U.S. 318 (1914). See also notes 34–41 to Chapter 6.

51. *Id.*

52. See *Brown* v. *Gaston County Dyeing Machine Co.,* 457 F.2d 1377 (4th Cir.), *cert. denied,* 409 U.S. 982 (1972).

53. See *Williams* v. *Anderson,* 562 F.2d 1081 (8th Cir. 1977).

54. E.g., *Hill* v. *Nettleton,* 455 F.Supp. 514 (D.Colo. 1978).

55. *Carey* v. *Piphus,* 435 U.S. 247 (1978).

56. *Harkless* v. *Sweeny Independent School District,* 427 F.2d 319, 323–324 (5th Cir. 1970), *cert. denied,* 400 U.S. 991 (1971).

57. See *Zarcone* v. *Perry,* 572 F.2d 52 (2d Cir. 1978), where an individual in a successful lawsuit under 42 U.S.C. §1983 was awarded $80,000 in compensatory damages and $61,000 in punitive damages. See also cases cited in notes 46–49 to Chapter 6.

58.    *Id.* See also *Bradshaw* v. *Zoological Society of San Diego,* 569
       F.27 1066 (9th Cir. 1978).
59.    *Hill* v. *Nettleton,* 455 F.Supp. 514 (D.Colo. 1978).
60.    *Edelman* v. *Jordan,* 415 U.S. 651 (1974), reaffirmed in *Quern* v.
       *Jordan,* 440 U.S. 332 (1979); see also *Skehan* v. *Board of Trustees
       of Bloomsbury State College,* 590 F.2d 470 (3d Cir. 1978), *cert.
       denied.* 444 U.S. 832 (1979); *Bogard* v. *Cook,* 586 F.2d 399 (5th
       Cir. 1978).
61.    This standard, which is set forth in *Wood* v. *Strickland,* 420 U.S.
       308 (1975), and in *Scheuer* v. *Rhodes,* 416 U.S. 232 (1974), allows
       government officials a limited immunity from damages for ac-
       tions taken in good faith. This same qualified immunity also pro-
       tects individual officials of county, municipal, and other local
       governments from monetary damages for actions taken in good
       faith except where they knew or should have known that their
       actions violated protected rights. E.g., *Williams* v. *Andersen,*
       562 F.2d 1081 (8th Cir. 1977).
          Since there is no immunity of any kind that can be claimed by
       local governments themselves, see *Owen* v. *City of Indepen-
       dence,* 48 U.S.L.W. 4389 (U.S., April 15, 1980), local governments
       can easily be found liable for back pay, actual damages, compen-
       satory damages, and punitive damages.
62.    42 U.S.C. §1988.
63.    *Hutto* v. *Finney,* 437 U.S. 678 (1975).
64.    *Id.*
65.    This "bad faith" standard is set forth in the legislative history of
       the Civil Rights Attorneys Fees Awards Act of 1976, 42 U.S.C.
       §1988. See note 52 to Chapter 6.
66.    *Harkless* v. *Sweeny Independent School District,* 554 F.2d 1353,
       1357–1358 (5th Cir.), *cert. denied,* 434 U.S. 966 (1977).
67.    *Harkless* v. *Sweeny Independent School District,* 608 F.2d 594
       (5th Cir. 1979), *aff'g,* 466 F.Supp. 457 (S.D.Tex. 1979).

**8:  COMBINING THE LAWS TO WIN YOUR RIGHTS AND THE
BROADEST REMEDIES POSSIBLE**

1.    *International Union of Electrical, Radio and Machine Workers*
      v. *Robbins & Myers, Inc.,* 429 U.S. 229 (1976); *Johnson* v. *Rail-
      way Express Agency, Inc.,* 421 U.S. 454 (1975); *Alexander* v.
      *Gardner-Denver Co.,* 415 U.S. 36 (1974).
2.    *Id.* There is one major exception to the combining principle.

Where Title VII prohibits discrimination in federal employment, Title VII cannot be joined with other laws such as the 1866 Act but rather is an exclusive remedy. *Brown* v. *General Services Administration*, 425 U.S. 820 (1976).

3. See note 1, *supra*, and notes 5, 6, 8 & 12, *infra*.

4. See note 11, *infra*.

5. *Rudolph* v. *Wagner Electric Corp.*, 586 F.2d 90 (8th Cir. 1978), *cert. denied*, 441 U.S. 924 (1979). Cf., *International Union of Electrical, Radio and Machine Workers* v. *Robbins & Myers, Inc.*, 429 U.S. 229 (1976) (filing of union grievance does not toll Title VII time periods).

6. *Everson* v. *McLouth Steel Corp.*, 586 F.2d 6 (6th Cir. 1978).

7. 42 U.S.C. §2000e–5(f)(1).

8. *Prophet* v. *Armco Steel, Inc.*, 575 F.2d 579 (5th Cir. 1978); see also, *Minor* v. *Lakeview Hospital*, 421 F.Supp. 485 (E.D. Wis. 1976) (Title VII lawsuit filed on 91st day after receipt of a right-to-sue letter is untimely).

9. *Id.*

10. *Johnson* v. *Railway Express Agency, Inc.*, 421 U.S. 454 (1975).

11. 42 U.S.C. §2000e–5(e). If an individual first files a charge with a state or local human rights agency, the federal administrative charge must be filed with the EEOC within 300 days of the discriminatory action or within 30 days of receiving notice that the state or local agency terminated its proceedings, whichever is earlier. *Id.*

12. *Krzyzewski* v. *Metropolitan Government of Nashville and Davidson County*, 584 F.2d 802 (6th Cir. 1978); see also, *Bonham* v. *Dresser Industries, Inc.*, 569 F.2d 187 (3d Cir. 1977), *cert. denied*, 439 U.S. 821 (1978); *Green* v. *Carter Carburetor Co.*, 532 F.2d 125 (8th Cir. 1976).

13. 31 C.F.R. §51.62(a).

14. *Bradshaw* v. *Zoological Society of San Diego*, 569 F.2d 1066 (9th Cir. 1978). See also *Blake* v. *Los Angeles*, 595 F.2d 1367 (9th Cir. 1979).

15. *Hill* v. *Nettleton*, 455 F.Supp. 415 (D. Colo. 1978).

16. Another avenue of legal relief in this situation is a lawsuit challenging the union's breach of its duty of fair representation under the Labor Management Relations Act, 29 U.S.C. §§141, *et seq.* See, e.g., *Steele* v. *Louisville and Nashville R.R.*, 323 U.S. 192 (1944).

17. *Allen* v. *Amalgamated Transit Union Local 788*, 554 F.2d 876 (8th Cir. 1977), *cert. denied*, 434 U.S. 891 (1978).

18.   *Garner* v. *Giarrusso,* 571 F.2d 1330 (5th Cir. 1978).
19.   *Laffey* v. *Northwest Airlines, Inc.,* 567 F.2d 429, 445 (D.C. Cir. 1976), *cert. denied,* 434 U.S. 1086 (1978). See generally, *Gunther* v. *County of Washington,* 602 F.2d 882 (9th Cir. 1979).
20.   *Wetzel* v. *Liberty Mutual Insurance Co.,* 372 F.Supp. 1146 (W.D. Pa. 1974), *aff'd,* 508 F.2d 239 (3d Cir.), *cert. denied,* 421 U.S. 1011 (1975).
21.   *Wetzel* v. *Liberty Mutual Insurance Co.,* 449 F.2d 397 (W.D. Pa. 1978).
22.   *Id.* at 402.
23.   *Id.* at 405.
24.   See also, *Taylor* v. *Philips Industries, Inc.,* 593 F.2d 783 (7th Cir. 1979).
25.   *Laffey* v. *Northwest Airlines, Inc.,* 567 F.2d 429 (D.C. Cir. 1976), *cert. denied,* 434 U.S. 1086 (1978), *on remand,* 481 F.Supp. 199 (D.D.C. 1979).
26.   *Howard* v. *Ward County,* 418 F.Supp. 494, 500 (D.N.D. 1976).
27.   *Id.* at 500–501. This erroneous determination would have been reversed on appeal. See, e.g., *Pearce* v. *Wichita County,* 590 F.2d 128 (5th Cir. 1979); *Marshall* v. *Kent State University,* 589 F.2d 255 (6th Cir. 1978); *Marshall* v. *Owensboro-Daviess County Hospital,* 581 F.2d 116 (6th Cir. 1978); *Usery* v. *Charleston County School District,* 588 F.2d 1169 (4th Cir. 1977); *Usery* v. *Allegheny County Institution District,* 544 F.2d 148 (3d Cir. 1976), *cert. denied,* 430 U.S. 946 (1977).
28.   *Howard* v. *Ward County,* 418 F.Supp. 494, 506 (D.N.D. 1976).
29.   See, e.g., *Kyriazi* v. *Western Electric Co.,* 476 F.Supp. 335 (D.N.J. 1979), where, in addition to the remedies provided under federal law, punitive damages were awarded under New Jersey tort law.
30.   See generally, Section 815(c) of the Justice System Improvement Act of 1979, Pub.L. No. 96–157 (Dec. 27, 1979), 93 Stat. 1167, 42 U.S.C. §3789d(c). See also note 5 to Chapter 4.
31.   See, e.g., *Davis* v. *Passman,* 442 U.S. 228 (1979).


9:   FILING AN ADMINISTRATIVE CHARGE OF DISCRIMINATION

1.   *Novotny* v. *Great American Federal Savings & Loan Ass'n,* 584 F.2d 1235, 1237 (3d Cir. 1978) *(en banc), rev'd on other grounds,* 442 U.S. 366 (1979).
2.   *Mitchell* v. *Mid-Continent Spring Co. of Kentucky,* 583 F.2d

275, 277 (6th Cir. 1978), *cert. denied,* 441 U.S. 922 (1979). *EEOC* v. *Liberty Mutual Ins. Co.,* 346 F.Supp. 675, 677 (N.D. Ga. 1972); cf., *Drew* v. *Liberty Mutual Ins. Co.,* 480 F.2d 69 (5th Cir. 1973), *cert. denied,* 417 U.S. 935 (1974).

3. *Pantchenko* v. *C. B. Dolge Co., Inc.,* 581 F.2d 1052 (2d Cir. 1978). *Rutherford* v. *American Bank of Commerce,* 565 F.2d 1162 (10th Cir. 1977).

4. *Givhan* v. *Western Line Consolidated School District,* 439 U.S. 410 (1979).

5. *Novotny* v. *Great American Federal Savings & Loan Ass'n,* 584 F.2d 1235 (3d Cir. 1978) *(en banc), rev'd on other grounds,* 442 U.S. 366 (1979).

6. *Burdine* v. *Texas Department of Community Affairs,* 608 F.2d 563 (5th Cir. 1979).

7. Cf., *Parham* v. *Southwestern Bell Telephone Co.,* 433 F.2d 421 (8th Cir. 1970) (the mere filing of this Title VII lawsuit caused the employer to quickly comply with the law).

8. 42 U.S.C. §2000e–5(e). If a charge was first filed with a state or local agency, then the EEOC charge must be filed with the EEOC within 300 days of the discriminatory act or within 30 days of the termination of the state or local agency proceedings, whichever is first. *Id.* See generally notes 115–122 and 134–148 to Chapter 2. These time periods are *shorter* for federal employees. See note 151 to Chapter 2.

9. 29 U.S.C. §626(d). If the charge arises in a state where there is a state agency with age discrimination enforcement powers, then the time period for filing an EEOC charge is extended to 300 days or to 30 days after the termination of state proceedings, whichever is first. 29 U.S.C. §626(d). There still is some uncertainty about these extended periods. See generally notes 53–61 to Chapter 3.

10. See notes 8 and 9, *supra.*

11. 41 C.F.R. §60–1.22. See generally Chapter 5.

12. The enforcement section of the Equal Pay Act, 29 U.S.C. §216, like the Equal Pay Act itself, 29 U.S.C. §206(d), is silent on the matter of filing charges. See generally, Chapter 1.

13. 31 C.F.R. §51.52(a). See generally, Chapter 4.

14. 31 U.S.C. §1245; see generally, 31 U.S.C. §1242.

15. 42 U.S.C. §2000e–5(b).

16. This is not a statutory or regulatory requirement. Rather, it simply is a fact that the OFCCP ordinarily refers individual charges

to the EEOC, see 41 C.F.R. §60–1.24(a), while retaining for itself and investigating only charges of "systemic" discrimination. See generally, Chapter 5.

17. Title VII: 42 U.S.C. §2000e–5(b); Revenue Sharing Act: 31 C.F.R. §51.52; Executive Order 11246: 41 C.F.R. §60–1.23. Although there are no specific provisions under the Equal Pay Act or the Age Discrimination in Employment Act allowing charges to be filed by a "representative" of an aggrieved individual, initial federal enforcement ordinarily is undertaken without disclosure to the employer of the names of the aggrieved individuals, a practice upheld by the courts. See, e.g., *Usery* v. *Ritter,* 547 F.2d 528 (10th Cir. 1977), and cases cited therein.

18. 42 U.S.C. §2000e–5(b).

19. See 29 C.F.R. §1601.8 and §1602.12; see also the EEOC Compliance Manual, Charges, §1.5.

## 10: FINDING A LAWYER IF YOU ACTUALLY HAVE TO SUE YOUR BOSS

1. See, e.g., the cases cited in notes 16 and 29–31 to Chapter 8.

2. 29 U.S.C. §216(b) is part of the minimum-wage law and hence is part of the Equal Pay Act, and it is incorporated into the Age Discrimination in Employment Act by 29 U.S.C. §626(b). See notes 81–82 to Chapter 1, and notes 77–78 to Chapter 3.

3. Despite the lack of a statutory authorization for a fee award to a prevailing defendant, a court in its equitable powers can award fees to a prevailing defendant in the rare situation where a court finds that the plaintiff's lawsuit was brought in bad faith. See generally, *Alyeska Pipeline Service Co.* v. *Wilderness Society,* 421 U.S. 240 (1975).

4. Title VII: 42 U.S.C. §2000e–5(k); the Revenue Sharing Act: 31 U.S.C. §1244(e); the Civil Rights Acts of 1866 and 1871: 42 U.S.C. §1988. See notes 184–85 to Chapter 2, note 68 to Chapter 4, notes 50–51 to Chapter 6, and notes 62–63 to Chapter 7.

5. This is the undisputed standard under all civil rights fee-shifting statutes. See, e.g., *Northcross* v. *Board of Education of Memphis,* 412 U.S. 427 (1973); *Newman* v. *Piggie Park Enterprises, Inc.,* 390 U.S. 400 (1968); see also, *Christiansburg Garment Co.* v. *EEOC,* 434 U.S. 412 (1978).

6. This standard was applied under Title VII in *Christiansburg Garment Co.* v. *EEOC,* 434 U.S. 412 (1978). Although the more

stringent bad faith standard, see note 7, *infra*, might possibly apply under the Revenue Sharing Act, it is more likely that the courts will apply the Title VII standard under the Revenue Sharing Act in view of the similar interpretation of these laws.

7. The common law bad faith standard is articulated throughout the legislative history of the Civil Rights Attorney's Fees Awards Act of 1976, 42 U.S.C. §1988. See, e.g., S.Rep.No. 94–1011, 94th Cong., 2d Sess., 5 (1976); H.R.Rep. No. 94–1558, 94th Cong., 2d Sess., 7 (1976).

8. E.g., *Faraci* v. *Hickey-Freeman Co., Inc.*, 607 F.2d 1025 (2d Cir. 1979); see also *United States Steel Corp.* v. *United States*, 519 F.2d 359, 364 n.24 (3d Cir. 1975); *Sek* v. *Bethlehem Steel Corp.*, 463 F.Supp. 144 (E.D.Pa. 1979).

9. *Nadeau* v. *Helgemoe*, 581 F.2d 275, 278–279 (1st Cir. 1978); see also *Battle* v. *Anderson*, 614 F.2d 251 (10th Cir. 1980); *Burdine* v. *Texas Department of Community Affairs*, 608 F.2d 563 (5th Cir. 1979); *Bagby* v. *Beal*, 606 F.2d 411 (3d Cir. 1979); *Sethy* v. *Alameda County Water District*, 602 F.2d 894 (9th Cir. 1979); *Dawson* v. *Pastrick*, 600 F.2d 70 (7th Cir. 1979).

10. *Hutto* v. *Finney*, 437 U.S. 678 (1978).

11. E.g., *Johnson* v. *Mississippi*, 606 F.2d 635 (5th Cir. 1979).

12. E.g., *Prandini* v. *National Tea Co.*, 557 F.2d 1015 (3d Cir. 1977); *Parker* v. *Califano*, 561 F.2d 320 (D.C. Cir. 1977); see also *Nadeau* v. *Helgemoe*, 581 F.2d 275 (1st Cir. 1978), and cases cited therein.

13. E.g., *Fisher* v. *Adams*, 572 F.2d 406 (1st Cir. 1978); *Parham* v. *Southwestern Bell Telephone Co.*, 433 F.2d 421 (8th Cir. 1970).

14. E.g., *Perez* v. *University of Puerto Rico*, 600 F.2d 1 (1st Cir. 1979).

15. E.g., *Sethy* v. *Alameda County Water District*, 602 F.2d 894 (9th Cir. 1979).

16. E.g., *Cleverly* v. *Western Electric Co.*, 594 F.2d 638 (8th Cir. 1979); *Sargeant* v. *Sharp*, 579 F.2d 645 (1st Cir. 1978).

17. E.g., *Prandini* v. *National Tea Co.*, 557 F.2d 1015 (3d Cir. 1977).

18. E.g., *International Society for Krishna Consciousness* v. *Collins*, 609 F.2d 151 (5th Cir. 1980).

19. E.g., *Rodriguez* v. *Taylor*, 569 F.2d 1231 (3d Cir. 1977), *cert. denied*, 436 U.S. 913 (1978) (fees awarded to a legal services organization); *Reynolds* v. *Coomey*, 567 F.2d 1166 (1st Cir. 1978) (fees awarded to the NAACP Legal Defense and Education Fund); *EEOC* v. *Enterprise Association of Steamfitters*, 542 F.2d 579, 592–593 (2d Cir. 1976) ($50,000 in fees to the National Employment Law Project); cf., *Brandenburger* v. *Thompson*,

494 F.2d 885 (9th Cir. 1974) (fees to the ACLU); *Fairley* v. *Patterson*, 493 F.2d 598 (5th Cir. 1974) (fees to the Lawyers Committee for Civil Rights under Law); see also *Northcross* v. *Board of Education of Memphis*, 611 F.2d 624 (6th Cir. 1979); *Harkless* v. *Sweeny Independent School District*, 608 F.2d 594 (5th Cir. 1979).

20. *Cleveland Board of Education* v. *LaFleur*, 414 U.S. 632 (1974). See note 8 to Chapter 7.
21. *Carter* v. *Gallagher*, 452 F.2d 315 (8th Cir. 1971), *modified on other grounds*, 452 F.2d 327 (8th Cir.) *(en banc), cert. denied*, 406 U.S. 950 (1972).
22. *Dothard* v. *Rawlinson*, 433 U.S. 321 (1977).
23. *Monell* v. *Department of Social Services of the City of New York*, 436 U.S. 658 (1978).

# Appendix
## Charts
## of the Seven Major Federal Laws
## Prohibiting Employment
## Discrimination

# CHART 1
## THE FEDERAL LAWS PROHIBITING EMPLOYMENT DISCRIMINATION

| | Race, Color, National Origin | | | Religion | | | Sex | | | Age | | |
|---|---|---|---|---|---|---|---|---|---|---|---|---|
| | Private | State & Local | Federal | Private | State & Local | Federal | Private | State & Local | Federal | Private | State & Local | Federal |
| Winning Equal Pay<br>Equal Pay Act<br>(Chapter 1) | | | | | | | X | X | X | | | |
| Obtaining Basic Rights<br>Title VII<br>(Chapter 2) | X | X | X | X | X | X | X | X | X | | | |
| Coming of Age<br>Age Discrimination Act<br>(Chapter 3) | | | | | | | | | | X | X | X |
| Terminating Federal<br>Monies<br>Revenue Sharing Act<br>(Chapter 4) | | X | | | X | | | X | | | | |
| Terminating Federal<br>Contracts<br>Executive Order 11246<br>(Chapter 5) | X | | | X | | | X | | | | | |
| Obtaining Racial Rights<br>1866 Civil Rights Act<br>(Chapter 6) | X | X | | | | | | | | | | |
| Pursuing Equal Rights<br>1871 Civil Rights Act<br>(Chapter 7) | | X | | | X | | | X | | | X | |

# CHART 2
## ENFORCEMENT OF THE FEDERAL LAWS

| | Administrative Enforcement Agency | Latest Filing of Administrative Charge | Administrative Termination of Federal Aid | Earliest/Latest Filing of Lawsuits by Federal Gov't. | Earliest/Latest Timing for Filing Your Lawsuit |
|---|---|---|---|---|---|
| Winning Equal Pay Equal Pay Act (Chapter 1) | EEOC | No limitation | | No waiting/ Within 2–3 years of the discrimination | No waiting/ Within 2–3 years of the discrimination |
| Obtaining Basic Rights Title VII (Chapter 2) | EEOC | Within 180 days of the discrimination | | No waiting/ No limitation | After 180 days of filing charge/ Within 90 days of right-to-sue letter |
| Coming of Age Age Discrimination Act (Chapter 3) | EEOC | Within 180 days of the discrimination | | No waiting/ Within 2–3 years of the discrimination | State deferral/ within 2–3 years of the discrimination |

# CHART 2
## ENFORCEMENT OF THE FEDERAL LAWS (*Continued*)

| | | | | | |
|---|---|---|---|---|---|
| Terminating Federal Monies Revenue Sharing Act (Chapter 4) | ORS | No limitation | Revenue sharing | No waiting/ No limitation | After 90 days of filing charge/ No limitation |
| Terminating Federal Contracts Executive Order 11246 (Chapter 5) | OFCCP | Within 180 days of the discrimination | Federal contracts | No waiting/ No limitation | |
| Obtaining Racial Rights 1866 Civil Rights Act (Chapter 6) | | | | | No waiting/ Within state law limitation period |
| Pursuing Equal Rights 1871 Civil Rights Act (Chapter 7) | | | | | No waiting/ Within state law limitation period |

319

# CHART 3
## REMEDIES UNDER THE FEDERAL LAWS

| | Your Rightful Place | Back Pay For You | Other Monetary Awards | Punitive Damages | Attorney's Fees |
|---|---|---|---|---|---|
| Winning Equal Pay Equal Pay Act (Chapter 1) | No: only equal pay | Limited to 2–3 years from lawsuit | Double back pay | | Yes |
| Obtaining Basic Rights Title VII (Chapter 2) | Yes | Limited to 2 years from charge | | | Yes |
| Coming of Age Age Discrimination Act (Chapter 3) | Yes | Limited to 2–3 years from lawsuit | Double back pay | | Yes |
| Terminating Federal Monies Revenue Sharing Act (Chapter 4) | Yes | Yes | | | Yes |

## CHART 3
### REMEDIES UNDER THE FEDERAL LAWS (*Continued*)

|  |  |  |  |  |  |
|---|---|---|---|---|---|
| Terminating Federal Contracts Executive Order 11246 (Chapter 5) | Yes | Yes |  |  |  |
| Obtaining Racial Rights 1866 Civil Rights Act (Chapter 6) | Yes | Yes | Misc. damages | Yes | Yes |
| Pursuing Equal Rights 1871 Civil Rights Act (Chapter 7) | Yes | Yes | Misc. damages | Yes | Yes |

# CHART 4
## RACE, COLOR, NATIONAL ORIGIN: YOUR RIGHTS TO NON-DISCRIMINATION IN EMPLOYMENT

| | Covered Employers | | | Methods of Enforcement | | | | Remedies Available to You | | | | |
|---|---|---|---|---|---|---|---|---|---|---|---|---|
| | Private | State & Local | Federal | Admin. Resolution | Loss of Federal Aid | Gov't Lawsuits | Your Lawsuit | Rightful Place | Back Pay | Other Money | Punitive Damages | Attorney's Fees |
| Obtaining Basic Rights Title VII (Chapter 2) | X | X | X | X | | X | X | X | X | | | X |
| Terminating Federal Monies Revenue Sharing Act (Chapter 4) | | X | | X | X | X | X | X | X | | | X |
| Terminating Federal Contracts Executive Order 11246 (Chapter 5) | X | | | X | X | X | | X | X | | | |
| Obtaining Racial Rights 1866 Civil Rights Act (Chapter 6) | X | X | | | | | X | X | X | X | X | X |
| Pursuing Equal Rights 1871 Civil Rights Act (Chapter 7) | | X | | | | | X | X | X | X | X | X |

# CHART 5
## RELIGION: YOUR RIGHTS TO NON-DISCRIMINATION IN EMPLOYMENT

| | Covered Employers | | | Methods of Enforcement | | | | Remedies Available to You | | | | |
|---|---|---|---|---|---|---|---|---|---|---|---|---|
| | Private | State & Local | Federal | Admin. Resolution | Loss of Federal Aid Lawsuits | Gov't Lawsuit | Your Lawsuit | Rightful Place | Back Pay | Other Money | Punitive Damages | Attorney's Fees |
| Obtaining Basic Rights Title VII (Chapter 2) | X | X | X | X | | X | X | X | X | | | X |
| Terminating Federal Monies Revenue Sharing Act (Chapter 4) | | X | | X | X | X | X | X | X | | | X |
| Terminating Federal Contracts Executive Order 11246 (Chapter 5) | X | | | X | X | X | | X | X | | | |
| Pursuing Equal Rights 1871 Civil Rights Act (Chapter 7) | | X | | | | | X | X | X | X | X | X |

CHART 6
# SEX: YOUR RIGHTS TO NON-DISCRIMINATION IN EMPLOYMENT

| | Covered Employers | | | Methods of Enforcement | | | | Remedies Available to You | | | | |
|---|---|---|---|---|---|---|---|---|---|---|---|---|
| | Private | State & Local | Federal | Admin. Resolution | Loss of Federal Aid | Lawsuits Gov't Lawsuit | Your Lawsuit | Rightful Place | Back Pay | Other Money | Punitive Damages | Attorney's Fees |
| Winning Equal Pay Equal Pay Act (Chapter 1) | X | X | X | X | | X | X | | X | X | | X |
| Obtaining Basic Rights Title VII (Chapter 2) | X | X | X | X | | X | X | X | X | | | X |
| | | | | | | | | | | | | |
| Terminating Federal Monies Revenue Sharing Act (Chapter 4) | | X | | X | X | X | X | X | X | | | X |
| Terminating Federal Contracts Executive Order 11246 (Chapter 5) | X | | | X | X | X | | X | X | | | |
| | | | | | | | | | | | | |
| Pursuing Equal Rights 1871 Civil Rights Act (Chapter 7) | | X | | | | | X | X | X | X | X | X |

# CHART 7
## Age: Your Rights to Non-discrimination in Employment

| | Covered Employers | | | Methods of Enforcement | | | | Remedies Available to You | | | | |
|---|---|---|---|---|---|---|---|---|---|---|---|---|
| | Private | State & Local | Federal | Admin. Resolution | Loss of Federal Aid | Gov't Lawsuits | Your Lawsuit | Rightful Place | Back Pay | Other Money | Punitive Damages | Attorney's Fees |
| | | | | | | | | | | | | |
| | | | | | | | | | | | | |
| Coming of Age Age Discrimination Act (Chapter 3) | X | X | X | X | | X | X | X | X | X | | X |
| | | | | | | | | | | | | |
| | | | | | | | | | | | | |
| | | | | | | | | | | | | |
| Pursuing Equal Rights 1871 Civil Rights Act (Chapter 7) | | X | | | | | X | X | X | X | X | X |